INTERNATIONAL JOURNAL

OF

INTEGRATIVE HUMANISM

(INTEGRATIVE PERSPECTIVE)

Volume 9 Number 1

June 2018

International Journal of Integrative Humanism

First published, 2011

Volume 9 Number 1: Published June 2018.

Print ISSN: 2026 – 6286

© Faculty of Arts, University of Cape Coast, Ghana.

© Faculty of Arts University of Calabar, Calabar, Nigeria.

All right reserved.

Print ISBN: 978-0-244-10039-1

Journal website: https://ediomsric.com/international-journal-of-integrative-humanism/

Indexed by: **iSi** International society of Indexing

Publisher

Edioms Research and Innovation Centre Website: www.ediomsric.com
Email: jihumanism@ediomsric.com (JIH enquiry), helpdesk@ediomsric.com (General enquiry)

Note: The publisher is not responsible for the views, validity of findings, conclusions or quality of articles in this journal. Please, forward all queries about articles to the authors and the editorial team.

Why not let us publish your first Academic Journal or Book for FREE?

Our packages are flexible and we allow you to choose what you want.

Package A – You manage articles collection, editorial services and collation while we publish.

Package B (Recommended) – Our experienced editors manage every process of publication which include checking article for fitness, quality of research method, plagiarism and soundness of overall presentation.

Contact us now for more information! (helpdesk@ediomsric.com). *Free publication offer is subject to terms and conditions.*

International Journal of Integrative Humanism Vol 9. No 1. June 2018. ISSN: 2026 – 6286

Introducing Africa Research Database

AFREDAT

Free Research Database for African Researchers and Institutions

Africa Research Database (AfreDat) is a platform designed to preserve and widen access to research information in Africa. Our aim is to meet the need for increased global visibility of research publications originating from or pertaining to Africa. AfreDat makes it possible for users to search scholarly publications held in OAI-compliant institutional repositories scattered across Africa, through one interface. Our African service was launched with **246,505 publications** from **51 repositories** in **15 countries**. These numbers are expected to grow steadily over the coming months.

Our worldwide service gives users free access to **over 170 million publications** from **more than 200 million authors**. Whether you are using our African or worldwide service, you can save queries or selected records from query results on the platform, for future analysis.

AfreDat does not own copyright of any publication accessed via this portal. Copyright belongs to the host repository or the author(s) named in the publication. Therefore, we are not liable for copyright issues relating to any publication that is found using this portal.

It is our desire that this database meets your expectations. However, if it doesn't, please feel free to contact us at **info@afredat.com** with your queries and suggestions for improvement.

How you can sign up

Be assured that it's very easy to sign up for AfreDat services. *Go to* www.afredat.com. We have two sign-up routes; Institution and Individual routes. If you are representing an institution, read How can my Institutions Sign-up? If you don't belong to an institution that is registered with AfreDat, read Can I use Afredat without belonging to any institution?

How your institution can sign up

If you are representing an institution and would like to know how your institution join AfreDat, you are in the right place. So, relax while we take you through the following simple steps:

Go to www.afredat.com

On the home page, click the tab join for free.

Click Partner registration.

Fill out and submit the application form.

You should see a confirmation that your form was submitted successfully.

The AfreDat Team will contact you via email for details confirmation.

You will receive another email detailing how to set up AfreDat Login form on your institution's website.

If you have any further queries on partner registration that is not covered here, please contact support@afredat.com.

No portal covers research in Africa better than Afredat. Sign up now! Go to www.afredat.com

Editorial Board

International Journal of Integrative Humanism Vol 9. No 1. June 2018. ISSN: 2026 – 6286

Editorial Consultant

International Journal of Integrative Humanism Vol 9. No 1. June 2018. ISSN: 2026 – 6286

List of Contributors

1. Paul Appiah-Sekyere. *Department of Religion and Human Values, University of Cape Coast, Ghana. Email:* nkasp2@yahoo.com

2. Professor G. O. Ozumba, *Department of Philosophy, University of Calabar. Email:* goddyozumba@yahoo.com.

3. Idongesit Eshiet (Ph. D). *Department of Sociology, University of Lagos, Lagos, Nigeria. E-mail:* doshiet2@yahoo.com

4. Samson Fabian Nzuanke. *Department of Modern Languages & Translation Studies, University of Calabar, Calabar-Nigeria*

5. Olufumilayo Olukemi Ogbadu. *Higher Institute of Translation, Interpretation and Communication, Nkolbisson, Yaounde-Cameroon.*

6. Chukwuma Anyanwu, PhD. *Deparment Of Theatre Arts, Faculty of Arts, Delta State University, Abraka. Email:* bonnyanyanwu@yahoo.com/anyanwubc@delsu.edu.ng

7. Kanayo L. Nwadialor. *Department of Religion and Human Relations, Nnamdi Azikiwe University, Awka, Nigeria. Email:* Kl.nwadialor@unizik.edu.ng

8. Chris TasieOsegenwune Ph. D. *Department of Philosophy, University of Lagos, Akoka, Nigeria.*

9. T.V. Ogan PhD. *Department of Philosophy, University of Port Harcourt, Nigeria. E-mail:* tamunosikivictor@gmail.com

10. Adie Edward Ugbada PhD. *Department of Theatre, Film and Carnival Studies, University of Calabar, Nigeria.*

11. Yusuf Ninzim Shamagana, *Department of Theatre and Performing Arts, Ahmadu Bello University Zaria, Nigeria. :* yusufshamagana232382@gmail.com

12. Adie Margaret Funmilayo. *Unical International Demonstration Secondary School, Calabar, Nigeria. E-mail :* raimifunmi@yahoo.com .

13. Adeseye, Bifatife Olufemi (Ph. D). *Department of Theatre and Media Arts, Federal University, Oye, Ekiti State, Nigeria. Email: bifatife.adeseye@fuoye.edu.ng,* touchbfatfe@gmail.com

14. Lamidi, Ishola Kamorudeen. *Department of Mass Communication, Adekunle Ajasin University, Akungba – Akoko, Ondo State, Nigeria. Email:* isholalamidi@yahoo.com

15. Prof. John A. Onimhawo. *Department of Religious Management and Cultural Studies, Ambrose Alli University, Ekpoma, Edo State, Nigeria.*

16. Dr. Peter O. O. Ottuh. *Department of Religious Studies and Philosophy, Delta State University, Abraka, Delta State, Nigeria, Email: pottuh@delsu.edu.ng; ottuhpeter@gmail.com*

17. Joseph Agofure Idogho. *Dept of Theatre and Media Arts, Federal University, Oye Ekiti, Ekiti State, Nigeria. Email: agofurei@gmail.com, agofure4u@yahoo.co.uk*

18. Dennis A. Mordi. *International Centre of Excellence on Development Communication, Department of Theatre and Performing Arts, Ahmadu Bello University, Zaria, Nigeria. Email-* damordi@yahoo.com

19. Felix A. Akínṣípẹ̀. *Department of the performing arts, university of ilorin, ilorin, kwara state, Nigeria. Email: felisipe@yahoo.com*

20. 'Bùnmi Babárìndé-Hall. *Administrator, Digital and Emerging Technologies, The Community College of Baltimore County, USA.*

21. Apeh, Columba Ph. D. *Department of Theatre and Media Studies, University of Calabar, Calabar – Nigeria. E-mail: apehcolumba@gmail.com,* Apehcolumba1976@gmail.com

22. Imoh Obot Sunday PhD. *Department of Theatre and Performing Arts, Ahmadu Bello University (ABU), Zaria, Nigeria. Email:* imohobot2000@gmail.com

23. Ogakason, Rasheed Oshoke. *Department of Theatre and Performing Arts, Ahmadu Bello University (ABU), Zaria, Nigeria. Email:* rashmanson@yahoo.com

24. Dr Chris Nwaru. *Department of Theatre Arts, Faculty of Humanities, Imo State University, Owerri, Nigeria. Email:* chrisnwaru@yahoo.com

25. Oshega Abang Ph. D. *Department of Mass Communication, University of Calabar, Nigeria. Email:* abangoshega@unical.edu.ng

26. Effiong Edet Okon. *Department of Linguistics and Communication Studies, University of Calabar, Nigeria. Email:* effiongedetokon54@gmail.com

27. Chibuzo Ikechi Nwanguma PhD. *Dept of Philosophy Religion, Mountain Top University, Km 12 Lagos-Ibadan Expressway, Ibafo, Ogun State, Nigeria. Email: chibuzonwanguma@gmail.com*

How to Publish an Academic Article in This Journal

We like you to know the processes involved in publishing with us in case you are seeing our journal for the first time.

Core Requirements
- An original article of a good quality having good presentation, reliable method and referencing (check before you submit).
- Name(s) of author(s) with correspondent email address(es) and phone number(s). If the article is authored by more than one person, please put name of the lead author first or we will take the first name as the lead author. We may contact you by phone call or email if necessary.
- Name of author's institution or current place of employment.
- *Relax, we are here to help you get through the process. If your article is not of the required standard, we will support you.*

Stage 1: Preliminary
- Article submission.
- Acceptance/rejection of article.
- Notification of the status of submission.

Stage 2: Payment for article publication
- For payment enquiries, send an email to jihumanism@ediomsric.com.
- **Payment for article publication in the International Journal of Integrative Humanism is non-refundable.**
- You can direct all complaints about article publication to jihumanism@ediomsric.com and your case will be handled adequately.
- Please, note that your article will not pass to peer-reviewers until your payment is confirmed.
- Authors who are members of our peer-review team receive 10% publication discount for every publication. If you which to join us, send an email to jihumanism@ediomsric.com.

Stage 3: Peer-review
- Check for plagiarism, ethical issues, presentation issues, fitness for publication and accuracy of findings if possible.
- Notification of outcome of review process.
- Please, note that you are responsible for the accuracy of data and findings of your work. Our peer-review team will not take the responsibility of making your work more accurate but will only suggest corrections if necessary.
- Authors are expected to make their corrections and return them within a week or the stipulated deadline. Corrected versions of articles not received within the deadline will be rejected or kept for the next publication.
- *If you need our high-quality proofreading services to make your more suitable for publication send a separate email to jihumanism@ediomsric.com and request for the service. You will be told the cost which will depend on the size of your work.*

Stage 4: Publication
- Authors will view their articles, accept them for publication and confirm the correctness of their details on the page.
- After resolving all complaints, the final journal print copy will be released and online versions will be updated.
- Late request for changes on already published journal will attract extra charges.

Stage 5: Request for print version
- Authors who live in Nigeria will get printed journal copies from Prof G. O. Ozumba at the Department of Philosophy, University of Calabar, Nigeria. Authors who live in other countries should send their requests to jihumanism@ediomsric.com. If you want your copy to be delivered to a private address, please let us know in time.

If you need further clarification or help with preparing your article for publication, please contact us via jihumanism@ediomsric.com.

Table of Contents

International Journal of Integrative Humanism Vol 9. No 1. June 2018. ISSN: 2026 – 6286

Humanism, Human Dignity and the Right to Die: A Critical Ethical Analysis

Paul Appiah-Sekyere[1]

Department of Religion and Human Values, University of Cape Coast, Ghana
Email: nkasp2@yahoo.com

Abstract

Given the various abuses to human dignity in our contemporary times, a discussion that deals with respect for the dignity of humans has significant importance. Without respect for human dignity, the quest for human well-being risks ending up as a mere wishful thinking. Humanism`s endeavour to promote human dignity is a very laudable idea. However, there seems to be a contradiction for Humanism to promote human dignity and concurrently allow the right to die through euthanasia, and suicide. This paper, critically analyses this apparent contradiction in Humanism`s attempt to promote Human dignity whiles endorsing the right to die.

Keywords: *Humanism, Human dignity, Right to die, Suicide, euthanasia*

Introduction

One of the current issues bothering the mind in contemporary society is the rate at which human dignity is disrespected and degraded. Human dignity is increasingly at risk. Humanity has witnessed terrible events such as wars, slave trade, civil un-rests; terrorist attacks coupled with environmental degradation in several parts of the globe that threaten human dignity.[2] There are undeniable cases of abuse of the fundamental human rights of people and constant violations of the dignity of humans on daily basis in different parts of the world.

In fact, over the years, humans have developed ideas and theories that will help liberate us and restore human dignity.[3] One of such theories that endeavours to promote human dignity and human well-being is Humanism.[4] Some critics, such as Dukor, argue that Humanism without theism loses more than half of its values pursuing human dignity; and that to be really human, one must have one's beginning and end in God. Thus, humanity and deity are inseparably related (Dukor, 2010).

This paper endeavours to analyse Humanism`s efforts to promote human dignity while accepting the right to die.

Definition of Terms

Different people have defined Humanism differently. However, each definition captures the basic principles and stance of Humanism.[5] The following are a few of the definitions. The American Humanist Association (AHA) is of the view that "Humanism is a progressive life stance that, without supernaturalism, affirms our ability and responsibility to lead meaningful, ethical lives capable of adding to the greater good of humanity."[6]

Humanism, according to the International Humanist and Ethical Union, (IHEU) is a democratic and ethical life stance which affirms that human beings have the right and responsibility to give meaning and shape to their own lives. It stands for the building of a humane society through an ethics-based on human and other natural values in a spirit of reason and free inquiry through human

---

[1]Paul Appiah-Sekyere, Ph.D., Department of Religion and Human Values, University of Cape Coast, Ghana. Main research fields: Ethics, Humanism, Religion, Poverty, Environment. Email: nkasp2@yahoo.com.

[2]For instance Paul Kurtz and Edwin H. Wilson also affirm this fact in the following way, "Nazism has shown the depths of brutality of which humanity is capable. Other totalitarian regimes have suppressed human rights ….." See Kurtz, P. and Wilson, E. H. (1973). *Humanist Manifesto II*, Preface.

[3] Edward Shills describes this as a deep primordial experience of being alive, the fear and awe of extinction. See Shills, E. (1968). The Sanctity of Life in *Life or death, ethics and options*. Labby, D. H. (ed.). Seattle, University of Washington Press, pp. 2-38.

[4]Cf. The American Humanist Association, (1973). *Humanist Manifesto II*, fifth article which states that "The preciousness and dignity of the individual person is a central humanist value."

[5] See Appiah-Sekyere, P. (20…). Humanist ethics: Its relevance for Ghana today, in*Integrative Humanist Journal*, p. 3.

[6]See http://www.americanhumanist.org

capabilities. It is not theistic, and it does not accept supernatural views of reality.[7]

Defining Humanism, the Bristol Humanist Group says, "Humanism is an approach to life based on reason and our common humanity, recognizing that moral values are properly founded on human nature and experience alone."[8] Paul Kurtz (2000) is regarded as the father of secular Humanism. He sees Humanism as a eupraxophy. For Kurtz, eupraxophy is derived from the following root words: eupraxis and sophia. Eu is a prefix that means "good," "well" or "advant-ageous." Praxis refers to "action or practice. Eupraxia means "right action" or "good conduct". The suffix sophia is derived from sophos ("wise") and means "wisdom". Humanism as a eupraxophy is a philosophy of good and wise action. In Humanism, the action is not only good and wise but also philosophical, scientific, and ethical (Kurtz, 2000).

Human Dignity

Dignity is a word for "worth or value". Thomas Aquinas in his Thomistic synthesis asserts that dignity/value is imbedded in substance, an objective reality distinct from, though related to, any subjective reaction to it. The honour due dignity does not lie in the object, but it is a reaction to some excellence in that object of honour (Aquinas I-II, q.2). Human dignity therefore is intrinsic, inherent or innate worth in every human being.[9]

This intrinsic and innate dignity is also implied in Kant's categorical imperative, "Any action that can be universalized can be accepted as ethical… Act only on the maxim whereby thou canst at the same time will that it should become a universal law."[10]

The humanist quest to safeguard human dignity and the well-being of the human person is a central core of the stance of Humanism. A lot of the teaching of Humanism on human dignity can be found in the Manifestoes. These documents spell out the vision and the mission of Humanism. For an example, Humanism asserts that

> Using technology wisely, we can control our environment, conquer poverty, markedly reduce disease, extend our lifespan, significantly modify our behavior, alter the course of human evolution and cultural development, unlock the vast new power, and provide humankind with unparalleled opportunity for achieving an abundant and meaningful life.[11]

In fact, Humanism stands for human dignity and the great importance of human life here and now. "Humanism further affirms that human life has meaning because we create and develop our futures. Happiness and the creative realization of human needs and desires, individually and in shared enjoyment, are continuous themes of Humanism. Humanists strive for the good life, here and now. The goal is to pursue life's enrichment despite debasing forces of vulgarization, commercialization and dehumanization."[12]

In 1933, a group of thirty-four liberal humanists in the United States defined and drafted the first Humanist manifesto which was concerned with expressing a general philosophical outlook that rejected orthodox and dogmatic positions and provided meaning and direction, unity and purpose to human life. It was also committed to reason, science, and democracy (Kurtz, 1973). The first Humanist manifesto reflected the general optimism of the time immediately after the First World War. Humanism was convinced that humans are capable and the sole determinants of the present and future destiny of humanity.

In summary, the first Humanist manifesto dealt with 15 major themes of Humanism. It affirmed that the universe is self-existing and not created; that man is a result of a continuous natural evolutionary process; that the human mind is a projection of the body; that there is nothing supernatural; that man has outgrown religion and any idea of God; that man's goal is the development of his own personality, which ceases to exist at death; that man will continue to develop to the point where he will look within himself and to the natural world for the solution to his problems; that all institutions and/or religions that in some way impede this "human well-being" are not serving the interest of humanity.[13]

The denigrating events of the Second World War, coupled with the numerous atrocities against

[7]Cf. http://www.iheu.org/amsterdamdeclaration

[8]Cf. http://www.nfuu.org/definitionsofhumanism.htm

[9]See United Nations,(1948). Universal Declaration of Human rights, preamble. Accessed on 17/07/2017. Retrieved from http://www.un.org/events/humanrights/2007/hrphotos/declaration%20 eng.pdf

[10]Cf. Christian, J. L. (1998). *Philosophy: An introduction to the art of wondering*. California: Harcourt Brace College Publishers, p. 307.On the categorical character of the moral demand See Peschke, K. H. (1996). *Christian ethics: Moral theology in the light of Vatican II, Vol. I*, Bangalore: Theological Publications, pp. 53-57.

[11]See The American Humanist Association, (1973). *Humanist Manifesto II*, Preface.

[12]The American Humanist Association, (1973). *Humanist Manifesto II*, third article.

[13]SeeThe American Humanist Association, (1973). *Humanist Manifesto II*, first article.

human dignity presented another set of heinous challenges to humanity.[14] Humanism issued a second manifesto in 1973. There are 17 propositions contained in the second manifesto. These propositions can be grouped under six themes, namely, religion, ethics, the individual, democratic society, world community and humanity as a whole.[15]

In the second manifesto, the Humanists affirmed that traditional theism, especially faith in the prayer-hearing God that is believed to love and care for persons, to hear and understand our prayers, and to be able to do something about them, is an unproved and outmoded faith. For them salvationism expressed in belief in everlasting life appears harmful, diverting people's attention from the present needs and challenges of this life here and now, while creating false hopes of heaven hereafter.[16]

According to Humanism, for humanity to survive, it requires bold and daring measures. Humans need to extend the uses of scientific method not renounce them, to fuse reason with compassion in order to build constructive social and moral values. Furthermore, for Humanists, humanity is confronted by many possible futures and we must decide which one to pursue. The ultimate goal, however, should be the fulfillment of the potential for growth in each human personality, not for the favoured few but for all humankind since only a shared world and global measures will suffice.[17]

A Humanist outlook will tap the creativity of each human being and provide the vision and courage for humans to work together. These outlooks emphasize the role human beings can play in their own spheres of action. The decades ahead call for dedicated, clear- minded men and women able to marshal the will, intelligence, and cooperative skills for shaping a desirable future. Humanism claims that it can provide the purpose and inspiration that so many people seek; it can give personal meaning and significance to human life (Kurtz, 1973).

The discussion above gives us an insight into the vision of Humanism. The dignity of the individual person is a central humanist value. According to Humanism,

The preciousness and dignity of the individual person is a central humanist value. Individuals should be encouraged to realize their own creative talents and desires. We reject all religious, ideological, or moral codes that denigrate the individual, suppress freedom, dull intellect, and dehumanize personality. We believe in maximum individual autonomy consonant with social responsibility. Although science can account for the causes of behavior, the possibilities of individual *freedom of choice* exist in human life and should be increased.[18]

In line with human dignity, Humanism abhors all kinds of discrimination be it religious, tribal, racial and the like.[19] Certainly, this is a noble and profound rational vision. However, some worrying questions can be raised to offer Humanism a further opportunity to respond to these issues for perhaps the education and edification of humanity as well as provide additional justification and substantiation for the tenets of Humanism.

Among the worrying issues that seem to undermine Humanism's promotion of human dignity is the humanist stance on the right to die, "... The individual's right to die with dignity, euthanasia, and the right to suicide."[20] This position, namely, the "right to die with dignity, euthanasia and the right to suicide" is a stance of Humanism that creates a delicate debate. How can one promote human dignity and at the same time claim that killing oneself is ethically right? This seems to be a controversial paradox that deserves a critical ethical examination, rationalization and justification.

The right to die

The term *right* can be understood from varied perspectives.[21] If *right* is considered from the ethical concept of *oughtness*, then the following two meanings can be identified, namely, *right* as that which is morally good (how I *ought* to act); and *right* as that which is opposed to wrong (how others *ought* to act towards me, thus right as a correlative of duty).[22]

Fagothey (1959) further opines that

---

[14]Cf. footnote 2 above.

[15]Cf. The American Humanist Association, (1973). *Humanist Manifesto II*, first to seventeenth articles and closing.

[16]The American Humanist Association, (1973). *Humanist Manifesto II*, Preface.

[17]Cf. The American Humanist Association, (1973). *Humanist Manifesto II*, Preface. See also Lamont, C.

(1997). The philosophy of Humanism. (Eight Edition). Amherst, New York, Humanist Press, p. 317.

[18] See The American Humanist Association, (1973). *Humanist Manifesto II*, fifth article; See also *Humanist Manifesto II*, in Lamont, C. (1997). The

philosophy of Humanism. (Eight Edition). Amherst, New York, Humanist Press, pp. 320-321.

[19]Cf. The American Humanist Association, (1973). *Humanist Manifesto II*, eleventh article.

[20] Cf. The American Humanist Association, (1973). *Humanist Manifesto II*, seventh article.

[21]For a *more* comprehensive understanding of rights, see Fagothey, A. (1959). *Right and reason: Ethics in theory and practice based on the teachings of Aristotle and St. Thomas Aquinas*. Rockford, Illinois: Tan Books and Publishers, INC., pp. 238-258.

[22]*Ibid*. 238.

in ethics *right* means that which squares with the norms of morality, and so is morally good. In this sense, it is equivalent to the Latin rectus, from which we derive such words as rectify, rectitude, erect, direct, correct... *Right* is also used as the equivalent of the Latin *jus*, from which we derive such words as just, justice, justify, jurist, juridical that, injure, perjure. In this sense, right means that which is just: a just law, just deed, just debt, just claim...[23]

For Humanism, an individual has the right to die with dignity through euthanasia and suicide.[24]Albeit some people may subscribe to Humanism's stance that suicide enables a person to leave this life with dignity, instead of enduring useless suffering, becoming a burden to others and, or to oneself, (especially in the situation of a disgraceful and dishonorable disease such as mental disorder, or HIV/AIDS), the other side of the coin needs to be considered. For instance, a cure[25] may be discovered after one has killed oneself. The hope for a better tomorrow is a great moral value in human life.[26]

Furthermore, some people argue that suicide can be utilized as a form of protest against social injustice. But are there no alternatives or better avenues for responding to injustice than to kill oneself?

From another perspective, some may argue that it is the individual's prerogative to assess one's life and acknowledge the worth or otherwise of one's life. Actually, it is morally unacceptable for the individual to be a law to himself/herself, making his/her own rules and values (including the value or worth of his/her life or another person's life). Is it justifiable for one to be an arbiter to oneself? If this is the case, then moral values will be subjective and thereby lose their objective and universal characteristics.[27]

Next, is it ethically right for the individual to claim that he/she is free to do whatever he/she pleases? Even to take one's life? Is freedom a life without limits? True freedom has limits such as respect for the rights and freedom of others as affirmed by the United Nations Universal Declaration of Human Rights as follows:

> In the exercise of his rights and freedoms, everyone shall be subject only to such limitations as are determined by law solely for the purpose of securing due recognition and respect for the rights and freedoms of others and of meeting the just requirements of morality, public order and the general welfare in a democratic society.[28] This implies that an individual is morally obliged to examine his/her action whether or not the effect of the said action will be for the good of the community/society or not. Deductively then, "those who kill themselves because they believe this will benefit others are following an exaggerated sense of moral obligation, while at the same time they are failing to fulfill their social obligations to continue to participate in the life of the community.[29]

Albeit some philosophers[30] such as the Stoics, Epicureans and agnostics saw suicide as permissible, generally monotheistic religions such as "Judaism, Christianity and Islam have always opposed suicide ... because they regard life as God's gift..."[31]

Those who do not belong to any religion, notwithstanding possible philosophical and ideological differences, are aware of the rights of the human person. Among these rights is each person's first and fundamental right to life. Recourse to arguments that deny the universal value of these rights ultimately undermines the good of the human community. Human life is seen as the basis of all

---

[23]*Ibid.*, p. 239.

[24] See the American Humanist Association, (1973). *Humanist Manifesto II,* seventh article.

[25]Humanism expresses a lot of hope in human reason, intelligence and science. The American Humanist Association, (1973). *Humanist Manifesto II,* fourth article.

[26]See Ashley, B. M. & O'Rourke, K. D. (1982). *Health care ethics: A theological analysis.* St. Louis: Catholic Health Association of the United States, pp. 327-379.

[27]For Kant, an action is ethical or morally right if it can be universalized. Cf. Christian, J. L. (1998). *Philosophy: An introduction to the art of wondering.* California: Harcourt Brace College Publishers, pp. 305-307, 420.

[28]See United Nations, (1948). *Universal declaration of human rights,* Article 29, section 2. Retrieved on 17/07/2017from http://www.un.org/events/humanrights/2007/hrphotos /declaration%20 eng.pdf

[29]Ashley, B. M. & O'Rourke, K. D. (1982). *Op. Cit.,* p. 378.

[30]Some philosophers, such as Plato and Kant oppose suicide. While the former regarded "suicide as a rejection of duty to one's body, to the community of which the person is a part, and to God who gave the person life," the latter, Kant, "argued that suicide is the greatest of crimes because it is a man's rejection of morality itself, since man must be his own moral lawgiver...." Ashley, B. M. & O'Rourke, K. D. (1982). *Op. Cit.,* p. 376.

[31]For Christians, Christ, (his life, death and resurrection) has given a new meaning to human existence and especially to the death of a Christian. Cf. Ashley, B. M. & O'Rourke, K. D. (1982). *Op. Cit.,* p. 376. Furthermore, in accordance with what St. Paul says: "If we live, we live to the Lord, and if we die, we die to the lord; so then, whether we live or whether we die, we are the Lord's" (Romans 14:8 NRSV). Therefore, the deliberate taking of one's life or the life of an innocent person is incompatible with this faith in Christ. Even if one is not a Christian, for example African Traditional Religion believers, to profess a God/Supreme Being who is a creator and provider and lord of life implies that the lofty dignity of every human person and the respect for each person and his life have some reference to that Creator. In this context then the deliberate destruction of one's life connotes a rejection of God's gift of life and his love which comes with this gift. For an example, among Akans, one who kills himself proclaims himself an enemy of everybody. He refuses to confide in anybody in times of difficulty. Suicide therefore is an anti-social act... anyone who commits suicide cannot be regarded as an ancestor and his/her name will never be passed on to any child at a naming ceremony. Hence, African Traditional Religion believers also abhor suicide, see Sarpong, P. (1974).

goods and therefore, it is the necessary source and condition of every human activity and of all society.

With reference to the Slippery Slope argument, one can posit that if the right to die, as suggested by the humanists is endorsed, it can lead to an irreversible situation that will not be in the interest of humanity. For example, if in a family of five, A, B, C, D and E, A decides to exercise his right to die through suicide or euthanasia and B also follows suit, and likewise C and D and E, what will be the ultimate end of the said family if not extinction? If this example is expanded to cover a whole community or village, town, city, nation and the entire human family, one can deduce that the right to die may not ultimately benefit humanity.

From a further perspective, one can argue that even if people may have genuine reasons[32] to exercise their right to commit suicide, the risk is that this can set a volatile precedence and as a result, other humans without similar genuine reasons may also end up taking their lives until the situation ends up in an irreversible disaster for humanity. Hence, to prevent a possible slippery slope whose consequences will ultimately not be in the interest of humanity, Humanism will need to review its stance on the right to suicide and euthanasia.

According to Boss (1999, p. 269), it is better for ten guilty men to go free than for one innocent man to be unjustly convicted. In other words, it will be a lesser evil to deny humans the right to suicide and euthanasia than to permit the said right and end up in an irreversible disaster for humanity, including innocent people. Furthermore, Boss (1999) unequivocally affirms "Justice requires that rights to avoid the worse of the two evils be honored first, before others come into play."[33] One can deduce from the analysis of Boss that the denial of the right to suicide and euthanasia is a lesser evil compared to its opposite.

Evaluation

Humanism has introduced to us a new worldview, a new social and moral order. Unlike Christianity and other religions that promote human dignity but do not endorse the right to die, Humanism promotes human dignity, freedom and liberty while permitting the right to die through euthanasia and suicide.[34] Will this right to kill oneself not result in creating unbridled immoral behaviours after which one will evade or escape being held responsible for one's actions by killing oneself?

For Humanism, man is the measure of all things.[35] Man, not God, is the determiner of reality, meaning and ethics (Geisler, 1982). With reference to suicide/assisted suicide, for example, how does Humanism respond to the pain, trauma, unexpected shock, disgrace, and loss experienced by the community, loved ones or family members of the suicider?

In another perspective, considering the emotional, psychological, social etc. impact of suicide on the loved ones of the suicider, one can argue that even if the suicider is exercising his freedom or right to live or die, if and only if the suicider would consider the afore-mentioned impact on his loved ones, family or community[36] then he/she may not commit suicide. In this light, the exercise of the freedom/right to suicide/euthanasia would not be considered an absolute freedom/right but a limited one. In other words, my right to commit suicide is not absolute because my child also has a right to parental care which is my moral responsibility.

Actually, in terms of morality, one ought not to act in a way that the action will bring pain, suffering and the like to others.[37] If one's action such as suicide relieves one from pain and suffering but the said act also inflicts pain and suffering on one's relatives, family, community and loved ones, how justifiable is such an act which relieves the subject's pain and causes similar pain to others? In this context, suicide appears to be a form of egoism or self-centeredness. This undermines Humanism which promotes altruism[38] and not egoism and self-centeredness.

In another perspective, the right to die expressed through suicide or euthanasia may be seen as something in accordance with respect for one's autonomy and one's freedom of choice as claimed by Humanism. Thus, one can choose to live or die, (to be part of society or reject it). The same Humanism also claims that everybody is important in society, meaning society needs each person. This appears

---

[32]This argument is porous if one questions who determines the yardstick for measuring the so called "genuine reasons."

[33]Boss, J. (1999). *Analyzing moral issues*. California: Mayfield Publishing Company, p. 270.

[34]For a more comprehensive understanding of the arguments for and against suicide and euthanasia, cf. Ashley, B. M. & O'Rourke, K. D. (1982). *Op. Cit.*, pp. 375-388.

[35]Protagoras the father of Humanism who claimed "that man is the measure of all thing..." See Geisler, N. L. (1989). *Christian ethics*. Grand Rapids, MI: Baker Book, p.18.

[36] For instance, the famous Greek philosopher, Plato argued that suicide is a rejection of duty to one's body, to the community of which the person is a part..." See Ashley, B. M. & O'Rourke, K. D. (1982). *Op. Cit.*, p. 376.

[37]For Kant's categorical imperative cf. Christian, J. L. (1998). *Op. Cit.* p. 305; See also Olen, J. and Barry, V. (1992). *Applying ethics*. Belmont, California: Wadsworth Publishing Company, p. 31.

[38]For the altruistic nature of Humanist ethical values, see The American Humanist Association, (1973). *Humanist Manifesto II*, "A humanist outlook will tap the creativity of each human being and provide the vision and courage for us to work together," preface; "Happiness and creative realization of human needs and desires, individually and in shared enjoyment, are continuous themes of Humanism," third article ; "We are concerned for the welfare of the aged, the infirm, the disadvantaged, ... humanize personal relations," eleventh article; "We must learn to live openly together or we shall perish together," seventeenth article; Cf. also "The Humanist combines self-interest with altruism. The Humanist wants to preserve his/her own life as well as the lives of his/her fellow humans," Lamont, C. (1980). The affirmative of Humanism, in *The Humanist Magazine, Vol. 4*, 2, March-April, pp. 4-5.

to be self-contradictory since to decide to kill oneself is to deny one's family, friends and society of one's company, contribution, presence, love and the like.

In fact, for humanists to dismiss the God factor, it becomes more difficult to employ only human reason to substantiate human dignity. Actually, the transcendental perspective of human dignity reinforces its promotion, substantiation and justification. To deny this transcendental dimension renders it extremely difficult to substantiate and prioritise the lofty and inviolable dignity due humans.

In a similar sense, St. Thomas Aquinas cogently argues that since God is the source and ground for all human values and thus human dignity (Aquinas, I, 892), any attempt to pursue the well-being of man in its totality outside God or without reference to God, may be doomed to failure. Affirming the transcendental factor in human dignity, John Paul II emphatically states that *"the root of modern totalitarianism is to be found in the denial of the transcendent dignity of the human person who, as the visible image of the invisible God, is therefore by his very nature the subject of rights which no one may violate – no individual, group, class, nation or state."*[39]

It is very significant therefore for Dukor (2010) to assert "that humanism without theism loses more than half of its values" pursuing human dignity… In fact, the belief in a Supreme Being's role in human life reinforces the dignity due humans. To detach the Supreme Being factor from human life and human dignity may be tantamount to detaching the worth/value that intrinsically belongs to humans.

From the aforementioned analysis, one can deduce that a God factor in human life is very crucial in discussing human dignity. Therefore, any life outside God or any attempt to understand humanity fully outside God will end up in meaninglessness and futility. For Dukor (2010) then, when life ends in futility and meaninglessness, it loses its dignity.

Conclusion

There is no gainsaying the fact that respect for human dignity cannot be overemphasized in our contemporary times given the various abuses purported by humans against humans. It is also worth noting that without respect for the dignity of humans, the quest for human well-being can seriously be undermined and may end up as a mere wishful thinking without the hope of its realization.

Humanists' attempt at promoting human dignity is therefore a very significant step in the right direction. However, as discussed above, this Humanist attempt is a quest in futility given the logic of atheistic humanism. This paper therefore agrees with Dukor (2010) "that humanism without theism loses more than half of its values" pursuing human dignity. In fact, the belief in a Supreme Being's role in human life reinforces the dignity due humans.[40] Perhaps one of the greatest miracles to be witnessed by humanity would be for all humans to acknowledge, accept and treat each other as human beings with human dignity while disassociating humanity and deity.

Hence, this paper is of the view that it is extremely difficult and self-undermining (almost "suicidal") for Humanism to affirm and promote human dignity and simultaneously reject the supernatural component or factor in humans while endorsing the right to kill oneself.

Probably, Humanism's staunch effort or zeal to promote human dignity, and further defend and protect the individual's life from being destroyed[41] by another person (single or group) with more power, Humanism resorts to placing the power to take one's life in the hands of the individual himself/herself and no one else. If this is the case, then it may be convincing to affirm that the dignity of each human being is so precious that no one should temper with it, except the individual himself/herself. In this context, it may be seen as a "just claim," (right in terms of *jus*) for one to assert that the right to live/die should belong to the individual and not society nor anyone else. However, it is not "morally right" (right in terms of *rectus*) for one to kill oneself since one's life is in relation to other humans and the effect of killing oneself is not only on the suicider but also on the living relatives especially the suicider's loved ones.

References

Abbagnano, N. (1967). Humanism. In *Encyclopedia of Philosophy* (Vol. 4). New York: Macmillan and Free Press.

Adler, M. (1973). *The difference of man and the difference it makes.* Downers Grove, IL: Intervarsity Press.

---

[39]*Cf. John Paul II, (1993). Encyclical letter: Veritatis splendor, The splendour of truth. Vatican City: Libreria Editrice Vaticana, p. 99.*

[40]All people, without any distinction as to sex, race, or social position, can say that Genesis 1:26-27 speaks of them. All people are created equal and are called to share, according to their capacities, in this dominion over the earth. In the perspective of Genesis, this is the deep root of human dignity and the respect. That is due to all human beings. Cf. **HAMEL, E. (1989). The Foundations of Human Rights in Biblical Theology Following the Orientations of *Gaudium et spes*, in LATOURELLE,R. (Ed.), *Vatican II assessment and perspectives,* Vol. Two., New York/Mahwah: Paulist Press, p. 461.**

[41]As it happened in World War 1 and World War 2; See also other threats to human dignity such as the slave trade and Nazism. Cf. footnote 2above.

Appiah-Sekyere, P. (2011). Humanist ethics: Its relevance for Ghana today, in *Integrative Humanist Journal*, pp. 1-14.

Aquinas, T. (1892). *Summa theologica,* Vol. 1. Rome: Leonine.

Ashley, B. M. & O'Rourke, K. D. (1982). *Health care ethics: A theological analysis.* St. Louis: Catholic Health Association of the United States.

Battin, M. P., "The Case for euthanasia," in Boss, A. J. (1999). *Analyzing moral issues.* California: Mayfield Publishing Company.

Boss, J. (1999). *Analyzing moral issues.* California: Mayfield Publishing Company.

Christian, J. L. (1998). *Philosophy: An introduction to the art of wondering.* California: Harcourt Brace College Publishers.

Dukor, M. (2010).*Theistic humanism of African philosophy.* Germany: Lambert Academic Publishing.

Fagothey, A. (1959). *Right and reason: Ethics in theory and practice based on the teachings of Aristotle and St. Thomas Aquinas.* Rockford, Illinois: Tan Books and Publishers, INC.

Geisler, N. (1982). *Is man the measure? An evaluation of contemporary Humanism.* Grand Rapids, MI: Baker Book House.

Geisler, N. L. (1989). *Christian ethics.* Grand Rapids, MI: Baker Book.

Peschke, K. H. (1996). *Christian ethics: Moral theology in the light of Vatican II, Vol. I,* Bangalore: Theological Publications.

Sarpong, P. (1974).*Ghana in retrospect: Some aspects of Ghanaian culture,* (reprint 2006). Accra: Ghana Publishing Corporation.

Shills, E. (1968). The sanctity of life, in Labby, D. H. (ed.), *Life or death, ethics and options.* Seattle: University of Washington Press, pp. 2-38.

United Nations (1948). Universal Declaration of Human rights, preamble. Accessed on 17/07/2017. Retrieved from http://www.un.or g/events/humanrights/2007/hrphotos/declarat ion%20 eng.pdf

http://www.americanhumanist.org

http://www.iheu.org/amsterdamdeclaration

http://www.nfuu.org/definitionsofhumanism.htm

Hamel, E. (1989). The Foundations of Human Rights in Biblical Theology Following the Orientations of *Gaudium et spes,* in Latourelle, R. (Ed.), *Vatican II assessment and perspectives,* Vol. Two. New York/Mahwah: Paulist Press.

John Paul II, (1993). Encyclical letter: Veritatis splendor, (The splendour of truth). Vatican City: Libreria Editrice Vaticana.

Kurtz, P. (1973). *Humanist manifesto I and II.* Buffalo: NY Prometheus Books.

Kurtz, P. (2000). *Embracing the power of Humanism.* New York: Row-man &Littlefield Publishers Inc.

Lamont, C. (1980). The affirmative of Humanism, in *The Humanist Magazine, Vol. 4,* 2, March-April, pp. 4-5.

Lamont, C. (1997). The philosophy of Humanism. (Eight Edition). Amherst, New York, Humanist Press.

McDowell, J. (1983). *Handbook of today's religions: Secular human-ism.* New York: Amazon Publishers.

Olen, J. and Barry, V. (1992). *Applying ethics.* Belmont, California: Wadsworth Publishing Company.

Pascal, B. (1894). *Thoughts on religion and philosophy.* Edinburgh: John Grant.

Integrative African Metaphysics

Professor G. O. Ozumba

Department of Philosophy, University of Calabar. Email: goddyozumba@yahoo.com

Abstract

Metaphysics is the encapsulation of reality. It is all embracing and all denoting. Metaphysics is one of the central branches of philosophy that is concerned with reality, existence and their multidimensional constitution and nature. Reality is both physically and spiritually immanent and transcendent, corporeal and incorporeal. This means that metaphysics should be studied in its essentialist, existentialist, phenomenological, religious (theological) psychological, sociological and relational ambience. We are interested in understanding the omni-comprehensiblity of the universe and entire reality. To have a full view of reality we must do so in their omni-dimensionality in essence, relations and evidence. This is why we are saying that African metaphysics can only be fully studied from the integrative perspective. The African uniquely views, reality from an all-encompassing, all-integrated whole. This is why we have identified "empirico-ratio-spiritocentricism" as the best metaphysical approach to the issue of African metaphysics and this is the view that is canvassed in this essay.

Keywords: *Integrative Metaphysics, African Metaphysics, existentialism, essentialism, phenomenology, psychology, cosmology, relationism and empirico-ratio-spiritocentricism.*

Introduction

African philosophers are called upon to maintain meaningful detachment from western metaphysical architecture. Though the metaphysical infrastructure may be similar but the overall metaphysical architecture cannot be seen. The chief reasons for this are obvious, namely; dissimilarities in worldview, in interpretation of reality arising from different existential experience, different cosmological, cultural, psychological and spiritual perceptions. Perception is key in those differences. It is like a gestalt switch where a lion can be seen as a tiger, hyena fox or zebra. Reality may remain the same largely in some areas but different in other areas. We can talk about similarities in material content but different in their formal characterization.

African metaphysical is both heterogeneous and homogenous. This means that the African has the capacity to keep disparate things disparate, this heterogeneity on the other hand he has the capacity and acumen to integrate reality and present an always seamless interconnectedness (interrelationship), between the physical and spiritual dimensions of reality (this is the harmonized view of reality). For the African, reality should not be viewed or conceived in its apertness but should be understood in their integratedness. This is why we have been advancing the philosophy of integrative humanism which we belief is the

way to go if we must make sense of the African metaphysical worldview.

African metaphysics is cosmological, socio-centric in relations, cultural, spiritual, physical and psychological. In our essay on African metaphysics, we discussed the African conception of such concepts as Being, potentiality and actuality, the cosmos, spiritual beings, God, divinities, spirit, ancestors, totems, reincarnation, soul, body, immortality, personhood, cause and effect, witchcraft, appearance and reality, oracles, communalism, substance, mystical experience, ancestral world, mediumism and religious mainstreaming from man through ancestors to the omnipotent God.

The above shows that mainstreaming African metaphysics must be done horizontally, man-ma, man-plant, man-animal, man-mineral world. We have vertical relationship which is man-physical, man-ideas, man-spiritual, man divinities (God of gods). Then we have crisscrossity of relations – this is mostly in the realm of ideas and spiritual trafficking. The African mind is very active, creative and inventing. This may not be wholly in the area of science and technology or in the western conception of it. But this is not to say that metaphysical potentiality of the African is limited to theory. The environmental needs of the Africans have always detected the direction to which his innate metaphysical energies are directed.

This explains why in craft, in smelting, farming implements, wrestling, dressing, dancing, war and hunting, the Africans have made their contributions and have displayed resilience by showing that the African can survive under very hard conditions.

Our attempt in this work is to examine in outline what constitutes the core issues as far as integrative African metaphysics is concerned. We examine some of the key concepts that are pivotal in understanding the point we are making, such concepts are metaphysics, African metaphysics, integrated African metaphysics, "empirico-ratio-spiritocentricism" in integrative African metaphysics. The relationship between causality, relations, soul, spirit, body and God have been examined.

Examination of Key Terms

Metaphysics as a philosophical term is always or in most cases defined from the background of Aristotle's conception. Metaphysics is said to have been coined by Andronicus of Rhodes who while chronicling the works of Aristotle named the corpus of works which came after those of physics as metaphysics. This means meta – after (physis), physics which as a whole means after physics. The contents of these corpus of works treated of such subjects as transcendental metaphysical realities. It is from this denotation that metaphysics has come to, be associated with ideas that are transcendental, spiritual, mystical, magical and astrological. The idea of the philosopher's stone that turns base metals into gold became the aspiration of metaphysical alchemists, metaphysics from this point gained notoriety as a branch of philosophy that is concerned with outlandish extra sensory, extra psychical and extra physical abstractions.

But this characterization is not true of what metaphysics is all about, though it deals with spiritual realities but it also deals with physical realities. Metaphysics deals with existences, objects, nature and attributes, substances, the essentials and the composition of these objects in their material and formal aspects. For example, it is the metaphysical dimension of science, that has driven science to probe into the nature of substances leading to the discovery of atoms by the atomists and subatomic particles by Einstein and his fellow-quantum physicists like Bohn, Planck, Heisenberg etc.

For Leibniz, he talked about monads as the most fundamental component of matter. We have currents of electricity and all the integral composition of nuclear physics, electromagnetic physics, particle, wave, and quantum physics. This is, to show how far metaphysicians have gone in their attempt to unravel the deep mysteries that enshroud reality either as physical or spiritual reality.

African Metaphysics

African metaphysics is African man's way of perceiving reality, decoding, denoting, interpreting or making sense out of what is presented in observation, feeling, introspected, dreamed, experienced and inspired Knowledge comes to the African through sense experience, ratiocination and extra sensory perception. There is dimension of knowledge which comes purely from intuition or through the pure light of the mind.

African metaphysics deals with the highlight, foresight and present sight with which the African interrogates the universe around him. Metaphysics is the outcome of man's clash with the environment and the entire universe with the perspectival discoveries that ensue from that clash or confrontation. Now, man begins to ask why am I here? What is my end? Of what purpose? What am I made up of? What am I made up of? Can I understand the universe? Can I control it? When will different seasons take their turn? How do I survive in this world into which I have been thrown? What are the reasons for all the created things water, air, fire, Earth, animals, plant, minerals? Why do men die? Is human soul mortal or immortal? Is there reincarnation? Do spirits exist? Do gods exist? Where does man fall into in the nexus of this humongous reality? This is why for the African, there is metaphysics about every conceivable thing whether physical or spiritual. He tries to understand the nexus between all things and tries to leave nothing to chance. Chance is the most dreaded phenomenon in the African metaphysics. Humans must not allow chance to cheat and overthrow them. All means possible must be sought to unravel all mysteries. This can be done through oracular, divinational, mystical, mediumistic, revelational means or by soothsaying or witchcraft, necromancy, spiritism or unceasing/unremitting investigations. The African world is concerned more about the phenomenon of survival than of conquest, comfort and relaxation. Though they had their cultural ways of releasing tension like dances, wrestling, cultural displays, competitions, and so on. African's lived a life of contentment and circumspection, rather than expansionism, and world conquest. This may have hamstrung the development of science and technology to the same frenzy as the west. With cozy and comfortable environment there was very little far overly scientific exploration and expedition of the unknown world or the deep world of matter.

Integrated African Metaphysics

African metaphysics is necessarily integrated. By this we mean that to have a holistic understanding of the African worldview we must perceive in an interconnected fashion. Many have seen this as the three-dimensional view of reality – that is body, soul and spirit. The world or universe is a continuum of interrelated causes and effects. Sometimes starting from the physical via physical to the spiritual and at other times start from the spirit via the psychological to the physical. An event in the physical reverberates until it gets to the spiritual and vice versa. To seek a wholly spiritual solution to a physical problem is anathema to the African. All avenues must be explored and exploited – the medical practitioner, the para-psychologist, the soothsayer, the spiritualist and the Witch are all involved in unraveling and providing cure for an ailment. Every aspect of reality is integral to the whole. To understand any piece of reality, we must do so from the three or multidimensional aspects of reality.

Empirico-Ratio-spiritocentricism

This is the key phrase or coinage underpinning all integrativist approaches to understanding reality. Empirico-represent the empirical-physical dimension, the ratio-represents the psychical and reasoning dimensions of reality while spiritocentricism has to do with the spiritual and transcendental dimensions of reality. In integrative humanism we outline the following

-    What is the nature of the problem
-    To what degree do we want to seek for solution – physical,   spiritual or   both?
-    What are the physical dimension of reality?
-    How do we apply the integrative method to explore, understand, explain   and   provide panacea?
-    How do we handle recalcitrant cases?
-    The resignation to ultimate authority as the end of the process.

Integrative metaphysics therefore has as *sine-qua-non* the momentous inquiry into the various aspects and dimensions of reality which embrace the tripartite nature of the human constitution as body, soul and spirit. This has led to the argument that African logic is three dimensional. We have explained our position in the text: (Njikoka: Further Discussions on the Philosophy of Integrative Humanism and Udo Etuk's Festschrift).

The Vital Role of Principle of Causality in Integrative African Philosophy

For the Africans the principle of cause and effect stand as the nexus that provide the thread of discernment, interrogation and inquiry into reality whether in the physical realm or the spiritual realm. The proof of the interconnectedness between the physical and the spiritual is traceable to the fact that in the phenomena of cause and effect Africans discover that in the event of an occurrence, at times the root is not traceable to physical causes. At times they end up with spiritual origin after they have exhausted the physical possibilities.

The cardinal streak in African ontological belief system is that "nothing happens without a cause". These are captured by such aphorisms as "if an animal is dancing at the middle of the road, then a drummer is near by". "A toad does not run in broad day light for nothing". "He that brings home ants infested firewood has willy-nilly, invited the lizards for unsolicited visit". "Any traditional sacrifice without vulture portends that all is not well in the land of the spirits". All these aphorisms indicate that nothing happens without a cause. The principle of causality runs through the epistemology, metaphysics, science, spiritually, psychology and ethics of African people. This shows the principal place the principle of causality occupies in our entire epistemological and metaphysical schema. The principle of causality helps us to explore existences, relations, the essence, the nature and attributes of things. It helps us to discern the potency and importance of discrete existent things depending on how they are able to affect or are affected by other things.

For example, there are certain objects, trees, plants, rivers, places, artefacts that are highly valued in the African ontological scheme of things. Examples are kolanut, bitter kola, moringa "Dogon yaro, Agulu lake, Arochukwu Oracle shrine, native chicken, Alligator pepper, etc. These objects, things or places symbolize peace, healing, mystical power, etc. We are talking about all these because metaphysical beliefs are the thread with which the African ontology is sewn and are the principles that undergird why we do what we do and hold certain beliefs. To understand the life style, culture of the African people we must understand the whole architecture of belief system, the principle of cause and effect and the reasons why we project, relate, avoid, pursue, emphasise certain actions at the expense of others.

We have been able to hint that the principle of causality is very central to the entire African metaphysical architecture. African metaphysics is therefore "spirito-humano and ratio-centric". Cause and effect cannot be explained away because of want of physical evidence. Where physical evidence is lacking a spiritual evidence will be contrived.

Understanding Cosmology Psychology and Theology in Integrative African Metaphysics

Cosmology is the study of the cosmos, to wit, the universe. The universe remains at the centre of man's existence, inquiry and attention. To gain mastery over the universe, the African man displayed deep interest in the knowledge of the universe including the flora and the fauna of the universe.

Cosmology is the scientific study of the universe and its origin and development (Oxford Dictionary 329). In the words of Ikenga Metuh, Igbo traditional worldview embraces the totality of Igbo world of human experience which is seen as fluid, coherent with spirits, men, animals, plants and the elements are engaged in continuous interaction. The invisible and visible realms of reality shade into and mutually influence each other (Metuh 1-3). For Uzodimma Nwala the Igbo cosmology consists of the complex of beliefs, habits, laws, customs and traditions of a people. It includes the overall picture they have about reality, the universe, life and existence. (Nwala.26). The cosmos for the Africans is a huge and complex but interrelated mechanism that is sustained on the principles of deism and theism. God has created an intricate and an internected machine with part of it ordered with a mixture of dynamism and fixity and the other parts continually subject to the mechanistic control of the Almighty God – called Chukwu Okike in Igbo, "Onyankopon" in (Ghana) and so on. We have other line of beings in the pantheon of spirits that populate the earth. The entire cosmos according to Metuh will include the Earth, the Sky, the Seas (streams, rivers, water, bodies) forests, plants, animals. All these constituents of the cosmos are composed of spiritual forces. we have stones, running waters, trees, are said to constitute spirits, powers, forces, etc. What the African does is to learn through inspiration, intuition, experience, trial and error, mystical insight and revelation on how to harness, manipulate, reorganize and apply the forces in order to achieve the overall harmony necessary for peaceful existence on the Earth.

There is the integrated use of the mind (psychology), and how the mind is deployed to worship God (theology) in order to get protection, provision, preservation, direction, leadership, control of the forces of nature. Through worship, God, the spirits, deities are moved to come to the aid of man. There is therefore the interplay of cosmology, psychology and theology in man's existence. Understanding the laws, principles and nature of cosmos through the application of the mind's (intellect's) abilities through divine help opens up the secret of the universe to man and makes it possible for him to exercise some existential control over the cosmos.

Metaphysics is an aspect of philosophy which is concerned with providing us with an overview of the architech tonics of all that exist. Quine calls it "all there is", Russell calls it "appearance and reality". G. E. Moore calls it the "common world of sense experience", the Igbo call it "Uwa" ((the world) and Pantaleon Iroegbu calls it "uwa-ontology", all that exist in the world.

Important Cultural Beliefs in Integrated African Metaphysics Reincarnation

From what we have seen so far, metaphysics is a philosophical framework that reveals "all that there is" and thein interconnectedness one with another. It gives us the picture of the web of integration among things. It helps to know the things that exist, why they exist, what their natures are and how they are related one with another. The entire outlay enables man to know how to live his life in harmony with all existent beings. It embraces the rules, regulations, laws, guidelines, programmes, pathways that man must tread in order to master the laws of nature, know the usefulness of all that exist and how to understand them in order to harness their usefulness.

This is why the concept of reincarnation is part of the aftermath of a vigorous understanding of what revealed truth for the African is. The Africans believe that life is an endless continuum of birth and rebirth. Children are born, die at old age, given full burial rites, return to the world of ancestors and then return to the earth through new born babes. This cycle of birth and rebirth which the Hindus call "Samsara" is called "reincarnation". However, only those who fulfilled the requirements for reincarnation are allowed by the gods to reincarnate. The living must live a good life, be a titled man, have children, die at old age, given full burial rites. The theory of reincarnation reinforces moral beliefs and propriety. It tells us that life is not a onetime affair. There are other beings entitled to reincarnate. The Ogbanje's (Abiku) children, children who are possessed by malevolent spirit who torture parents by untimely circle of death at each arrival through birth.

Witchcraft is the practice of wickedness through the manipulation of a wicked spirit that inhabits a person. A person so inhabited becomes willy nilly an agent serving as a medium for the perpetration of wicked acts like killing, sucking of blood, aborting, pregnancy and causing accidents. The atrocities are endless. The person so possessed can be delivered through exorcisim by powerful "dibias" (native doctors) or delivered by anointed ministers of God.

Witchcraft as the name goes is also a craft which can be used for good deeds. Because of extra ordinary endowments, witchcrafts practitioners (can heal the sick). Witches can discover things that can be useful to mankind.

Immortality of the Soul

Immortality of the soul is another pillar in the metaphysical architecture of the Africans. The Africans as a follow-up from reincarnation believe that the soul of man/woman is immortal. The concept of immortality holds that the soul does not die, continues to live after the physical death of the body. For the Africans the soul is the real man in man. The concept of soul is often used interchangeably with spirit. However, in different African communities we may have minor or wide differences. While some view the concept of human PERSONALITY from dichotomistic perspective, others hold trichotomistic or, pentachomustic view. That is two, three and five dimensional views. Soul/spirit and body, soul, spirit and body, soul/spirit, body, spiritual component from the father and spiritual component from the mother.

However, we can reduce all to a dualistic reality of the physical and the spiritual. What is of interest to us is that man is made up of the earthy (dust) and of the godly, that is, the spirit. The spirit continues to exist after death. Most people of the earth hold this view except for those who think that man is a useless passion with no recourse to God who created man.

ANCESTOR WORSHIP is again part of the chain of reality running from immortality of souls. Ancestors are dead members of the society who by qualification are honourable and are said to continue to exist in the underworld from where they continue to play their innocuous role in guiding, protecting, providing, revealing privileged information to the living.

Ancestor worship is the reverence and sacrifice to dead ancestors in order to maintain the relationship they have with the living and to continue to implore them (the ancestors) to continue to fulfill their functions to their living relatives. The relative can sacrifice cocks, hens, children, goats, bits of food, kola nut, palm wine, hot drinks to this ancestors as a way of feeding them with what humans eat. In some cultures, some kings have people buried with them who continue to serve the kings in the great beyond.

Ancestor worship occupies a central place in African traditional religion. These ancestor sare called living dead because though dead physically are spiritually alive and play a role in the activities of the living. These ancestors can be consulted to know about mysteries, they can be manipulated through necromancy to kill and harm enemies.

Contemporary Syncretism

Today African metaphysics has become a hotchpotch of syncretism. We have a mixture of Christian metaphysics and African metaphysics. For instance, what the Roman Catholics call saints, the Africans call ancestors. What Catholics call purgatory is what the Africans call the ancestral underworld. What Africans call reincarnation, they call apparitions etc. The Africans hold that Africans who lived well are admitted into the world of ancestors which is somewhat like the place of Rest (heaven) of Christians. The Catholics pray to saints, and seek the intervention in the Virgin Mary, the same way the Africans seek the help of their ancestors.

However, the Pentecostals hold that the above parallels drawn between Christian and African Metaphysics are unacceptable. They hold that there is nothing like reincarnation because it is appointed unto men once to die and after that is the judgment. There is no place for dead saints interceding for the living. Only Jesus remains our intercessor and High Priest. The soul of man remains immortal in both Christian and African metaphysics, however, life after death exists for different reasons. While the wicked go to hell, the righteous go to heaven. It is important to keep these worldviews distinct to make rewarding deductions and analysis which yield to truth which better secures man's eternity.

Critical Analysis of African Metaphysics

A close analysis of African metaphysics has shown a very closely knit or interconnectedness among existent beings. There is hardly any break in the essentialism and existentialism of being whether as Dasein, Being in-itself, Being for-itself, whether physical or spiritual beings.

However, with better insight and better revelation, there are adjustments that need to be done. For example, the living dead (ancestors) do not automatically go to heaven except those who fulfilled the requirements for heavenly existence. Again, they do not interfere in the affairs of the living as believed in African metaphysics.

The belief that the spiritual dimension can be divined through oracles, diviners, fortune, tellers, witch doctors is not always true or exact. There exists the gap of the unknown which only the Almighty can supply because secret things belong to God but revealed things belong to man. There is therefore the need to streamline and fulfill African metaphysics through insightful modification through the revealing word of God. This will bring truth and fullness to the deep and rich surmises inherent in African metaphysics.

Conclusion

We have examined the entire gamut of African metaphysics. We have defined African metaphysics as the African's way of depicting his architecture of being, existence, essence, nature, possibilities, potentialities, visions, explanations, understandings of the entire gamut of reality. Reality includes cosmology, psychology, theology, culture, relationships and interpretations of these realities.

African worldview, African metaphysics means (Weltanchung) perception, meanings, interpretation of reality, understanding, culture, coordinated and integrated picture of the universe. It has to do with explaining of the whys, whats, hows and whens of existence.

We have shown that the best way of viewing African metaphysics is through integrated pigeonhole. Therefore, we describe African metaphysics as integrative metaphysics.

References

Anyacho, Ernest O. "Igbo Traditional Religion and Cosmology" in *Igbo Traditional Religion, Culture and Society.* Ed. Etim E. Okon. Calabar: Afri Pentecost Press, 2016.

Awolalu, Umosade J. Sacrifice in Yoruba Traditional Religion in African Traditional Religion and Philosophy. Ed. Etim, E. Okon, Calabar: University of Calabar Press, 2013.

Mbiti, John S. "The Nature, Works and Attributes of God in African Traditional Religion" in *African Traditional Religion and Philosophy* Ed. Etim E. Okon. Calabar: University of Calabar Press, 2013.

Metuh, Emefie Ikenga *God and Man in African Religion.* London: Chapman, 1981.

Mudimbe, V. Y. *The Invention of Africa: Gnosis, Philosophy and the Order of Knowledge.* Bloomington: James Currey Ltd, 1988.

Nwala, Uzodimma T. *Igbo Philosophy.* Lagos: Lan Tern Books 1985.

Onwdanibe, Richard C. "The Human person and Immortality in Igbo (African Metaphysics" in *African Philosophy* Ed. Richard A. Wright. New York: University Press of America 1984.

Opoku, Kofi Asare. *West African Traditional Religion.* Accra: Fep International Ltd. 1978.

Ozumba, G. O. Philosophy and Method of Integrative Humanism. Calabar: Jochrisam publishers, 2010.

Ozumba, Emele M. "The Theology of African Traditional Religion" in *African Traditional Religion and Philosophy* Ed. Etim E. Okon. Calabar: University of Calabar Press, 2013.

Uchendu, Victor C. *The Igbo off Southeast Nigeria.* New York: Holt, Rinehart and Winston, 1965.

Wirendu, Kwasi. *Philosophy and an African Culture.* Cambridge: Cambridge University Press, 1980.

Socio-economic Predictors of Maternal Healthcare Uptake by Women in Makoko Community, Lagos, Nigeria

Idongesit Eshiet (Ph. D)

Department of Sociology, University of Lagos, Lagos, Nigeria. E-mail: <u>doshiet2@yahoo.com</u>

Abstract

The study investigated the socio-economic predictors of maternal healthcare uptake in Makoko community (an urban slum) within the Lagos metropolis, Nigeria. A cross sectional survey was conducted on a sample size of 250 women of child bearing age (15 – 49 years), randomly drawn from the community, using the multi-stage sampling technique. Specifically, the study sought to unravel if age, marital status, education, employment status, income, birth order, husband's education and distance to health facility mediated on the uptake of maternal healthcare by women in Makoko community. Conflict and symbolic interactionism perspectives serve as the theoretical underpinnings of the study. Findings reveal that age, education, income, birth parity and husband's education are positively correlated with the uptake of maternal healthcare. The study recommends targeted campaigns by government and non-governmental organizations on the dangers of lack of maternal healthcare, skill training for unemployed women and improvement of health facilities in Makoko community.

Key words*: antenatal, safe delivery, postnatal, family planning, mortality, death*

Introduction

Maternal healthcare refers to pregnancy related care. It is healthcare provided for women, especially during pregnancy, childbirth and the postpartum period in order to prevent maternal morbidity and mortality (WHO, 2012[a]). Maternal morbidity and mortality have remained an endemic health issue for women through the ages. Globally, maternal deaths stand at 216 deaths per 100,000 live births with the approximate lifetime risk of maternal death being 1 in 180 (WHO, 2015). However, the burden of maternal deaths is unevenly shared between the developed and developing worlds. While the developed world has been freed from the shackles of maternal deaths, the developing world is still grappling with the challenge. A majority of the deaths still occurs in the developing world. The developing world currently accounts for about 99% (302,000) of maternal deaths and has a maternal mortality ratio of 239. This is 20 times higher than the 12 deaths per 100,000 live births in the developed world. Similarly, the estimated lifetime risk of maternal death in the developed world is 1 in 3,300, as compared to 1 in 41 in the developing world (WHO, 2015). Regionally, sub-Saharan Africa has the highest maternal mortality ratio. It accounts for about 66% (201,000) with a maternal mortality ratio of 546. Equally, a woman's life time risk of dying during or following a pregnancy is estimated at 1 in 36 in sub-Saharan Africa as compared to 1 in 4,900 for the developed world (WHO, 2015). At the country level, Nigeria and India account for over one third of all maternal deaths globally. Nigeria accounts for 19% (58,000) with a maternal mortality ratio of 814, while India accounts for 15% (45,000) of the deaths (WHO, 2015).

The World Health Organization says these deaths are needless, as there are health-care solutions to prevent or manage maternal health issues (WHO, 2012[a]). In view of this, the United Nations, through its Development Goals has taken steps to curtail maternal deaths. Hence, both Millennium Development Goal (MDG) 5 and Target 3.1 of Sustainable Development Goal (SDG) 3 focus on reducing the global maternal deaths. Specifically, MDG 5 aimed at reducing maternal mortality ratio by three-quarters between 1990 and 2015 (UN, 2005) while Target 3.1 of SDG 3 aims at reducing maternal mortality ratio to less than 70 per 100,000 live births by 2030 (UN, 2016). These goals have encouraged national governments to take actions to stem maternal deaths. These have resulted in a reduction in maternal deaths however, the achievements still remain a far cry from the targets of the goals. A majority of women in the developing world still lack access to maternal healthcare. Poor women in the rural areas and urban slum settlements are particularly vulnerable, as their access and uptake of maternal healthcare is marred by political, socio-economic, and demographic factors among others. This study therefore, aims at investigating the socio-economic predictors of maternal healthcare uptake in Makoko community (an urban slum) in the Lagos metropolis, Nigeria.

Statement of Problem
Nigeria ranks as the second contributor to maternal deaths globally, accounting for 19% (58,000) of the overall deaths and having a maternal mortality ratio of 814 deaths per 100,000 live births (WHO, 2015). This fact though alarming is however, not surprising due to the revelations of the National Demographic and Health Survey. The National Demographic and Health Survey (NDHS) 2013, findings reveal a gloomy picture about the maternal health situation in Nigeria. The survey reveals that contraceptive usage by married women stands at 15%. The aftermath of this is Nigeria's high fertility rate, which stands at 5.5 children per woman. However, despite this high fertility rate, access and uptake of maternal healthcare is limited. The survey reveals that only 38% of births are delivered by a skilled health provider (midwife, doctor or nurse), while only 36% of them are delivered in a health facility. On the other hand, only 51% of mothers receive at least four antenatal care visits during pregnancy, while equally, only 40% of them receive a postnatal check-up within the first two days of giving birth (National Population Commission & ICF International, 2014). Similarly, UNICEF (2013) observes that less than 20 per cent of health facilities in the country offer emergency obstetric care.

In response to the then MDG Goal 5 and now SDG Target 3.1 of Goal 3, the Nigerian government like other national governments has taken steps to curb maternal deaths. Among such steps is the adoption of the UNICEF/WHO Integrated Management of Newborn, Infant, and Childhood Health (IMNCH) strategy, which was designed to fast-track the achievement of MDG Goals 4 and 5. The strategy is an all-encompassing evidence-based approach, which incorporates all aspects of maternal and child healthcare

system, including material and human resources, health governance, health information, strengthening of clinical services and community engagement (Findley *et al,* 2013). The strategy was adopted in 2007, under the auspices of the Federal Ministry of Health (Federal Ministry of Health, 2007).

Despite this intervention, much progress has not been achieved in tackling maternal deaths. Nigeria still ranks as one of the countries with the highest maternal mortality ratio globally with a mortality ratio of 814 deaths per 100,000 live births. Part of the reason adduced for this is due to the lack of access of a majority of women to maternal healthcare. Access may be limited by a myriad of factors, which include cultural, political, religious, socio-economic, demographic and geographical. This calls for micro level studies such as the intended study to unravel some of the factors that mediate access and uptake of maternal healthcare by women.

This study therefore, aims at investigating the socio-economic predictors of maternal healthcare uptake in Makoko community in the Lagos metropolis. Specifically, the study aims at unraveling the relationship between age, marital status, education, employment status, income, birth order, husband's education and distance to health facility and uptake of maternal healthcare in Makoko community.

Theoretical Frameworks
The analysis of the socio-economic predictors of the uptake of maternal healthcare in Makoko community is situated within an eclectic theoretical approach namely the sociological conflict and symbolic interactionism perspectives.

The conflict perspective pioneered by the classic works of Karl Marx explains the structuring of society from the viewpoint of historical materialism. It argues that at all times, human society is structured into two classes – the dominant and the dominated. In the capitalist society, the dominant class comprises the ruling class and the owners of the means of production, who use their power to make policies that protect its class interest (Haralambos and Heald, 2008). From this viewpoint, urban slums are manifestations of the lopsided policies, of the ruling class. The urban fringes become haven to the less privileged who have no access to housing in the planned areas. Hence urban slums are dirty, overcrowded and lack basic amenities including healthcare facilities, and this limits the access of women to maternal healthcare.

The symbolic interactionism perspective is concerned with the social psychological dynamics of individuals interacting in small groups. The perspective has its origins in the works of George Simmel, Charles Cooley, George Herbert Mead and Erving Goffman (Haralambos and Heald, 2008). From the symbolic interactionism perspective, the social world could be explained from the basis of the social interactions that occur between individuals and the meanings derived from such interactions by the individuals. Thus, the meanings that individuals give to their interactions with one another and to the symbols within their socio-cultural environment, affect their response to such symbols. For example, the meanings that people give to orthodox healthcare vis-à-vis unorthodox care affects their response to either healthcare system. Where the meaning given to orthodox healthcare is positive, people will make use of the facilities but if it is negative, they will not make use of it. In urban slums, where there is high level of poverty and low level of literacy, much importance may not be attached to maternal healthcare. Thus, child bearing women may not subscribe to maternal healthcare even where such healthcare services are available within the community. They may still prefer unorthodox maternal care such as drinking herbs, visit to traditional birth attendants, etc. This is attributed to the positive meaning they attach to such practices.

Dimensions of Maternal Healthcare

Maternal healthcare seemingly a unified system of healthcare nevertheless, has different components. The World Health Organization (WHO, 2012[a]) outlines the components of maternal healthcare as encompassing family planning, preconception, prenatal, delivery and postnatal care.

Family Planning – refers to a conscious effort by a couple to limit their family size or space their children using contraceptives. The World Health Organization (2012[b]) observes that prevention of unwanted and too-early pregnancies is vital to tackling maternal deaths. The organization argues that satisfying the unmet need for family planning of women alone could reduce the number of maternal deaths by almost a third (WHO, 2012[b]). Yet, WHO observes that globally, over 10% of women do not have access to or are not using an effective method of contraception. Thus, it advocates that all women including

adolescents should be given access to family planning (WHO, 2012[a]). In Nigeria, the National Demographic and Health Survey (2013) data reveals that only 15% of married women use a contraceptive method, while 16 per cent has an unmet need for family planning services. On the overall, contraceptive prevalence among women in Nigeria is 16 per cent (National Population Commission & ICF International, 2014).

Antenatal Care (ANC) - refers to the medical care of a woman during pregnancy. The major objective of antenatal care is to ensure optimal health outcomes for the mother and child. Antenatal care from a trained healthcare provider helps to monitor the pregnancy and reduce morbidity risks for mother and child during pregnancy and delivery. It has been observed that ANC provides the following benefits for mother and child – (a) it enables early detection of complications and prompt treatment (for example, detection and treatment of sexually transmitted infections), (b) it enables the prevention of diseases through immunization and micronutrient supplementation, (c) it enables birth preparedness and complication readiness and (d) it enables health promotion and disease prevention through health messages and counseling (National Population Commission & ICF International, 2014:128). The World Health Organization recommends a minimum of four ANC visits for every pregnant woman who has no complications. The first visit should occur by the end of 16 weeks of pregnancy, the second visit should be between 24 and 28 weeks of pregnancy, while the third visit should be by 32 weeks and the fourth visit by 36 weeks. However, women with complications, special needs or conditions beyond the scope of basic care may require additional visits (National Population Commission & ICF International, 2014). Nigeria's ANC policy aligns with the WHO's approach. However, statistic reveals that only 51 per cent of pregnant women in Nigeria have four antenatal visits while 34 per cent do not have antennal care (National Population Commission & ICF International, 2014).

Delivery Care – entails delivery in a health facility and by a skilled attendant – skilled attendance at delivery encompasses the presence of health professionals such as doctors, midwives, and nurses as well as an enabling environment, where the equipment, drugs and other resources required for effective and efficient management of complications are available. Evidence from the developed world shows that delivery in health facility and by a skilled attendant are the major factors that have led to the drastic reduction in maternal deaths (Adamu, 2011; Kruk *et al,* 2007). In Nigeria, only 36 per cent of births are delivered in health facilities, while 63 percent are delivered at home (National Population Commission & ICF International, 2014).

Postnatal Care (PNC) – The postnatal period is the time from immediately after birth up to 40 days. The postpartum period is particularly important for women, because during this period, they may develop serious life-threatening complications, especially in the interval immediately after delivery. Evidence shows that a large proportion of maternal and neonatal deaths occur during the first 48 hours after delivery (National Population Commission & ICF International, 2014; Adamu, 2011). Thus, receiving postnatal care is critical in making a difference between life and death for mother and child. It prevents death from preventable causes such as hemorrhage, infections and hypertensive disorders, which are common diseases during this period (WHO, 2012[a]).

Postnatal care visits also provide opportunity to learn and acquire information on issues such as family planning, maternal and child nutrition, immunization, hygiene and sanitation, etc. (USAID, 2009). WHO recommends that all women receive a health check within two days of giving birth. But statistic show that 58 percent of women in Nigeria do not have postnatal checkup (National Population Commission & ICF International, 2014).

Barriers to Maternal Healthcare in Developing Countries
There is a great disparity in the healthcare systems of the developed and developing world. While the developed world has a viable healthcare and referral system in which pregnant women can receive emergency obstetric care when needed, this is absent in the developing world (Adamu, 2011). However, apart from the lack of a viable healthcare and referral system, evidence from studies reveal some other socio-economic, demographic, cultural and geographical factors that mediate access to maternal healthcare in developing countries. For example, studies reveal mother's age at child birth as influencing access and utilization of maternal healthcare, although there are contradictory findings with regard to the direction of the effect of mother's age and utilization of maternal healthcare services. While some studies show a lack of association

between mother's age and utilization of maternal healthcare services (Magadi*et al,* 2007; Celik& Hotchkiss, 2000), some others show higher utilization for younger women than older women (Abou-Zahr&Wardlaw, 2001), yet some others show a higher utilization for older women than younger women (Tsawe*et al,* 2015; Reynolds *et al,* 2006).

Similarly, parity or birth order is shown as a predictor of maternal healthcare services utilization. Evidence shows that women who have more than three living children are more confident about their ability to handle their maternal health issues and so do utilize maternal health services less frequently than those who have had less than three children (Tsawe*et al,* 2015; Raj Baral*et al,* 2012; Simkhada*et al,* 2008).

Maternal education is also shown as a factor influencing access and utilization of maternal healthcare services. Studies reveal that the higher a woman's level of education, the more likely she is to access and use maternal healthcare services (Tsawe*et al,* 2015; Ononokpono&Odimegwu, 2014: Ayele*et al,* 2014). However, some other studies do question the independent effect of education on maternal health utilization, arguing that some other factors such as husband's educational level, socio-economic environment do mediate on the association between education and utilization of maternal healthcare services (Gage &Calixte, 2006; Raghupathy, 1996).

Studies similarly show a relationship between women's employment status and access to and utilization of maternal healthcare services. While it could be assumed that working women who earn income would have more autonomy and the financial wherewithal to seek maternal healthcare services, in reality this is not always so, as the context in which women are employed does impact on their access to maternal healthcare services. Thus, the contextual differences in women's employment have given rise to different findings on the association between employment and access to and utilization of maternal health services. Studies reveal a positive relationship between a woman's formal employment and utilization of maternal healthcare services as such healthcare provisioning are part of the official employment benefits (Ononokpono&Odimegwu, 2014; Dalal*et al,* 2012), however, in context where women have no control over their earnings and where women do not earn money for the work they do or where employment is poverty-induced, employment is found not to be associated with maternal healthcare services utilization (Lowe *et al*, 2016; Furuta&Salway, 2006; Addai, 2000; Nwakoby 1994).

The place of residence similarly plays a significant role in access to and utilization of maternal healthcare services. Studies show that women who reside in urban areas are more likely to have access to and utilize maternal healthcare services than those who reside in the rural areas (Muchabaiwa*et al*, 2012; Dagne, 2010; Babalola &Fatusi, 2009). This may be attributed to the lopsided healthcare provisioning in developing countries in which sophisticated health facilities are often situated in the urban areas (Peltzer*et al*, 2005). Thus, issues of accessibility and affordability have been critical factors in determining maternal healthcare utilization as rural women often have to travel long distances before accessing the nearest heath facility (Tsawe&Susuman, 2014; Silal*et al*, 2012; Ensor & Cooper, 2004).

Household wealth quintile is also associated with the use of maternal healthcare services. This is however, not surprising, as the use of maternal healthcare services entails some monetary costs such as cost of transportation, medication, user fees, etc. Thus, women from rich families are more likely to utilize maternal healthcare services than women from poor families (Gabrysh& Campbell, 2009). Likewise, the use of maternal healthcare also increases with the wealth quintile of women themselves, thus women from the rich quintile use maternal healthcare services more than those from the poor quintile (Fotso*et al*, 2009).

Religion also mediates access to and utilization of maternal healthcare services. For example, studies reveal a higher use of maternal healthcare services by non-Muslim women, and a lower rate of use by Muslim women (Babalola&Fatusi, 2009; Ethiopian Society of Population Studies, 2008; Addai, 2000). Similarly, cultural factors such as the traditional gender division of labour, patriarchy, which denies women autonomy in decision making, etc. are associated with non-utilization of maternal healthcare services (Lowe *et al*, 2016; Ayele*et al*, 2014).

The factors that mediate on women's access to maternal healthcare services are complex, numerous and varied, hence this review is not exhaustive, as it has only discussed some of the variables.

Methods

Research Design and Setting – The study utilized a cross sectional survey to gather quantitative data from Makoko community, an urban slum settlement within the Lagos metropolis of Nigeria. Makoko is a multi-ethnic fishing community with a population size of 85,840 comprising of 43,280 males and 41,540 females. A third of the community is built on stilts along the lagoon and the rest on land. Makoko is made up of six distinct 'communities' spread across land and water - OkoAgbon, Adogbo, Migbewhe, Yanshiwhe, Sogunro and Apollo. The first four are the floating communities, known as 'Makoko on water' while the rest are based on land. Makoko has a non-functional government primary health centre located within the community. However, there is a network of privately owned hospitals and some informal, unregistered clinics that attend to the health needs of the community. There are also a number of traditional birth attendants (Ogunlesi, 2016).

Study population – The study population comprised of child bearing women (15-49 years) who were single and never married and those who have been ever married and who gave at least one live birth in the five years prior to the time of the survey and were resident in the community.

Sample Size and Technique – A sample size of 250 women was drawn using the multi-stage sampling technique. Makoko comprises of 6 communities - OkoAgbon, Adogbo, Migbewhe, Yanshiwhe, Sogunro and Apollo. Four of the communities are floating communities on water, while two are on land. The two communities on land - Sogunro and Apollo, were purposively selected for the study to allow for convenience of gathering the data. Twenty-four streets were identified in the two communities and houses on the streets were enlisted. Respondents were randomly selected from the enlisted houses.

Data Collection- Quantitative data was gathered using the questionnaire. Questions were asked on socio-demographic characteristics of respondents, access to and uptake of family planning; antenatal care; delivery care and postnatal care. In collecting the data, a face-to-face interview technique was used.

Ethical considerations - such as anonymity, confidentiality, as well as informed consent were obtained from respondents.

Data Analysis - The Statistical Package for Social Sciences (SPSS) version 20 was used to analyze the data. Findings are presented in descriptive and inferential statistics. The independent variables are age, marital status, education, employment status, income, birth order, husband's education and distance to health facility while maternal healthcare is measured by - antenatal care (ANC) (compliance with WHO prescribed minimum of four ANC visits); delivery care (delivery in a health facility and by a skilled attendant); and postnatal care (PNC) (received from a skilled medical professional within two days of delivery).

Results

The results are analyzed and presented in descriptive and inferential statistics. Findings are discussed under the various dimensions of maternal healthcare – family planning, antenatal care, delivery care and postnatal care.

Uptake of Family Planning by Women in Makoko Community

Variables that measure the reproductive health practices of respondents were analyzed using descriptive statistics and presented in simple frequency and percentage distributions.

Findings reveal that 21.2% of the respondents have had one or more abortions. Similarly, 58.0% do practice family planning. For those who practice family planning, 90.3% practice modern family planning, with a majority of them using condom. However, 9.7% practice traditional type of family planning such as withdrawal method, the use of herbs, and other unconventional substances such as alcoholic drink, lime, salt, etc. Similarly, 66.2% of those who practice family planning had the onset of their first family planning after their first life birth. And about 14.0% of them obtained the family planning services in a government hospital, while 10.0% did so in a private hospital. However, 84.0% do so through diverse sources, such as chemists, herbs, condoms, withdrawal, etc.

Socio-economic Predictors of uptake of Maternal Healthcare by Women in Makoko Community

Table 1 is a summary of the chi square test of the socio-economic variables that mediate on the uptake of maternal healthcare (antennal care, delivery care and postnatal care) in Makoko community.

Table 1: Socio-economic Predictors of uptake of Maternal Healthcare by Women in Makoko Community

Variable	Four ANC Visits		Delivery in Health Facility		Postnatal Care (ANC)	
	X^2	P-Value	X^2	P-Value	X^2	P-Value
Age	21.372	.0000	3.122	0.210	5.579	.061
Marital Status	2.248	.134	4.083	.043	4.859	.027
Education	3.806	.283	10.376	0.016	14.385	.002
Employment Status	.008	.929	7.615	.006	17.401	.000
Income	8.192	.017	14.336	.001	7.362	.025
Birth Order	23.612	.000	4.621	.202	3.232	.357
Husband's Education	.902	.637	6.793	.033	19.881	.000
Distance to Health Facility	.249	.618	.087	.768	.792	.374

Uptake of Antenatal Care (ANC) by Women in Makoko Community

The descriptive analysis of uptake of ANC reveals a high level of utilization. About 92.2% of respondents admit to having had at least four ANC visits in their last pregnancy. However, the inferential statistics based on chi square test (see Table 1) reveals no association between marital status ($X^2 = 2.248$, df=1, P>.05); education ($X^2 = 3.806$;df =3, P>.05); employment status ($X^2 = .008$, df= 1, P>.05); husband's education ($X^2 = .902$, df= 2, P>.05); and distance to health facility ($X^2 = .249$, df= 1, P>.05) and uptake of ANC. On the other hand, age ($X^2 = 21.372$, df=2, P<.05);

income ($X^2 = 8.192$, df =2, P<.05); and birth order ($X^2 = 23.612$, df=3, P<.05) are associated with uptake of ANC.

In terms of age, younger women less than 30 years are more likely to utilize ANC. However, uptake tends to decline with age as women; ages 30-39 years also utilize ANC more than those who are 40 – 49 years. With regards to birth order, uptake is higher for women who have given birth to less than three children and less with those who have given birth to three children and above. Hence, parity is significant with uptake. The lack of association between distance to health facility as established in some other studies (Muchabaiwa*et al,* 2012; Dagne, 2010; Babalola&Fatusi, 2009) may be attributed to the fact that the gap between the nearest and farthest distance is not much. The farthest distance to a health facility is more than 1 Km (21.6%) while the nearest is less than 1 Km (78.4%).

The variables associated with ANC uptake (age, income and birth order) are further subjected to multivariate analysis using the logistic regression model as depicted in Table 2.

Table 2: Logistic Regression Model for uptake of ANC by Women in Makoko Community

Variable	B	S.E.	Exp(B)	95% C.I.for EXP(B)	
Age				Lower	Upper
< 30 years (Ref)					
30 – 39 years	-1.040	.426	.353**	.153	.815
40 – 49 years	-1.033	.716	.356	.087	1.448
Income					
N1 – N10,000 (Ref)					
N10,001 – N20,000	.967	.445	2.629*	1.098	6.294
N20,001 & above	1.832	.795	6.247*	1.315	29.672
Birth Order					
1 (Ref)					
2	-.724	.512	.485	.178	1.322
3	-.729	.589	.482	.152	1.529
4 & above	-1.458	.628	.233*	.068	.798

*p<0.5; **p<0.01; *** <0.001

Result of logistic regression as depicted in Table 2 further confirms that age, income and birth order are predictors of uptake of ANC. In terms of age, women between ages 30 – 39 years are less likely to uptake ANC than women who are less than 30 years. This means that uptake declines with age. With regards to income, uptake increases in the same direction with income. Thus, women with higher incomes (N10,001- N 20,000) are two times more likely to uptake ANC than those with less (below N10,000) incomes. Similarly, those with incomes that are higher than N20,001 and above are six times more likely to uptake than those with less (N10,000 and below) incomes. Uptake similarly declines with birth order. Women who have at least three and above live births are less likely to comply than those who have less than three live births.

Uptake of Delivery Care by Women in Makoko Community

Result of the chi square test in Table 1 reveals no association between age ($X^2 = 3.122$, *df=2, P>.05*); birth order ($X^2 = 4.621$, *df=3, P>.05*); and distance to health facility ($X^2 = .087$, *df=1, P>.05*) with delivery care. However, marital status ($X^2 = 4.083$, *df=1, P<.05*); education ($X^2 =10.376$, *df=3, P<.05*); employment status ($X^2 =7.615$, *df=1, P<.05*); income ($X^2 =14.336$, *df=2, P<.05*); and husband's education ($X^2 = 6.793$, *df=2, P<.05*) are associated with delivery care. In terms of marital status, the result reveals that married women are more likely to have delivery care than single women, while employed women are more likely to have delivery care than the unemployed. Similarly, women who earn higher income are more likely to have delivery care than those who earn less. Also, women whose husbands have a higher education are more likely to have delivery care than those with lower or no education.

The variables associated with delivery care (education, employment status, income and husband's education) are further subjected to a multivariate logistic regression analysis to see if they would be predictors of delivery care as depicted in Table 3.

Table 3: Logistic Regression Model for uptake of Delivery Care by Women in Makoko Community

Variable	B	S.E.	Exp(B)	95% C.I.for EXP(B)	
Level of Education					
None (Ref)					
Primary	-1.734	1.096	.177	.021	1.513
Secondary	-1.167	1.111	.311	.035	2.744
Tertiary	-1.225	1.364	.294	.020	4.257
Employment Status					
Unemployed/housewife (Ref)					
Employed	-.142	.661	.868	.238	3.170
Income					
N1 – N10,000 (Ref)					
N10,001 – N20,000	1.199	.497	3.318**	1.254	8.781
N20,000 & above	1.050	.807	2.859	.588	13.891
Husband's Education					
Primary (Ref)					
Secondary	.524	.482	1.688	.657	4.338
Tertiary	.921	.834	2.511	.490	12.866

*p<0.5; **p<0.01; *** <0.001

Result in Table 3 reveals that marital status, education, employment status and husband's education are not predictors of uptake of delivery care. However, income is a predictor of delivery care. Women who earn income, between N10,001 – N20,000 are three times more likely to uptake delivery care than those who earn N10,000 and less.

Uptake of Postnatal Care (PNC) by Women in Makoko Community

Result of the descriptive statistic reveals a high uptake of postnatal care (83.6%). However, result of the chi square test in Table 1 reveals that age ($X^2 = 5.579$, $df=2$, $P>.05$);

birth order ($X^2 = 3.232$, $df=3$, $P>.05$); and distance to health facility ($X^2 = .792$, $df=1$, $P>.05$) are not associated with uptake of PNC. However, marital status ($X^2 = 4.859$, $df=1$, $P<.05$); education ($X^2 = 14.385$, $df=3$, $P<.05$); employment status ($X^2 = 17.401$, $df=1$, $P<.05$); income ($X^2 = 7.362$, $df=2$, $P<.05$); and husband's education ($X^2 = 19.881$, $df=2$, $P<.05$) are associated with postnatal care.

The variables associated with uptake of postnatal care (marital status, education, employment status, income and husband's education) are further subjected to a multivariate analysis as depicted in Table 4.

Table 4: Logistic Regression Model for uptake of Postnatal Care by Women in Makoko Community

Variable	B	S.E.	Exp(B)	95% C.I.for EXP(B)	
Education					
None (Ref)					
Primary	-.730	.885	.482	.085	2.730
Secondary	-.032	.940	.968	.153	6.118
Tertiary	-.602	1.201	.548	.052	5.768
Employment Status					
Unemployed/housewife (Ref)					
Employed	.705	.663	2.023	.551	7.425
Income					
N1 – N10,000 (Ref)					
N10,001 – N20,000	.689	.617	1.992	.595	6.670
N20,001 & above	-.312	.742	.732	.171	3.136
Husband's Education					
Primary (Ref)					

Secondary	1.476	.551	4.374**	1.486	12.878
Tertiary	1.199	.900	3.317	.569	19.355

*p<0.5; **p<0.01; *** <0.001

Result of logistics regression in Table 4 reveals that marital status, education, employment status and income are not predictors of uptake of postnatal care; however, husband's education is a predictor of uptake of postnatal care. Women, whose husbands have a secondary education, are four times more likely to have postnatal care than those with no or primary education.

Discussion

This study investigated the socio-economic predictors of uptake of maternal healthcare by women in Makoko community, an urban slum within the Lagos metropolis of Nigeria, using a cross sectional survey of 250 women of child bearing age (15 -49 years), who gave at least one live birth in the five years prior to the time of the survey. The study sought to unravel the mediating influence of age, marital status, education, employment status, income, birth order, husband's education and distance to health facility on the uptake of maternal healthcare.

Descriptive and inferential statistics were utilized to analyze the quantitative data. Result of the descriptive statistics reveal an average level of uptake of family planning (58.0%); a high level of uptake of antenatal care (92.4%); delivery care (78.8%); and postnatal care (83.6%). These statistics are higher than those of the national average, which shows a contraceptive prevalence of 16 per cent; 51% antenatal care; 38% of delivery care; and 40 % of postnatal care.

Result of the bivariate analyses reveals that age, marital status, education, employment status, income, birth order, and husband's education are associated with uptake of maternal healthcare by women in Makoko community. This result aligns with the findings of other similar studies such as Tsawe*et al* (2015); Ononokpono&Odimegwu (2014); Ayele*et al* (2014); Gage &Calixte (2006); Raghupathy (1996); and Dalal*et al* (2012).

The multivariate analyses to investigate the association of these variables with the different dimensions of maternal healthcare reveals age, income and birth order as predictors of uptake of antenatal care. Uptake of antenatal care declines with age. Younger women are more likely to

utilize ANC than older women. Similarly, uptake of ANC increases as income increases while it declines with more live births. This result aligns with result of other studies such as Ononokpono&Odimegwu, (2014); Ayele*et al* (2014); and Fotso*et al* (2008). With regards to delivery care, result indicates income as a predictor of delivery care. Women with high income are three times more likely to deliver in a health facility and by a skilled attendant than those with lower income. This result is also in line with Ononokpono&Odimegwu, (2014); Ayele*et al*, (2014); and Tsawe*et al*, 2015 findings. For postnatal care, result reveals husband's education as a predictor of postnatal care. This is also in line with Ayele*et al* (2014) and Dalal*et al* (2012) findings.

The positive outcomes of this result should however, be cautiously interpreted. This is because maternal healthcare has standards as espoused by the World Health Organization. Thus, maternal healthcare could either be 'adequate' or 'inadequate' if it fails to meet the WHO's standards. Therefore, in situations where efficient healthcare delivery system is lacking, as it is often in urban slum settlements, adequate or quality maternal healthcare may be lacking. Makoko community has only one non-functional government owned primary health center located within the community. There is however, a network of private hospitals and informal, unregistered health clinics that attend to the health needs of the community. These private hospitals and clinics lack the WHO standards to provide 'adequate' or 'quality' maternal care for women, especially delivery care. Quality delivery care encompasses the presence of health professionals (doctors, midwives, and nurses) as well as an enabling environment, where the equipment, drugs and other resources required for effective and efficient management of complications are available. The health facilities in Makoko community lack the capacity to offer emergency obstetric care as well as an efficient referral system (although this was not part of the investigation of this study). However, this assertion could be supported by UNICEF (2013) report that less than 20 per cent of health facilities in Nigeria offer emergency obstetric care. From this vein, it could be argued that despite the high uptake of maternal healthcare services by women in Makoko community as revealed by this study, the reality is that these women are as good as having no maternal care.

This is particularly so as 88.0% of respondents admitted utilizing the health facilities within the community for their maternal healthcare services. This observation corroborates Fotso*et al* (2009) study of access to maternal healthcare in the slum settlements of Nairobi, Kenya, in which he raised the rhetorical question 'What does access to maternal healthcare mean among the urban poor? Fotso*et al* (2009) study found that although 70% of their respondents delivered in a health facility, only 48% of such deliveries were attended to by a skilled attendant. Therefore, the result of this study necessitates a further study to investigate the 'quality' of maternal healthcare services receive by women in Makoko community.

Recommendations

- To make the maternal health seeking behaviour of women in Makoko community to yield the desired result, government should scale-up the health facilities in Makoko community by ensuring adherence of both government and privately-owned facilities to the WHO standards of operation. Defaulting private facilities should be fined and sealed up until they comply.
- Government interventions should include a focused on improved access to emergency obstetric care as well as an efficient referral system.
- The reluctance of older women, as well as women who have many live births to utilize ANC services in Makoko community should be addressed through targeted campaigns by government and non-governmental organizations at such women, on the dangers of non-utilization of ANC services.
- Since employment and income are predictors of access to maternal healthcare, the government in conjunction with non-governmental organizations should empower poor unemployed women in Makoko community through skill acquisition trainings. Successful participants should be given seed money to start off after the training.
- In view of the importance of husband's education in influencing uptake of maternal healthcare by women in Makoko community, the family as a cohesive unit should be the main target of maternal healthcare interventions. Pregnancy should be perceived as an inclusive event, where both husband and wife should participate to ensure a healthy outcome for both mother and child.

- Furthermore, the findings of this study are based on the survey result of the part of Makoko community 'on land'. Therefore, further study is required on the part of Makoko community 'on water', to see if the result will be comparable.
- In view of the very high maternal mortality ratio in Nigeria, there is a need for more context specific studies, in order to unravel the diverse variables that mediate access and uptake of maternal healthcare in diverse settings in Nigeria. This will enable the adoption of appropriate policies to address the problem.

Conclusion

Maternal mortality ratio has remained all-time high in Nigeria over the years. Nigeria has consistently ranked as the second highest contributor to maternal deaths globally. This scenario makes maternal mortality to go beyond being an individual problem to a societal problem, due to the disruptive effect it has on the effective functioning of the society. Despite Nigeria's high fertility rate (5.5 children per woman), the uptake of maternal healthcare services is low. Contraceptive prevalence still stands at 16 per cent while only 51% of women receive antenatal care, only 38% delivery care and 40% postnatal care (National Population Commission & ICF International, 2014). However, contrary to the national picture, there is a high uptake of maternal healthcare services by women in Makoko community. Nevertheless, due to the poor quality of these services, they may not be adequate to address causes of maternal deaths. Thus, maternal healthcare uptake should be accompanied by quality services to enable it stem maternal deaths. In view of the findings of the study, the following recommendations are made.

References

AbouZahr, C. & Wardlaw, T. (2001). Maternal Mortality at the End of the Decade: What Signs of Progress? *Bulletin of the World Health Organization*, 79(6):561–573.

Addai, I. (2000). Determinants of Use of Maternal-Child Health Services in Rural Ghana.*Journal of Biosocial Science,* 32(1):1–15.

Adamu, H. A. (2011). Utilization of Maternal Health Care Services in Nigeria: An Analysis of Regional differences in the Patterns and Determinants of Maternal Health Care Use. University of Liverpool: Master of Public Health Dissertation.

Ayele, D. Z., B. Belayihun, K. Teji, & D. A. Ayana (2014). Factors Affecting Utilization of Maternal Health Care Services in Kombolcha District, Eastern Harare Zone, Oromia Regional State, Eastern Ethiopia. *International ScholarlyResearch Notices.*Retrieved from https://www.hindawi.com/journals/isrn/2014/91705 8/ on 2/8/2017.

Babalola, S. &Fatusi, A. (2009). Determinants of Use of Maternal Health Services in Nigeria - Looking Beyond Individual and Household Factors.*BMC Pregnancy Childbirth,* 9(43):1–13.

Celik, Y. & Hotchkiss, D.R. (2000). The Socio-Economic Determinants of Maternal Healthcare Utilization in Turkey.*Social Science Medicine,* 50(12):1797–1806.

Dagne, E. (2010). Role of Socio-Demographic Factors on Utilization of Maternal Healthcare Services in Ethiopia. Sweden: UMEA University Dissertation.

Dalal, K., J. Shabnam, J. Andrews-Chavez, L. B. Mårtensson&T. Timpka (2012). Economic Empowerment of Women and Utilization of Maternal Delivery Care in Bangladesh.*International Journal of Preventive Medicine,* 3(9) 628-636.

Ensor, T. & Cooper, S. (2004). Overcoming Barriers to Health Service Access: Influencing the Demand Side.*Health Policy Plan,* 19(2):69–79.

Ethiopian Society of Population Studies (2008). Maternal Healthcare seeking Behavior in Ethiopia: Findings from EDHS 2005. Retrieved from http://ethopia.unfpa.org/drive/Maternal Health.pdf.

Federal Ministry of Health. (2007). *Integrated Maternal, Newborn and Child Health Strategy Nigeria.* Abuja, Nigeria: Federal Ministry of Health.

Findley, S. E., Uwemedimo, O. T., Doctor, H. V., Green, C., Adamu, F. &Afenyadu, G. (2013). Early Results of an Integrated Maternal, Newborn and Child Health Program, Northern Nigeria, 2009 to 2011. *BMC Public Health,* 13: 1034-

Fotso, J. C., A. Ezeh, N. Madise, A. Ziraba& R. Ogollah (2009). What does Access to Maternal Care Mean among the Urban Poor? Factors Associated with Use of Appropriate Maternal Health Services in the Slum Settlements of Nairobi, Kenya. *Maternal and Child Health Journal,* 13(1): 130–137.

Fotso, J. C., A. Ezeh, &R. Oronje (2008). Provision and Use of Maternal Health Services among Urban Poor Women in Kenya: What Do We Know and What Can We Do? *Journal of Urban Health, May* 85(3): 428–442.

Furuta, M. &Salway, S. (2006). Women's Position within the Household as a Determinant of Maternal Health Care Use in Nepal.*International Family Planning Perspective,* 32(1):17–27.

Gabrysch, S. & Campbell, O.M (2009). Still too Far to Walk: Literature Review of the Determinants of Delivery Service Use.*BMC Pregnancy Childbirth,* 9:34.

Gage, A.J. &Calixte, M.G. (2006). Effects of Physical Accessibility of Maternal Health Services on their Use in Rural Haiti. *Population Studies,* 60(3): 271-88.

Haralambos, M. &Heald, R. M. (2008). *Sociology: Themes and Perspectives.* New Delhi: Cambridge University Press.

Kruk, M. E., S. Galea, M. R. Prescott & L.P. Freedman (2007). Healthcare Financing and Utilization of Maternal Health Services in Developing Countries. *Health Policy and Planning 22*:303-10.

Lowe, M., D. R. Chen & S. L. Huang (2016). Social and Cultural Factors Affecting Maternal Health in Rural Gambia: An Exploratory Qualitative Study. *PLoS ONE* 11(9): e0163653. https://doi.org/10.1371/journal.pone.0163653.

Magadi, M. A., A. O. Agwanda& F. O. Obare (2007). A Comparative Analysis of the Use of Maternal Health Services between Teenagers and Older Mothers in sub-Saharan Africa: Evidence from Demographic Health Surveys. *Social Science and Medicine 64*:1311-25.

Muchabaiwa, L., D. Mazambani, L. Chigusiwa, S. Bindu, & V. Mudavanhu (2012). Determinants of Maternal Healthcare Utilization in Zimbabwe.*International Journal of Economic Science Application Res.* 5(2):145–62.

National Population Commission & ICF International (2014). *Nigeria Demographic and HealthSurvey 2013.*Abuja, Nigeria and Rockville, Maryland, USA: NPC & ICF International.

Nwakoby, B. N. (1994). Use of Obsteric Services in Rural Nigeria.*Journal of Rural Social Health,*114(3): 132-36.

Ogunlesi, T. (2016). Inside Makoko: Danger and Ingenuity in the World's Biggest Floating Slum. Guardian Lagos Week.Retrieved from https://www.theguardian.com/cities/2016/feb/23/ma

koko-lagos-danger-ingenuity-floating-slum on July 3, 2017.

Ononokpono, D. N. &Odimegwu, C. O. (2014). Determinants of Maternal Health Care Utilization in Nigeria: A Multilevel Approach. *The Pan African Medical Journal,* 17 (1):2. Retrieved fromhttp://www.panafrican-med-journal.com/content/series/17/1/2/full on July6, 2017.

Peltzer, K., D. Skinner, S. Mfecane, O. Shisana, A. Nqeketo, & T. Mosala (2005). Factors Influencing the Utilization of Prevention of Mother-to-Child-Transmission Services by Pregnant Women in the Eastern Cape, South Africa. *Health SA Gesondheid,* 10(1):26–40.

Raj Baral, Y., K. Lyons, J. Skinner , E. R. & van Teijlingen. (2012). Maternal Health Services Utilization in Nepal: Progress in the New Millennium? *Health Science Journal* 6(4):618-33.

Raghupathy, S. (1996). Education and the Use of Maternal Health Care in Thailand.*Social Science & Medicine* 43(4):459-471.

Reynolds, H. W., E. L. Wong, & H. Tucker (2006). Adolescents Use of Maternal and Child Health Services in Developing Countries.*International Family Planning Perspectives* 32(1):6-16.

Silal, S., L. Penn-Kekana, B. Harris, S. Birch & D. McIntyre (2012). Exploring Inequalities in Access to and Use of Maternal Health Services in South Africa.*BMC Health Services Research*, 12:120, https://doi.org/10.1186/1472-6963-12-120.

Simkhada, B., Teijlingen, E. R., Porter, M., &Simkhada, P. (2008). Factors Affecting the Utilization of Antenatal Care in Developing Countries: Systematic Review of the Literature. *Journal of Advance Nursing* 61(3):244–60.

Tsawe, M., Moto, A., Netshivhera, T., Ralesego, L., Nyathi, C. &Susuman, A. S. (2015). Factors Influencing the Use of Maternal Healthcare Services and Childhood Immunization in Swaziland.*International Journal For Equity in Health,* *March*.Retrieved from https://www.ncbi.nlm.nih.gov/pmc/articles/PMC4391603/ on September 27, 2017.

Tsawe, M. &Susuman, A. S. (2014). Determinants of Access to and Use of Maternal Health Care Services in the Eastern Cape, South Africa: A Quantitative and Qualitative Investigation.*BioMed Central Research*

Notes, 7: 723. Retrieved from https://www.ncbi.nlm.nih.gov/pmc/articles/PMC4203863/ on August 2, 2017.

United Nations Children's Fund (UNICEF) (2013). Maternal and Child Mortality.Retrieved from http://www.unicef.org/nigeria/children_1926.html on May 1, 2013.

United Nations (2016). Transforming Our World: The 2030 Agenda for Sustainable Development.ARES/70/1.Retrieved from sustainable development.org.on August 2, 2017.

United Nations (2005). *The Millennium Development Goals Report 2005.* New York: United Nations.

USAID (2009). Maternal and Child Health.Retrieved from http://www.usaid.gov/our_work/global_health/mch/mh/techareas/post.html.on August 2, 2017.

World Health Organization (2015). *Trends in Maternal Mortality: 1990-2015.* WHO, UNICEF, UNFPA, World Bank Estimates.Geneva, Switzerland: World Health Organization.

World Health Organization (2012[a]). *Trends in Maternal Mortality: 1990-2010. WHO, UNICEF, UNFPA,*

World Bank Estimates. Geneva: World Health Organization.

World Health Organization (2012[b]). MDG 5: Improve Maternal Health. Retrieved from http://www.who.int/topics/maternal_health/en/ on May 31, 2013.

International Journal of Integrative Humanism Vol 9. No 1. June 2018. ISSN: 2026 – 6286

Translation and Interpretation in Providing Assistance to Refugees: The Case of Central Africa Republic Refugees in Cameroon

Samson Fabian Nzuanke
Department of Modern Languages & Translation Studies, University of Calabar, Calabar-Nigeria
&
Olufumilayo Olukemi Ogbadu
Higher Institute of Translation, Interpretation and Communication, Nkolbisson, Yaounde-Cameroon

Abstract

This study seeks to highlight the relevance of translation and interpretation in providing assistance to refugees and builds on a case study of refugees from Central African Republic who sought refuge in the Republic of Cameroon. The study also seeks to find out the extent humanitarian workers need and use competent translators and interpreters to provide assistance to refugees. This study adopts the sociolinguistic theory of translation which underscores the adaptation of information to the culture and ethnic origin of the target audience. To this end, primary data were collected through questionnaires, interviews and observation while secondary data were collected through relevant textbooks, journals and websites. Questionnaires were administered to 120 refugees in Gado refugee site, to 45 humanitarian workers that provide assistance to refugees and to 15 translators and interpreters who have worked with agencies handling refugee matters. Descriptive Statistical Method was used to analyze the data collected. The results of the findings show that Central African Republic refugees in Cameroon are in real need of translation and interpretation services as the majority of the respondents, that is 90% of the sample population indicated the fact that they needed translation and interpretation services in different areas ranging from registration with the UNHCR, to receiving health services, and other forms of assistance.

Key-words: Translation/Interpretation, Assistance, Refugees, Cameroon, Central Africa Republic

Introduction

Cameroon, officially the Republic of Cameroon, is a country in West Central Africa. It is bordered by Nigeria to the west; Chad to the north-east; the Central Africa Republic to the east; and Equatorial Guinea, Gabon, and the Republic of the Congo to the south. Cameroon's coastline lies on the Bight of Bonny, part of the Gulf of Guinea and the Atlantic Ocean (Neba, 1999). The country is called "Africa in miniature" for its geological and cultural diversity. Historically, Cameroon is a bilingual country with over 200 different ethnic and linguistic groups. English and French are the official languages, a heritage of Cameroon's colonial past under the rule of the United Kingdom and France from 1916 to 1960.

The United Nations High Commissioner for Refugees (UNHCR) Cameroon Global Appeal update for 2014 indicates that Cameroon is a signatory to the 1951 Convention relating to the Status of Refugees and its 1967 Protocol, as well as the 1969 OAU Convention governing the Specific Aspects of Refugee Problems in Africa. At the national level, the Government adopted the Law Defining the Legal Framework for Refugee Protection in July 2005. A decree to implement the 2005 Refugee law was signed in November 2011, and this was followed by the creation of the Eligibility and Appeals Commissions in July 2012. It is therefore not surprising that Cameroon accepts refugees from countries in distress situations.

The influx of refugees into Cameroon has become more pronounced in recent years due to armed conflicts and unrest in neighbouring countries (especially Chad, Nigeria and Central Africa Republic). The Integrated Regional Information Network (IRIN) reported on the 30 of October

2013, that Cameroon is grappling with the influx of over a hundred thousand refugees whose presence is causing tensions with the local population. On Thursday 20 March 2014, the same Network reported that the tumult in the neighbouring Central African Republic and North-Eastern Nigeria has made Cameroon to become a safe haven for some 266,880 refugees, fleeing from conflict zones in these two neighbouring countries. According to *Cameroon Tribune* of 14 March 2014, an inter-ministerial ad-hoc committee under the leadership of Cameroon's minister of the Interior was set up by a presidential decree issued on 13 March 2014 to manage the refugee emergency situation in Cameroon, most likely, because of security concerns.

Before refugees get to the level of seeking durable solutions to their problems, they should have already undergone numerous experiences that need various forms of basic assistance from food, water, shelter, sanitation, medicine among many other needs. For instance, the *Voice of America* site reported on the 11 September 2014, that the United Nations refugee agency warned that a food and humanitarian crisis is looming over Cameroon, where hundreds of thousands of people have taken refuge, fleeing violence in Nigeria and the Central Africa Republic. The representative of the UNHCR in Cameroon, Ndeye Ndiougue Ndour, said people fleeing terrorist activities in Nigeria and carnage in the Central Africa Republic were arriving in Cameroon in bad shape. Some had wounds inflicted by Boko Haram (Nigeria) and anti-Balaka militias (Central Africa Republic). It would require effective communication for humanitarian workers to relate easily with the refugees; such relations could be impaired if there is a language barrier.

For its part, the Central Africa Republic (CAR) is a landlocked state situated in Africa's geographical centre (Mandryk, 2010). The Central Africa Republic is situated about 805 km north of the equator. It is bordered by the Republic of Chad to the North, Sudan to the North-East, South Sudan to the East, both Republic of Congo and the Democratic Republic of Congo to the South, and Cameroon to the West. It is a nation with a population of 4.7 million inhabitants and with about 80 ethnic groups. French and Sango are the official languages. Sango is the trademark language used by most Central Africans. The various religious groups are Christians 76.37%, Muslims 13.8% and others 9.83% (Mandryk, 2010).

Though rich in natural resources, CAR has remained chronically poor. It is ranked 185 out of 187 countries in the 2013 Human Development Index (UNDP, 2014) and has been suffering from chronic instability since its independence from France on the 13th of August 1960. The latest of the crises in CAR was the one that started in March 2013.

At the end of 2012, the alliance of militias known as Séléka ("coalition" in Sango, the national language) took up arms against the Bozizé government, alleging the state was not respecting the 2008 agreement signed in Libreville, Gabon, which had brought to an end the conflict between the government and the two major rebel militias (IRIN, 2014). Séléka seized several towns in the north and north-central areas, thus sparking the most extensive of CAR's multiple displacement crises (ACAPS, 2014). It left about half the population fleeing for their lives in all directions, thus needing assistance for internally displaced persons by the end of 2013 (UNHCR, January 2014) as well as triggering cross-border flights of refugees.

In January 2013, a government-Séléka peace agreement was signed but the coalition accused the government of not putting sufficient political will into its implementation. Séléka supporters alleged the army and the Presidential Guard committed such abuses as enforced disappearances, torture and killings against those judged to be Séléka supporters. Séléka took up arms again and, led by Michel Djotodia, took control of Bangui on 24 March 2013.

In January 2014, international pressure forced Djotodia to resign, bringing short-lived relief for some and tremendous fear for the Muslim population (Reuters, 2014). Following Djotodia's resignation. Catherine Samba-Panza was selected as the new interim president.
according to UNHCR estimates, as of mid-May 2014, 554,800 persons had been displaced inside the CAR and 359,834 had sought refuge in neighbouring countries.

Refugees from Central Africa Republic come into Cameroon through three main entry points. That is: Kentzou, Garoua-Boulai and Gbiti. Most of them arrive in very precarious conditions, tired, sick, without food or water. When they enter Cameroon, they meet with the Police at the border. The Police will alert the Divisional Officer who will inform the Senior Divisional Officer of their presence. The latter (Senior Divisional Officer) will notify the Governor who will in turn inform the UNHCR of the presence of the refugees. The UNHCR will then visit the site in conjunction with State Officials. This procedure will give room for the initial registration of the refugees which will involve communicating with the people who, in most cases, speak only Fulfuldé and Sango.

Fulfuldé is spoken in the Northern part of Cameroon while Sango is uniquely spoken in the Central Africa Republic. Humanitarian workers are from different ethnic groups and some are of other nationalities. To what extent can translators and interpreters aid these humanitarian workers (who are hindered by language barrier) to assist the refugees who are seriously in need? This is what this study seeks to find out.

Methodology

A case study approach has been adopted with the target population being primarily the Central Africa Republic refugees fleeing from their war-torn country into Cameroon and needing assistance from humanitarian agencies. Some refugees from the Central Africa Republic, who have been uprooted from their habitual environment, found themselves among the people of Eastern Cameroon with a different language and culture. This study also covers humanitarian workers who render various forms of humanitarian assistance on a regular basis to these refugees who need to overcome language barriers for effective communication to take place. Some of these workers also need to overcome language barriers while interacting with each other. Services rendered to refugees are in the areas of registration with UNHCR, advocacy, provision of educational facilities, aid distribution, health care delivery, provision of water supply, and toilet facilities.

In like manner, the views of translators and interpreters who have worked with or are working with refugees or organizations that are linked to refugees from the Central Africa Republic were sought in order to investigate the impact of the services they render.

Sample Population and Sample Size

The sample population consists of three categories. The first consists of the refugees, the second is made up of humanitarian workers, and the third sample consists of translators and interpreters. The study sought the views of 120 refugees in UNHCR Gado refugee site in the Eastern Region of Cameroon. The choice of this refugee site is due to accessibility and safety concerns as compared to other sites located either in remote areas or in the forest areas of the East where Central Africa Republic refugees are found. The Gado refugee site is the most densely populated with about 17,000 refugees in an area of 80 hectares.

Another group of respondents were 45 humanitarian staff of organizations working in the Gado refugee site in various domains of humanitarian assistance offered. And the third category of people served with questionnaires were 15 translators and interpreters who are working with governmental and non-governmental organizations handling refugee matters or those who have worked with such organizations before.

The three sets of questionnaires were designed and adapted to each group in order to achieve the objectives set for the study.

Sampling Techniques

Non-probability sampling or convenience sampling was applied. Participants were selected on the basis of easy accessibility to the researcher in a procedure which involves drawing representative data from the target population.

Data Collection

Two approaches of data collection were adopted to ensure an excellent understanding of the research theme. Primary as well as secondary data were used in the study.
Primary data: Research instruments used in collecting primary data included:

1. Interviews

2. Questionnaires

3. Observation

Secondary data: The secondary data for this study were collected from relevant textbooks gotten mostly from the UNHCR staff and website. Information was also gotten from the Cameroon Tribune, international journals, unpublished lectures, other related websites. The Cameroon Red Cross library and the Summer Institute for Linguistics (SIL) Library in Yaoundé were also visited for books on refugee assistance and on translation.

Method of Data Analysis

The Descriptive Statistical Method through the use of simple frequency tables was used to analyze the quantitative data collected through questionnaires for the study. This method was appropriate for most of the questions found in the questionnaires. The responses were counted as the numbers and the percentages were used in displaying the data in tables. Furthermore, a pie and two-bar chart were used to analyse the data. The percentages were calculated using the following formula:

$$\frac{\text{Number of response}}{\text{Total number of respondents}} \times \frac{100}{1}$$

Literature Review

According to Social Care Institute for Excellence (SCIE) one of the pointers for good practice in social care for asylum seekers and refugees include ensuring effective communication between local interpreting agencies and service providers in order to gain a better knowledge of each other's work. The interpreters should understand the situation of asylum seekers and refugees and the context for service delivery (SCIE-Guide 37, 2015). This is because, communication between health and social care givers and the refugees may be affected by language and cultural differences as well as different social, economic and political experiences (Promoting Refugee Health, 2007, p. 34). It is particularly important that a professional interpreter is offered to the refugee to preserve confidentially and to assure health officials that the information they are provided with is correct, thereby avoiding misdiagnosis.

According to Clune and Hosey (2003, p. 16), a community that is receptive to the needs of refugees' resettlement must among other things make available interpreters' and translators' services at public agencies, have materials and signs.

The function performed by translators/interpreters which is that of overcoming the barrier of language is vital in this context. Professional translators/interpreters are essential in all these meetings, because asylum investigations like any specialized field require a particular terminology. Of the numerous settings in which the services of translators/interpreters are needed, the most important is that of the interview for refugee status determination. Being recognized or not recognized as a refugee will have direct consequences for the life and well-being of the applicant and his or her family.

The role that translation and interpretation play in providing assistance to refugees cannot be overemphasized. There is however a need to distinguish moments when interpretation or translation is most suitable, and provide assistance accordingly. Barsky (2012) is of the opinion that the most important moment for refugees and asylum seekers occurs in the initial interactions with the authority which tends to take the form of conversations with border guards and law enforcement agents. He argues that it is essential at this point to have sympathetic and culturally sensitive interpreters, rather than strict translators, to help beyond translating the meaning of words. The idea of "assistance" he said needs to come in the form of "knowledge interpretation" and "knowledge translation" that harness the interpreters' knowledge as a means of improving the conditions of illegal refugees and asylum seekers' interaction with authorities.

According to Refugee Advice Centre (2010), a heavy burden of responsibility lies on the interpreter in the asylum process. The ease and accuracy of communication are of great importance, and it is in this that the interpreter has a vital role to play. Persons who are called upon to provide interpreting services, especially those with little previous experience of UNHCR's work, need guidance on how to perform their role effectively. The asylum seeker's matter must be interpreted into another language comprehensively and accurately, so that the authorities can reach a fair decision in the matter of a person seeking international protection. Therefore, the interpreter is in a key position, communicating messages in situations which have a bearing on the rest of the asylum seeker's life.

The interpreter's task is to faithfully and accurately interpret the message from one language to another.

On the whole, all the studies discussed above tend to insist on the need for translation and interpretation services for asylum seekers and refugees purely from a Western perspective. None of the works attempted to discuss a similar need from an African perspective with a view to looking at the specific language challenges and needs of African asylum seekers and refugees within Africa. That is what this study seeks to achieve.

Theoretical Framework

The focus of sociolinguistics is on language use, that is, on what can be said in a particular language, by whom, in whose presence, when and where, in what manner and under what social circumstances. The torchbearers of this theory, Nida and Taber (1969, p. 7), insist on the fact that information should be manipulated to enable target receptors to understand the message. In order to achieve this, the sociolinguistics element of the text must be analysed. Parameters such as ethnic origin, profession and living conditions of the target audience must be taken into consideration.

The relationship between translation and sociolinguistics is an obvious one since by definition sociolinguistics refers primarily to the use of language in society in communicating. Since society differs from one another and the way language is used in these societies for interpersonal relations differs, sociolinguistics becomes indispensable for translation and interpretation. Nida (1991, p. 25) is also of the opinion that the different ways in which societies employ language in interpersonal relations are crucial for anyone concerned with translating. The translator or interpreter is viewed as a facilitator between the structure of the source text and the transformation to be effected in the target text. Humanitarian workers providing assistance to refugees have different linguistic and cultural backgrounds necessitating the translator or interpreter to bridge the gap for effective communication to take place.

Regarding language change and sociolinguistics focus on variation in time, on how a given change spreads internally within a language and possible correlations between that change and concepts such as prestige. The natural changes in a language can promote translation activity while translation can also be a promoting agent for language change (Kranich et al, 2011).

Data Presentation, Analysis and Discussion
Profiles of Respondents – Refugees
Gender

Of the 120 refugees that filled the questionnaire, 40% are male while 60% are female. At the time of administering the questionnaire, women gathered around the researcher. This could be explained by the fact that women constituted a sizable percentage of the site population. They were more enthusiastic than men. The gender of the respondents is shown in Table 1.

Table 1: Gender

Gender	Frequency	Percentage
Male	48	40%
Female	72	60%
Total	120	100%

Age

The ages of the respondents range from between 20 to 60 years. Of the 120 respondents, 35% are within the ages of 20-30 years, 35% within 30-40 years, 21.7% within 40-50 years and 8.3% within 50-60 years. This shows that the dominant age group is adult. The age distribution of the respondents is shown in Table 2.

Table 2: Age

Age	Frequency	Percentage
20-30	42	35%
30-40	42	35%
40-50	26	21.7%
50-60	10	8.3%
Total	120	100%

Ethnic background

Of the 120 respondents, 87% are of the Mbororo tribe, 5% are Gbaya, 5% are Hausa, while the other tribes are 3%. Most of the refugees from Mbororo tribe were farmers or shepherds. This accounts for the fact that interpretation into their local language is of utmost importance for effective communication to take place with them. The tribes of the respondents are shown in Table 3.

Table 3: Ethnic background

Ethnic background	Frequency	Percentage
Mbororo	104	87%
Gbaya	6	5%
Hausa	6	5%
Others	4	3%
Total	120	100%

Languages spoken

It is worthy of note, that besides the French language, Sango is the second official language of the Central Africa Republic. According to the site officials, about 98% of the site population speaks Sango, while 10% could communicate in French language. This implies that a sizable number of the refugees could communicate among themselves in Sango, but not with most humanitarian workers who are Cameroonians or of other nationalities. Of the 120 respondents 87% spoke Fulfulde which they call Fulata. And a total of about 13% of the sample population spoke minority languages like Gbaya, Hausa and others. This shows the need for translation for humanitarian agents who neither spoke Fulata or Sango languages.

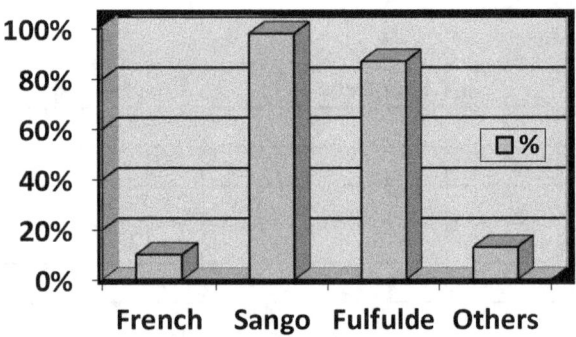

Figure 1: Languages spoken

Registration with UNHCR

All the 120 respondents were registered with the UNHCR. This also implies that they have been screened and have had an interview with the humanitarian officials. It goes further to show that most of them would have had the services of interpreters.

Need for translators and interpreters

Those who needed the services of interpreters were 90% of the total number of respondents. It was observed that the 10% that did not need interpreters were those who could communicate in the French language. The need for interpretation services is reflected in Table 4.

Table 4: Need for translators and interpreters

Need for Interpreters	Frequency	Percentage
In need of interpreters	108	90%
Not needing interpreters	12	10%
Total	120	100%

Communication with humanitarian workers

Out of 120 respondents, 90% interacted with the humanitarian officials through local interpreters. Some of the local interpreters are themselves refugees who were hired to render other services alongside interpreting. Those who spoke French were usually co-opted as volunteers to interpret and serve in other areas. Some refugees missed dates of events previously communicated to them because they were written in the French language. Some argued that if the information were written in Arabic they would have been able to read them.

Areas of assistance needing translation and interpretation

Interpretation services were needed in three of the four areas mentioned in the questionnaire. Advocacy was not applicable at the time of the collection of data. Of the 120 respondents, 90% needed interpretation during registration, health care delivery and aid distribution.

Evaluation of translation and interpretation services received

When asked to assess the services of interpreters/translators received, 5% of respondents evaluated the services as excellent, 20% evaluated them as good, 45% said it was average, 20% said it was poor, while 10% was not applicable. The respondents for which interpretation was not applicable were those who spoke the French language alongside Fulfuldé or Sango. The interpreters were from the local community and those co-opted from among the refugees. This shows that competent translators and interpreters were not used by the humanitarian agencies. This is revealed in table 5 below

Table 5: Evaluation of translation and interpretation received

Quality of service	Frequency	Percentage
Excellent	6	5%
Good	24	20%
Average	54	45%
Poor	24	20%
Not applicable	12	10%
Total	120	100%

Hypothesis testing

The hypotheses proposed in this study are subjected to empirical test to determine whether to accept or reject them as the case may be.

The first hypotheses proposed in this study states that:

H1: Newly arrived refugees from Central Africa Republic into Cameroon are in real need of translation and interpretation in receiving assistance from humanitarian workers.

From the findings of this study, we accept that newly arrived refugees from Central Africa Republic into Cameroon are in real need of translation and interpretation services to enable them to receive necessary assistance from humanitarian workers.

Respondents' answers revealed that 90% of the respondents needed interpretation/translation to get registered. 90% needed interpretation/translation in order to interact with the humanitarian workers while receiving assistance. This is further confirmed by the fact that interpretation was needed in all the areas in which humanitarian workers provided assistance to the refugees.

Profiles of Respondents

a. Humanitarian workers Nationality

The survey sample for humanitarian workers comprised predominantly of Cameroonians. Out of a total of 60 questionnaires which were handed out, 45 were filled and returned. Of the 45 respondents 39, representing 87%, were Cameroonians. Other nationalities included three Central Africans representing 7%, one Togolese representing 2%, one Ugandan representing 2% and one Ivorian representing 2%. This is understandable because most operational partners depended on national staff to implement their policies. Female respondents were slightly more than the male (55%). This is of no particular importance as the researcher noticed the presence of both male and female workers at the Gado refugee site.

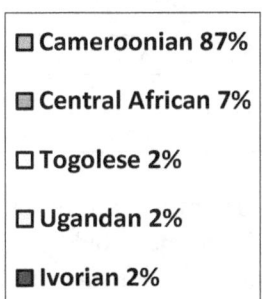
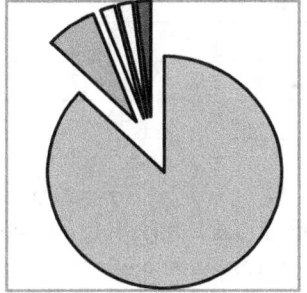

Figure 2 – Nationality

Official languages spoken

As regards the official languages, of the 45 respondents, 47% speak only French, 38% speak French and English, 11% speak French, Arabic and Sango, and 4% speak French, English and Sango. This shows that those who could effectively communicate with refugees without

interpretation are a total of 15% while 85% would obviously need interpretation.

Table 6: Official languages spoken

Languages spoken	Frequency	Percentage
French	21	47%
French, English & Sango	2	4%
French and English	17	38%
French, Arabic & Sango	5	11%
Total	45	100%

Organization represented in the survey

The staff of these humanitarian agencies returned the questionnaire to the researcher in the following percentages as reflected in table 7 below:

Table 7: Organizations represented in the survey

Organization	Frequency	Percentage
International Federation of Red Cross/Cameroon Red Cross	23	51%
Plan Cameroon	6	13%
Doctors Without Borders	3	7%
International Relief & Development	5	11%
World Health Organization	3	7%
United Nations High Commissioner for Refugees	3	7
World Food Program	2	4%
Total	45	100%

The International Federation of the Red Cross and Red Crescent Societies (IFRC)/Cameroon Red Cross (CRC) has the highest number with 51%. The Red Cross is an important implementing partner of the UNHCR. They are directly responsible for managing some refugee sites including Gado site where the researcher did the field work.

Types of services provided

Concerning the services provided, it is shown that in relative terms, the highest number of humanitarian workers (16 respondents) representing 35% came from the health and nutrition sector. 13 workers representing 29% in agro-pastoral and socio-community service sector, 12 workers representing 28% in education while the other sectors with four respondents accounted for 8% of the workers.

Position and Period of Service

The survey included humanitarian workers with different responsibilities such as Camp manager, medical doctor, nurses, midwife, information management coordinator, health coordinator, veterinary nurse, volunteers as teachers, interpreters, aid distributors, among others. The longest serving humanitarian worker is the respondent that builds shelter for refugees. He has been doing this job for about 20 years; the shortest serving humanitarian worker is an intern who has only worked for one month. They are both of the Cameroon Red Cross.

Need for Translation and Interpretation

Of the 45 respondents, those who needed the services of interpreters in the discharge of their duties were 85%, 10% did not need interpreters at all, 5% sometimes needed interpreters. It was observed that the 10% that did not need interpreters spoke Fulfulde which is the major language spoken by the refugees. The need for interpretation services is reflected in Table 8 below.

Table 8: Need for translation/Interpretation

Need for Interpretation	Frequency	Percentage
Need Interpreters	38	85%
No need of interpreters	5	10%
Sometime need interpreters	2	5%
Total	45	100%

Language Unit

Of the seven organizations from which the 45 respondents came, only one organization, representing 14% has a language unit. Six of the organizations do not have language units. The organization with a language unit is the International Federation of the Red Cross and Red Crescent Societies.

Table 9: Language unit

Organization/language unit	Frequency	Percentage
Have language unit	1	14%
Don't have language unit	6	86%
Total	7	100%

From the above table, we see that most of the humanitarian agencies have not yet seen the need to have language units in their organizations.

Evaluation of translation and interpretation services received

When asked to assess the services of interpreters /translators received, 11% indicated that they were excellent, 20% said they were good, 22% said they were satisfactory, 25% evaluated the services as poor while 22% left the space blank.

Table 10: Evaluation of translation and interpretation services received

Evaluation	Frequency	Percentage
Excellent	5	11%
Good	9	20%
Satisfactory	10	22%
Poor	11	25%
Blank	10	22%
Total	45	100%

It is worthy of note that 10% of the respondents who did not fill anything indicated that they could speak Fulfuldé (as indicated in question 4 concerning local languages spoken), which may be the reason why they did not need the services of interpreters. Based on the interaction of the researcher with the respondents, the remaining 12% found it difficult to evaluate the services they received since they could not measure the quality of these services. This therefore calls for someone to supervise the translation and interpretation services rendered.

Hypothesis testing

H2 –Humanitarian organizations providing assistance to refugees from the Central African Republic in Cameroon do not use competent translators and interpreters to facilitate communication.

From the findings of this study, we accept that humanitarian organizations providing assistance to Central Africa Republic refugees in Cameroon do not use competent translators and interpreters to facilitate communication with them. In testing this hypothesis, respondents' answers revealed that 90% of the respondents do not use the services of professional interpreters and translators. 86% do not have a language unit.

Profile of Respondents
b. Translators and Interpreters
Gender
Of the 15 translators and interpreters that filled the questionnaire, 53% were female and 47% were male. This shows that females are more represented in the translation and interpretation work among refugees.

Table 11: Gender

Gender	Frequency	Percentage
Male	7	47%
Female	8	53%
Total	15	100%

Working Experience
Of the 15 respondents, 27% have been in the translation business for 2-5 years, 53% for 5-10 years, and 20% for 11 years and above.

Table 12: Working experience

Working experience	Frequency	Percentage
0-1	-	-
2-5 years	4	27%
5-10 years	8	53%
11 and above	3	20%
Total	15	100%

Type of Training Received
Of the 15 respondents, eight, representing 53% were trained in translation and interpretation while seven others, representing 47% are linguists as reflected in table 13 below:

Table 13: Type of training received

Type of training	Frequency	Percentage
Translation & Interpretation	8	53%
Linguist	7	47%
Others	-	-
Total	15	100%

Contact with refugees and area of service

We observed that 13 of the respondents had been hired to provide translation and interpretation services to humanitarian agencies including the UNHCR. The remaining two of the respondents are employed as in-house translators in the only humanitarian organization that has a translation unit.

Table 14: Contact with refugees and area of service

Contact with refugees	Frequency	Percentage
Worked with refugees	13	87%
Staff of IFRC	2	13%
Total	15	100%

Evaluation of services
All the 15 respondents are of the opinion that translation and interpretation are important in providing assistance to refugees.

Table 15: Evaluation of service

Evaluation of services	Frequency	Percentage
Important	15	100%
Total	15	100%

Appreciation of translators/interpreters in refugee context
Out of the 15 translators, 14 respondents representing 93% are of the opinion that translators and interpreters are underutilized in Cameroon while one person, representing 7% feels they are not underutilized.

Table 16: Use of translators/interpreters

Opinion about translators/Interpreters	Frequency	Percentage
Underutilized	14	93%
Not underutilized	1	7%
Total	15	100%

Challenges encountered in discharging duties

Out of the 15 respondents, only one in-house translator, representing 7% did not indicate having a particular challenge in the discharge of his duties. However, the remaining 14 respondents, representing 93% indicated that they encountered problems in the discharge of their duties. The summary of the problems highlighted are seen below:

i. Lack of adequate working tools such as office space;

ii. Lack of appreciation of translators;

iii. The challenge of having to combine translation work with other duties;

iv. Emotional trauma arising from pathetic stories recounted by refugees and the need to overcome stress associated with consecutive translation in a formal setting.

Hypothesis Testing

H3 – Translators and interpreters play key roles in helping the humanitarian agencies provide assistance to the refugees in Cameroon.

From the findings of this study, we accept that translators and interpreters play key roles in helping the humanitarian agencies provide assistance to the refugees in Cameroon.

Respondents' answers revealed that 100% of the respondents were involved or have been involved in translation/interpretation in helping the humanitarian workers provide assistance to the refugees in Cameroon. Furthermore, 100% of the respondents are of the opinion that translation/interpretation is really important in providing assistance to refugees.

Conclusion

This study was carried out based on three objectives. The first was to highlight the importance of translation and interpretation in providing assistance to Central Africa Republic refugees in Cameroon. This objective required the formulation of the first research hypothesis that guided the collection of data through questionnaires for refugees. The study proved that Central Africa Republic refugees are in need of translation and interpretation services as the majority of those from the research sample (87%) are essentially agro-pastoralists of the Mbororo tribe with no formal education. Sango, the second official language in Central Africa Republic is more widely spoken (by 90% of the population) than the French Language. This makes it imperative to overcome the language barrier between refugees and the humanitarian agents who neither speak Fulfulde nor Sango. Besides, 90% of the population sample indicated the fact that they needed translation and interpretation services in different areas ranging from registration with the UNHCR, receiving health services, and other forms of assistance.

The second objective of the study was to identify the efforts of humanitarian workers to overcome language and cultural barriers through translation and interpretation in providing assistance to Central Africa Republic refugees in Cameroon. This objective led to the formulation of the second research hypothesis that guided the collection of data through questionnaires for humanitarian workers. The results indicated that even though 85% of the humanitarian workers could not effectively communicate with refugees without translation and interpretation services, only local interpreters recruited from amongst the refugees or from the local community were available to assist them in the discharge of their duties. Some of these humanitarian workers were not even sure of the reliability of the services they were receiving from these interpreters as reflected in the fact that 22% gave no response when asked to evaluate the translation and interpretation services they had received from the makeshift local interpreters. Moreover, out of seven humanitarian organizations surveyed, only one had a translation unit.

The third objective of the study was to examine the role of translators and interpreters in helping humanitarian agencies to provide assistance to refugees. This objective also led to the formulation of the third research hypothesis that guided the collection of data through questionnaires for translators and interpreters. All the 15 translators and interpreters surveyed (100%) have been involved in rendering services to humanitarian agencies and they are of the opinion that translation and interpretation services are important in helping humanitarian workers provide assistance to refugees. In addition, they are of the opinion that competent translators and interpreters are underutilized in providing assistance to refugees in Cameroon. Out of the 15 translators and interpreters, 14 of them representing 93% believe that translators and interpreters are underutilized in the above-named context in Cameroon.

Even though local interpreters have been recruited to help solve the problems of language barrier, there is need for professional translators and interpreters to coordinate these efforts and make sure that these volunteers are adequately trained for the job they are to do.

References

ACAPS. (2014). "Analyse des besoins de crise République Centrafricaine", *Conflit,*
Décembre 2013 – Fevrier 2014.

Barsky, R. F. (2012). "First encounters: Knowledge interpretation on the frontlines of
cross-cultural encounters", *Global Media Journal* Canadian Edition, 5 (1), 53-74.

Cameroon Tribune. (2014, March 14). "Arrêté no 269 du 13 mars 2014 portant création d'un
comité interministériel ad hoc chargé de la gestion des situations d'urgence concernant
les réfugiés au Cameroun".

Clune, D. and Hosey, J. (2003). "New Neighbours, New Opportunities, Immigrants and
Refugees in Grand Rapids". Michigan: Dyer-lves Foundation.

Integrated Regional Information Networks-IRIN. (2014, February 12). "Who are the Anti-
Balaka of CAR ? ". Retrieved from www.irinnews.org at 11:00 am (2014, April 23).

Kranich, S., Beeher, V., Hoder, S. and House, J. (2011). Multilingual Discourse Production:
Diachronic and Synchronic Perspectives. Amsterderm/Philadelphia: John Benjamins.

Mandryk, J. (2010). *Operation World*. Colorado Springs: Biblica Publishing.

Neba, A. S. (1999). *Modern Geography of the Republic of Cameroon*. Bamenda:
Neba Publishers.

Nida, E. and Taber, C. (1969). *The Theory and Practice of Translation*. London:
United Bible Society.

Nida, E. (1991). "Theories of Translation". *TTR : traduction,terminologie, redaction,* 4 (1),
19–32. doi:10.7202/037079ar

Refugees Advise Centre & Finnish Immigration Service. (2010). *Interpretation in the Asylum*
Process : Guide for Interpreters. Retrieved from http://www.refworld.org/docid/5449fe6a4.html at 11:45am (2014, August 22).

Reuters. (2014, January 15). *Central African Republic Religious Hatred was Underestimated.*
New York: United Nations Organisation.

Social Care Institute for Excellence. (2015, May). "Good practice in social care for refugees
and asylum seekers". In *SCIE Guide 37*. Retrieved from
https://www.scie.org.uk/publications/guides/guide37-good-practice-in-social-care-with-refugees-and-asylum-seekers/ at 10:35 pm (2017, June 13).

UNDP. (2014). Human Development Report 2013. Retrieved from http://www.undp.org at
12 :30 pm (2014, September 24).

UNHCR document. (2006). *The State of the World's Refugees, Human Displacement in the*
New Millennium. New York: Oxford University Press Inc.

UNHCR. (2007). *Protecting Refugees and the Role of UNHCR*. Geneva: United Nations
Organisation.

UNHCR. (2011). UNHCR *Refugee Resettlement Handbook*. Retrieved from
http://www.unhcr.org/resettlementhandbook at 1:50 pm (2014, September 24).

UNHCR. (2014). *Rapport interagences sur la situation des réfugiés centrafricains.* Geneva:
United Nations Organisation.

UNHCR. (2014). *Global Appeal for 2014.* Country operations Profile. Geneva:
United Nations Organisation.

VOA News. (2014, September 11). "Crisis Looming in Cameroon for Refugees".
Retrieved from www.voanews.com/content/cameroon at 8pm (2014, September 11)

The Influence of Cross Cultural Communication on Communication Research in A Changing World

Chukwuma Anyanwu, PhD

Deparment Of Theatre Arts, Faculty of Arts, Delta State University, Abraka

Email: bonnyanyanwu@yahoo.com/anyanwubc@delsu.edu.ng

Abstract

Communication is said by experts in the field to be the wheel that drives the engine of the society; that neither society nor communication can operate meaningfully without the other. It has also been observed by communication scholars that every society gets the kind of media it deserves. The implication is that the ideology which a given society has inevitably rubs off on its culture and communication and inevitably determines the mode and type of communication education in such society, hence of its research. No doubt, the world of the 21st century is remarkably different from the worlds of past centuries. It is particularly so as it has not only manifested the predictions of Herbert Marshall McLuhan about the global village, the media being the message and the extensions of man; it has transcended such predictions beyond imagination. This paper discusses how a people's culture, the society they live in and the kind of ideology they live by affect the communication research in such a society even as the world continues to change on a daily basis, with particular emphasis on Nigeria. The paper uses library research method by looking at extant materials on the subject. Arising from the findings, conclusion is made and recommendations were suggested.

***Key words**: Communication, Society, Research, Culture, Education.*

Introduction

The main concerns of life are constituted not only of the major events of human existence which dominate media attention but also includes those apparently insignificant events that never ever get noticed or are deliberately ignored by the media. Yet, most times it is these neglected issues and events that fester and over the years convolute and burst forcing attention on themselves. Human beings are very unique in several ways. While being basically the same in every facet of their being, they are nevertheless eminently different. This difference is a product of the culture which they have developed over the years; the society they live in and the ideology which drives their overall world view. These put together affect and determine how these human beings relate and communicate with one another within the same cultural and ideological space and beyond. They also have impact on how they (human beings) work towards improving, inventing, maintaining their means of communication and of course how the communication process is evolved. It is an intricate business as the concepts in the foregoing discourse are intertwined. That is, society, culture, ideology and communication, are interrelated and even cyclical in their

relationship and have impact on communication research. It is therefore, the focus of this paper to attempt an explanation of how these elements fuse together collectively to influence and impact communication research especially so in a world that is not static. This is done with recourse to library research method where extant materials are utilized.

It must also be pointed out that the concepts mentioned above fuse together and intertwine in mutual interdependence to drive a society towards a social nexus, thus making the society progress or retrogress in accordance with the principal ideology prevalent at that point in time. In Nigeria where contending forces for and against education abound, and where the need for communication research is equally opposed by some as it is craved by others, it becomes necessary to make a case for cross-cultural research especially given the multi-ethnic nature of our country.

Definition of Concepts

It is necessary to explain the concepts which constitute the topic of this discourse in order to leave nothing to chance in comprehension. Culture entails the way and manner in which a people do things. It is what a people choose to be; how they see themselves, how other people see them irrespective of what the reality is. For instance, the world today sees Nigeria and Nigerians as corrupt; it thus becomes part of their culture notwithstanding that not every Nigerian is corrupt. Thus, like democracy which is said to be the rule of the majority, culture operates in much the same manner. Anyanwu (2015: 30) says that "communication is the sharing of information, ideas, knowledge, thought from one person to another, or from several people to one person. Necessarily, there must be something to be exchanged in the communication encounter." He goes on to say that communication is cyclical in nature with no clearly defined beginning and no end because both sender and receiver are constantly swapping roles, (Anyanwu, 2015). On the other hand, Bulus (2015: 258) draws her definition of communication from several sources when she says, "communication can be defined as interacting socially through messages and interacting socially through both human and technological messages. This means that communication can be achieved both through interpersonal and modern means of communication (radio, television, cinema and so on)." Again, on their part, Grossberg, WArtella, Whitney and Wise (2006), submit that:

> Communication is perhaps the most human of all human activities. Humans have been seeking new media through which to extend the possibilities of communications- their ability to transcend time and space-since the invention of writing paper, and much later, the printing press. (xvii).

Communication as noted above is also the most engaging of all human activities. It is such a compulsive act that even against the will, every human still communicates. This is why its study is very vital to man since it enables him to understand himself better.

On the other hand, culture as defined by Asigbo and Ejue (2012:65) "is a people's way of life; how they bring up their young, bury their dead, sing, dance, respond to insults, fight their battles, cook, eat their food and so on,". In other words, culture consists of how a people live their lives and interact both with themselves and their neighbours. On his part Gana draws his definition of culture when he quotes Aina as saying that:

> Culture can be seen as the principal equipment through which men and women in society cope and

interact with either material environment, which though also shapes them, but which depending on their specific level of social and economic development they shape to a greater or lesser degree for the provision of their basic and other needs. Through integrative roles culture is significant in the creation of a moral community within any defined society, providing the bonds and symbols for the existence of people within communities. (Gana, 2016:336).

The two definitions of culture above show that culture is a product of a people's accumulated manners and methods of doing things. It has direct impact on their successes and failures as well as influences their thinking process. It regulates the totality of their being and makes them to be what they eventually turn out to be in the eyes of those who relate with them as well as affects the nature of such relationship. Culture from the submissions above would comprise all the components of collective interaction and activities of people in a given society. We will now turn our attention to society.

Society has been variously seen by experts as an aggregate of people living together in a more or less ordered community, embracing a clearly defined geographical space. It is collective co-existence of persons within defined geographical or conceptual environments. Anyanwu (2015:31) cites UNESCO's definition of community as "an aggregation of groups which vary in social class, economic status, often in political or religious affiliation and also in outlook and opinion." He goes on to say that "any community, large or small, is held together by a nexus of communications." Going further, he enumerates the characteristics of society which have some similarities with those of communication. Having noted that neither society nor communication can do without the other he declares that, "the relationship between communication and society cannot always be cordial," (34). While writing on political communication, Anibueze (2015: 153) says that "one aspect of community experiencing (sic) is self-interest versus group interest. Community life implicates group life, but not all members of a community would agree every time, all the time, on how things are or on how thing should be." It is this attitude of members of a society/community not being in agreement on how things are or should be that necessitates communication research in order to arrive at conducive and misunderstanding free living environment or a gross reduction of disagreement in the way society is governed.

This now takes us to research and communication research in particular. Research in its simplest term is regarded as a thorough investigation designed to discover, confirm, prove, or disprove the veracity of things in the light of new discoveries. Research, however, has many definitions depending on the field of study or the aim for which it is embarked. We will extract a few from the joint work of Fawole, Egbokhare, Itiola, Odejide and Olayinka (2005:2), who give the following definitions of research:

- Research is an endeavour to study or obtain knowledge through the use of systematic approach with the intent of clarification.
- Research is a curiosity-driven activity that has the purpose of discovery and advancement of knowledge (Basic Research).
- Research is a systematic investigation designed to develop or contribute to general knowledge.
- Research is a form of inquiry that involves seeking of evidence to increase knowledge. It involves a systematic process for recognizing a need for information, acquiring and validating that information and deriving conclusions from it.

Research from the foregoing is an organized enquiry into phenomena. Having established that research is a systematic inquiry to increase knowledge, we turn now to communication research. As has been noted:

> Communication research is the application of the scientific method to the study of the process and effects of communication. Like all research, it frowns strongly at hunches, conjectures, unsystematic method of arriving at conclusions, and un-procedural writing of reports, (Tejumaiye, 2003: 48).

From the foregoing, it is quite plain that communication research follows a specific method and procedure in order to arrive at its objective. It does not align itself with things being done haphazardly or carelessly. It requires thoroughness and must be systematic to be accepted. Needless to state, ideology encompasses all the concepts which constitute the present topic. This is because it covers how a people live, communicate, their culture, their attitude to and reactions to change, among other things. *The Oxford Dictionary Thesaurus & Wordpower Guide* (2001: 634),

offers two definitions of ideology as: (1). "a system of ideas and ideals forming the basis of an economic or political theory." (2). "The set of beliefs characteristic of a social group or individual." Ideology would be from the above, a collection of ideas and beliefs governing the mindsets of people.

Both definitions clearly show that ideology is embedded in a society's manners and methods of doing things, their belief systems, their political systems, their religion, spirituality; intellectual and mental reflections. Indeed, a people's ideology covers their world view. It affects the totality of their being collectively as a people as well as individuals. It necessarily affects their communication research and their communication itself. Ideology permeates the worldview of a people and thus shapes their attitude, informs their decisions, guides their relationships and controls their temperament. If the ideology is good, it affects the entire comportment of a people progressively. And the reverse, if it is bad. What Helon Habila, cited in Okoroegbe (2016: 99), said about military regimes can help us get the impact of ideology or lack of it on the society:

> There was nothing to believe in: the only mission the military rulers had was systematically to loot the national treasury; their only morality was a vicious survivalist agenda in which any hint of disloyalty was ruthlessly crushed.

Ideology, then, helps to give focus and directive and points a people either to success or failure, depending on their set objectives. It provides ideas that enable them bear fruits of progress if the leadership is good and the opposite if otherwise. It is based on the values, beliefs and accepted norms of behaviour. Like culture, ideology is not static; different regimes operate different ideologies. There is group/national ideology as well as individual ideology. The former is projected by the government in power and it rubs off on the people. One can say that national or group ideology runs from top to down as the people ape what their leaders do. Ideology is also peculiar to professions and disciplines. While trying to explain business ideology, Professor Gerald Cavanaugh, cited in Sturdivant (1985), defines it as, "a coherent, systematic, and moving statement of basic values and purposes. It is a constellation of values generally held by a group, and those in that group tend to support one another in that ideology," (p.79). Going further, Sturdivant notes that, "ideologies evolve over time as realities force changes in basic beliefs," (p. 80). Thus, different governments and or institutions can change the way they do things based on the new ideology which they choose to identify with. This can naturally affect communication research and communication in general, to align with what they believe in or value. The concepts espoused in this work are all intertwined in interdependent relationships where none can be clearly separated from the others.

Now, that we have taken care of these conceptual details, we will now turn our attention on how these concepts impact and influence communication research and affect a society's reaction to change and changing. Change is of course seen as the quality of being dynamic or different; not constant, the ability of not remaining the same for any significant length of time, while changing is the process which brings about the said change. Indeed, while it is said that change is constant, that is, it has the ability to always occur irrespective of the length of time it has remained unchangeable, it must happen. One major characteristic of change is that it is almost always gradual, except when and where things go contrary to their natural state, at such times, change can be sudden.

The influence of Cross-Cultural Communication on Communication Research in a Changing World

Cross-cultural communication as the name implies, is communication across cultures, embracing the different peoples and their cultures. It is appropriate in a multi-ethnic nation such as Nigeria. In this work, we have seen how culture, communication, ideology and research operate in a collectively and intertwined relationship. Even though they are interwoven, it would be pertinent to also discuss how the elements singly influence and are in turn influenced by communication research before discussing such influence in their collective. This would help to properly guide the paper as well as aid comprehension. We will therefore begin with society.

Society and Communication Research

Society has culture, communication and ideology as its elements. All of them operate in a sort of cyclical relationship where they fuse together to achieve relevance. Society is the catalyst to the others and is therefore the pulley that draws the rest together and engenders research. How is this done? By its nature, society which can be used interchangeably or substituted for public, community, masses or the people contains the germs which cause it to grow as well as to fall. Society seems simple yet complex. Its complexity arises from the people who dwell in it. And

these people are as different in their needs as they are in their wants and as their physical appearances, especially their faces are. In the same token, these people comprise those with high intelligent quotient (IQ), low IQ, medium and out-rightly dull even to the level of imbecility. Because of the nature of humanity, they must live together and work together. This makes it inevitable that there must be problems associated with both individual and collective needs, which must necessarily be addressed using communication. And when communication fails, the consequence is crisis. The complexity of these needs from these different individuals and societies and the necessity to live in a conducive, environment makes communication research unavoidable. Communication embraces the entirety of the media, print, electronic, non-verbal, etc. which are used to disseminate information in any given society.

> Broadcasting therefore, serves as the town hall where all segments of the society, the elite group and those who are not well educated, meet to speak their minds to the people in government and for the government to explain their actions in form of a report card for the people who voted them into power. (Okoduwa, 2014: 5).

Society therefore needs to embark on communication research for the purpose of serving its own needs better. Failure to do so would be paving way for chaos, anarchy, lawlessness, and indeed, making itself to being near unliveable as only the fittest are likely to survive. It is through communication research that society unknots the twine of misunderstanding, oppression, violence, corruption and all the negative tendencies which humanity are prone to and which make it difficult for peaceful coexistence. Communication research discovers what caused what, when, where, how, and provides the why. With these society is better off and life becomes meaningful, even enjoyable to live. Communication research also helps society to know which media, that is, which communication medium would serve any of its segments better as noted in the quotation from Okoduwa above. Adelabu cites Peskin by saying that there are three ways to look at how society is informed. These according to him are:

- that people are gullible and will read, listen to, or watch just about anything;

- that most people require an informed intermediary to tell them what is good, important, or meaningful, and;
- that people are pretty smart-given the means-they can sort things out for themselves-find their own version of the truth. (Adelabu, 2008: 365).

The above is evidence of communication research at work as it concerns what the society needs in order to understand itself. Thus, society influences communication research or rather, the nature of society as noted above makes communication research inevitable.

Culture and Communication Research
Culture cannot be discussed effectively without recourse to the media/communication nor can the reverse be possible. That may account for why Campbell, Martin and Fabos (2009), chose to link culture with mass communication in their explanation of the former. As they put it:

> Often, culture is narrowly associated with art, the unique forms of representational expression that give pleasure and set standards about what is true, good, and beautiful. Culture, however, can be viewed as a broader category that identifies the ways in which people live and represent themselves at particular historical times. The idea of culture encompasses fashion, sports, architecture, education, religion, and science, as well as mass media. Although we can study permanent cultural forms, such as novels or songs from various historical periods, culture is always changing. It also includes a society's art, beliefs, customs, games, technologies, traditions, and institutions. It also encompasses a society's modes of **communication:** the process of creating symbol systems that convey information and meaning (for example, language systems, dot-dash Morse code, motion pictures, or one zero-binary computer codes). (6).

They go further on the same page to explain that culture is made up of the products a society fashions and more importantly, the processes that forge those products and reflect a culture's diverse values. On the basis of the foregoing, they then define culture as "the symbols of expression that individuals, groups, and societies use to make sense of daily life and to articulate their values." They observe that culture "links individuals to their society, providing shared and contested values and the mass media

help circulate those values," (6). The foregoing clearly spells out the relationship between culture and communication. Culture cannot function effectively without the mass media to project and promote it. In the same token, communication is the link between the media and culture and it thus becomes necessary to involve communication research in order to ferret out how this relationship works and what it entails. Communication research here would focus on life in its entirety. This is because from the definition and explanation of culture above, culture is life. It then becomes the responsibility of communication research to find out everything about culture that makes it good or bad and its relevance or lack of it to society. Indeed, culture by its definition engenders communication research and since culture is always changing even as society too is in a flux, the necessity to determine what triggers this change; whether it is for better or worse, its impact on society etc., are all reasons for communication research.

Again, since mass media are essential part of culture, there is need to embark on communication research not only to find out the relevant medium to serve a particular aspect of culture, it is also important to research to discover the purpose of culture, its functions, its dynamism, as well as how the people relate to it. It is also needed to know how media workers see and treat culture and how they, (media workers) are treated against the backdrop of the culture where they work. All these are vital for the good of society and the betterment of mankind. It has been proved from the above that culture embodies in itself the reasons for research; therefore, communication research is influenced by culture as an aspect of society. In our culture where some people in authority exhibit clear apathy against research and new ideas especially where they concern investigating into bad governance and given our cultural multiplicity, the need for cross-cultural research cannot be over emphasized.

Ideology and Communication Research
Ideology is much subtler to comprehend than culture, society or communication yet none is complete without it. Indeed, none of the concepts can function effectively without ideology nor can anything in life be fruitfully and gainfully utilized where there is no ideology. It is the silent but inevitable presence of ideology that runs society, guides culture, controls communication and determines the success or failure of a people and their government and nation. Ideology is the invisible force that makes or mars a

people and makes them what they eventually turn out to be. If a people are corrupt, bad, good, progressive or retrogressive, whatever a people are, their worldview, culture, internal and international relations, government policies, everything, is a consequence of their ideology. This being so one would then ask; how does ideology affect and influence communication research and how does communication research fare in the light of ideology?

Before delving into the question raised above, it is necessary to reiterate the fact that ideology is belief, attitude and conviction driven which is why it is not easily perceivable except in physical manifestation of actions, inactions and utterances. Thus, for ideology to have influence and affect communication research, it must be predicated on government's policy on education and related fields. It is such policy and government's attitude to it based on its content that would impact on communication research. Recall also that communication permeates the entirety of man's life and as such whichever aspect of it that has challenges, should need to be researched on. But focusing specifically on academics as it relates to communication research; one needs to look at media research as it concerns print, electronic, social and related areas such as news agencies, public relation, advertising and all the adjuncts of the mass media and more.

Again, depending on the government's policy/ideology on education for instance, the nation's academic calendar and or, curriculum should be updated regularly to fit into modern needs. It is this ideology that affects curriculum development where education is regarded. As Okoye (2017p.6) has noted:

> Curriculum development is defined as planned, purposeful, progressive and systematic process carried out to create positive improvements in the educational system. Whenever there are changes or developments happening around the world, the school curricula are affected. There is then the need to update them in order to address society's need.

Ideology is central to how things are done in a nation or country and communication research is no exception. Beyond the academia however, government communications commission or the ministry of communication and or information should pilot the communication research effort. This is because government at all levels should be proactive on how information is packaged for their various interests. Again, the effects of certain communication with certain bodies-like external affairs, the military of all shades as it affects national and external relations/security-, among others are all subjects for communication research. It must be recalled that all the media-electronic and print, cable and satellite inclusive, invariably become coveted by governments once they are invented. In some cases, governments through their various security interests help to invent or improve the communications technology already in existence. If government does not take part in media invention, it inevitably features prominently in their control. As early as 1923, the trio of Campbell, Marin and Fabos, already cited, give instance of government's interference in broadcasting.

> As early as 1923, the Federal Trade Commission had charged RCA with violations of antitrust laws but allowed the monopoly to continue. By the late 1920s, the government, concerned about NBC's growing control over radio content, intensified its scrutiny. Then, in 1930, when RCA bought out the GE and Westinghouse interests in the two NBC networks, federal marshals charged RCA/NBC with a number of violations, including exercising too much control over manufacturing and programming. Although the government had originally sanctioned closely supervised monopoly for wireless communication, RCA products, its networks, and the growth of the mass medium dramatically changed the radio industry by the late 1920s. After the collapse of the stock market in 1929, the public became increasingly distrustful of big business. In 1932, the government revoked RCA's monopoly status, (P.129).

The foregoing is merely to illustrate how governments can interfere with the interest of communication thereby influencing communication research. It does not have to be stated in government ideology that it would censor communication, nor would it be necessary for government to do so. It suffices that governments universally are not comfortable with the operations of the media no matter the nature of such media. It is in this way that ideology subtly or otherwise influences communication research. On the other hand, communication research can be provoked by the media practitioners based on their own media policies. They may wish to find out how best to do their work; how to survive in the face of perceived threats and professional hazards, how to project a balanced view in their report; how to cover the various segments of society and what to do and why in all areas of their profession. These and more, are the various ways that ideology can influence and be influenced by communication research since it takes communication research to discover what ideology a particular government projects, in some cases. Unfortunately, the ethnic politics of our people is anti-research because the tendency for an Hausa led government for example to discredit or ignore the outcome of a Yoruba or Igbo led research is high, because such research would be accused of being bias on the basis of ethnicity, in spite of the objective of the researchers.

How Society, Culture and Ideology influence and are influenced by Communication Research

We have seen from the foregoing, the cyclical nature of the relationship between society, culture, communication and ideology. It is quite difficult if not out rightly impossible to consider one without the order. Even when they are not clearly spelt out, they still remain interwoven. This is because one concept dovetails into the others and helps to project them and make them more significant and clearer. It is however, research that unearths the underlying similarities and differences in all of them. Since all are driven by communication, it is communication research in its various types that connects them and also separates them in order to bring out their unique attributes. For instance, with the aid of communication research, one gets to know the appropriate media to serve each segment of the society. In the same vein, communication research determines the language, the culture, the ideology which governs a people's belief systems, their relationships, the religion and everything about them. In our specific focus, communication research helps to identify the best methods for teaching and imparting knowledge as well as the effects of such knowledge on the society. In this way communication research through its discoveries and recommendations engenders other forms of research. It must be noted here that the web which links culture with ideology is not easily perceivable in its physical form; it can however, be noticed in the ways and manners of doing things by the people; their attitude and response to old and new ideas and such tell-tale signs that give insights into society's pulse and impulse.

It is however, through communications research that these subtle and not so obvious signs are unearthed and decoded. Thus, communications research is the web that links

society, culture and ideology. Without communications research, little or nothing would be known about a society's culture, ideology and even methods and means of communication. Society, culture, ideology and communication, are therefore, a revolving disc that cannot be easily separated. They are catalysts to and for the institution of communications research, as much as communications research is catalyst to and for them.

Conclusion

The paper has exhaustively examined the relationship between culture, society, ideology, and communications research, noting that it is cyclical and intertwined such that the web of linkage cannot be easily discerned or separated. It was established that communication research determines and influences investigation into the other concepts, notably, society, culture and ideology. All the concepts are dynamic and are prone to change on the basis of the prevalent ideology as well as engender research into and about one another. For instance, the people's culture can cause research to be carried out on how they live, behave; their beliefs and values, their ideology, etc. The society both generates communications research and also fights against it especially when it appears that things are going contrary to how certain people in the society, including the government, want them to go. This in turn is dependent on the prevalent ideology which is operable by the powers that be in the society.

Recommendations

Arising from the findings above, the following recommendations are hereby proffered:

- Society by its nature breeds and generates the germs that lead to its growth as well as destruction. It therefore, needs communications research to guide it on the right part and protect it from itself.
- A society succeeds or fails based on the prevalent ideology which it adopts, it is thus recommended that the more positive the ideology, the more upward mobile such society would be.
- Research by its nature is ongoing. Society must always engage in one form of it or the other and ensure that all units are covered in order for it to be constantly up to date with current trends.
- Given the multi-ethnic nature of Nigeria as a nation prone to indulging to defend and condole evil on ethnic basis, cross-cultural research is recommended in order to accommodate all the

ethnic strands and address their communication needs.

- There is need for enlightenment of the people by government at all levels especially on the need to unanimously condemn whatever is worthy of condemnation without recourse to ethnic, religious or even political affiliations.

- Lastly, no society can afford to do without communications research since communication holds the key to its progress, therefore, communications research is necessary to help the society actualize itself.

References

Adelabu, O. (2008). Citizen Journalism Practice: The 21st Century Challenges for Nigerian Journalism, In E. M. V. Mojaye, O. O. Oyewo, R. M'Bayo & I. A. Sobowale (Eds.). *Globalization and Development Communication In Africa.* Ibadan: Ibadan University. Pp. 363-373.

Anibueze, S. (2015). Advertising and Political Communication: A Game of Euphemisms, Lies and Myths? In J. E. Aliede (Ed.) *Studies in Communication, Mass Media and Society: Discourses and Debates.* Lagos. Public Relations Mix (PR-Mix). Pp. 149-160.

Anyanwu, C. (2015). Communication and Society: An Introductory Overview. In J. E. Aliede (Ed.) *Studies in Communication, Mass Media and Society: Discourses and Debates.* Lagos. Public Relations Mix (PR-Mix). Pp. 28-37.

Asigbo, A. C. & O. G. Ejue. (2012). Evolving a Universal Culture for Peace, Good Governance and Sustainable Development in Nigeria. In. A. B. C. Chiegboka, T. C. Utoh-Ezeajugh, E. U. Ibekwe, C. C. Nwosu, N. C. Oguno & K. L. Nwadialor. (Eds.). *The Humanities And Good Governance.* Nimo. Rex Charles and Patrick Ltd. Pp. 65-69.

Bulus, C. S. (2015). African Communication Systems As Current Discourse in Mass Communication. In J. E. Aliede (Ed.) *Studies in Communication, Mass Media and Society: Discourses and Debates.* Lagos. Public Relations Mix (PR-Mix). Pp. 256-272.

Campbell, R., C. R. Martin, & B. Fabos. (2009). *Media & Culture: An Introduction to Mass Communication, 6th Ed.* New York. Bedford/St.Martin's.

Fawole, I., F. O. Egbokhare, O. A. Itiola, A. I. Odejide and A. I. Olayinka. (2005). Definition, Spectrum and Types of Research, In. Olayinka, A. I., V. O. Taiwo, A. Raji-Oyelade, and I. P. Farai, (Eds.). *Methodology of Basic and Applied Research.* Ibadan: The Postgraduate School. Pp. 1-17.

Gana, E. T. (2016). Nollywood and the New Media Interface: Exploring New Spaces for the Theatre. In. B. F. Ayakoroma. (Ed.). *Repositioning Nollywood for The Promotion of Nigeria's Cultural Diplomacy & National Security.* Ibadan. Kraft Books, Ltd. Pp. 334-341.

Grossberg, L., Wartella, E., Whitney, D. C. and Wise, J. M. (2006) *Media Making: Mass Media in a Popular Culture, 2nd Ed.* London. Sage.

Okoduwa, M.E. (2014). *Broadcasting and Politics In Nigeria.* Lagos: Mat-Emos Publishers.

Okoroegbe, F. N. (2016). The Angel as a Dictator: *Waiting for an Angel* and Postcolonial Military Politics in Nigeria. *ANA Review: New Series.* Vol. 4. Pp. 99-119.

Okoye, N. S. (2017) *The Curriculum of Higher Education in Nigeria: The Paradox of Having Everything and Lacking Everything.* 59th Inaugural Lecture, Abraka, Delta State University..

Oxford Dictionary Thesaurus & Wordpower Guide. (2001). Oxford: University.

Sturdivant, D. F. (1985). *The Corporate Social Challenge: Cases and Commentaries, 3rd Ed.* Illinois. Irwin.

Tejumaiye, A. (2003). *Mass Communication Research: An Introduction.* Lagos. Sceptre.

Trends and Tensions in Christian Missionary Enterprise in Africa, 1860-1930, And African Response: The Nigerian Example

Kanayo L. Nwadialor

Department of Religion and Human Relations, Nnamdi Azikiwe University, Awka

Email: Kl.nwadialor@unizik.edu.ng

Abstract

At a certain point in time, the history of the Church in Africa reached a turning point. This was when the spirit of separatism started within the Church due to white domination, maltreatment of the blacks by the white missionaries and the influence of education. It is quite obvious that as soon as the European missionaries, especially the British Protestants, were established in Africa, the white missionaries began to see themselves as belonging to a special group of rulers. Their safety was further guaranteed by the presence of colonial administrations and the breakthrough in European medicine with the discovery of quinine as an antidote to mosquito related malaria. This perhaps, added to what has made them to arrogate more powers to themselves. Furthermore, the missionaries could not bring to Africa the 'pure milk of the gospel', but like the majority of human beings, were unable to emancipate themselves from the cultural, emotional and social frame in which they were accustomed to living and expressing their religious lives in Europe. They lived in an age when European civilization and Christianity were believed to hang together as cause and effect, as root and branch. It was then natural that they considered their theological approach, their own forms of marriage and burial, their narrow concept of family and individualism as in the main the best for African converts as well. African culture on the other hand is essentially a religious culture and its customs and behaviour are geared towards religious concepts almost completely. African religion had silently, and over innumerable centuries entered a happy symbiosis with the ambient culture such that to be African in culture meant to be African in religion and to separate them was a most delicate operation whose equivalent in surgery might be the separation of Siamese twins. But the early missionaries had little patience for such finesse and delicacy. Since the missionaries were trying to convert the people to a new religion they could not escape condemning many practices as 'heathenism'. What else could they do but attack the traditional culture, which represented the rival religion they were trying to supplant? The resultant effect was a reaction by African converts that eventually shook the foundation of a universal Church in a similar way that the 16th century Reformation in Western Europe did to Christendom, and consequently, a new course was chatted for a distinctive African Christianity.

Introduction

The decade after 1850 marked the turning point in African history. Repeated attempts by the Europeans to penetrate the hinterland of Nigeria, for instance, since 1832 by way of the River Niger-signaled by the famous Niger expeditions-had failed disastrously after twenty-two years of continuous effort to accomplish their object. A similar fate greeted the earliest attempt to introduce Christianity to West Africa. The Roman Catholics were the first to send missionaries to West Africa in the 14th, 15th and the 16th centuries. These missionary endeavours were championed by the Portuguese. By 1487, the Portuguese, who had already opened up trading connection with Benin City two years earlier, sent out Portuguese Catholic Christian missionaries to Benin City and old Warri. These early missionaries laboured under difficult conditions. Despite the initial good reception, the mission to both Benin and Warri collapsed due partly to inadequacy of the numerical strength of the missionaries and partly to the cold feet which the traditional rulers and their people developed later. The military and political reasons for which the traditional rulers received the missionaries were no longer coming forth, so they lost the patronage of the kings. The unfriendly climatic conditions also contributed to the discontinuation of the missionary work. It finally collapsed as there were no natives strong and convinced to carry on, but the sites were identifiable.

The successful expansion of the Christian missions in West Africa began in the 19th century. The first half of that century witnessed a revolution in European attitudes and policies towards West Africa. The protracted struggle to end the Trans Atlantic slave trade registered its first decisive victory in 1807, when Britain, the most powerful industrial and maritime power of the day, proscribed the trade to her citizens. It would be expected that the abolitionists had won a legal victory, but legal enactment was not effective enough to put a final stop to the inhuman activity until 1833. This was because several notable African chieftains who had thrived on slave trade were not in a hurry to stop without any promise of an alternative profitable trade, and several other European nations like Spain, France, and Portugal had continued with a trade that had been proscribed by the British parliament. The British government decided to enter into treaties with United States of America (USA) and other European countries to enable them to enforce the parliamentary Act of May 1, 1807. Britain, therefore, authorized her Navy to capture foreign slave dealers on the high seas. The slaves thus captured were sent to Freetown in Sierra Leone. Thus, Freetown became a conglomeration of people from several Nigerian and West African ethnic groups. The Sierra Leone settlers were exposed to Christian doctrines and Freetown was

to serve as a nerve centre for the spread of Christianity and civilization in West Africa.

The anti-slavery movement did not only result in the founding of the settlement in Sierra Leone in 1787, but also in the entry of new missionary societies into West Africa. The Protestant missionary societies practically dominated the field during the first half of the 19th century. Through the vigorous activities of these missions, Churches were planted in major centres in Africa. The missionaries, at a point, had a strong desire to evangelize the interior of West Africa. Unfortunately, the Europeans had some difficulties. The most prevalent was the mortality of most of the missionaries through malaria attack, which had earned West Africa the derogatory appellation of "white man's grave". In addition to this were the acute shortage of funds to sustain the European staff, and finally, the language barrier. These predicaments propelled the leadership of

many of the missionary bodies to formulate a policy which would allow Africans to be given a measure of freedom to evangelize the interiors of Africa under the supervision of the European missionaries. African converts too, by and large, supported this policy and on the whole, there was good accord between them and the missionaries until the 1860s when strains began to be felt in their relationship and there were new developments in the African sentiment.

This study therefore aligns with the submission of Rieber (1977) that beginning from the 1860s there was a change in European relations with Africans which affected their relations in the Church as well as elsewhere. The reasons for the change may be attributed variously according to one's weighing of economic, political, or social influences. The thrust of this paper, therefore, is to investigate the factors behind the change in this erstwhile cordiality that characterized the relationship between African Christian converts and their European mentors. The research further seeks to understudy African response to this change with special reference to Nigeria and see if there is a connection between this incidence and the emergence of what may be considered a distinctive African Christianity.

Socio-Religious Background of the Nineteenth Century Missionaries to Africa

Since the history and behaviour of any missionary group in Africa cannot be fully understood unless an attempt is made to understand the prevailing theological, cultural, and political ideas, norms and values from which the missionary group developed. And since this study deals with British missionaries, particularly Protestant missionaries, an attempt is made to discuss briefly some of the prevailing theological, cultural, and political ideas and beliefs in Britain in the 18th and 19th centuries. The present researcher argues that these ideas and beliefs shaped the attitudes and behaviour of the British missionaries towards the Africans.

One of the major theological movements that shaped the ideas and beliefs of many British missionaries in the 18th and 19th centuries was the Evangelical movement. It is pertinent to note that since many of them were evangelicals, they shared some theological and political ideas. Kamuyu (1988) opines that the evangelical movement was started by a group of Christians at Oxford University in 1735. It involved mainly the Anglicans. Evangelical theology was selective, individualistic, pietistic, and often unreflective. He continues to say that the rise of the evangelical movement was prompted, among other things, by a reaction against an age which it felt to be an age not of faith but of atheism, deism, rationalism, secularism, doubts, skepticism and excessive materialism.

One of the leading men of the English Evangelical movement was John Wesley. Like other evangelicals, Wesley believed in the literal interpretation of the Bible, the importance of the spread of the gospel in the world. Through Wesley and other notables such as George Whitefield, Charles Wesley, William Booth, and Dwight Moody, the Evangelical movement spread like wild fire throughout Europe and America. It is out of this movement that some of the missionary groups arose.

The Evangelical theology contributed to the missionaries' attitudes towards what they considered to be African secular life. The evangelicals had developed the doctrine of two kingdoms, namely, the kingdom of salvation and sanctification, and the kingdom of the world. The first kingdom is headed by Christ while the head of the second is Satan. This doctrine of the two kingdoms had a substantial influence on the missionaries who perceived the African world as a world headed by Satan while their world was headed by God. This corresponds with what Baur (2005) considers as the Augustinian view of history as a fight between the kingdom of God and the kingdom of Satan. Hence missionaries saw the fight against African customs as a fight against Satan, and traditional religion simply as idolatry. Its sacrifices were "adoration of Satan", to be fought as Satan himself. This was due to two misconceptions: on the one hand, there was the unfortunate but suite general European prejudice that Africans were a primitive people without religion; on the other hand, it had become generally accepted in Europe that all magic and all spirits were devilish. Consequently, the missionaries, not knowing anything about ancestor and fertility and cults, or the African distinction between protective and harmful magic and between medicine man and witch, rejected all and everything as Satan's service. Hence all "fetishes" had to be burnt or buried. Consequently, the medicine men became their great adversaries, to be pursued mercilessly until they submitted. This ruthless attempt at rooting out all superstitions can only be explained by another European axiom: "There is no pact with the devil".

Once again, a common European prejudice, this time a misinterpretation of the Bible, hindered any deeper understanding of the African social situation. Africans were regarded as the "cursed sons of Ham", hence polygamy, and also trial marriage were understood as symptoms of their unbridled sensuality. Canon Law had to be strictly observed; customary marriage was to be regarded as concubinage. The fear of eternal damnation must have been the main motive for complying with the two basic religious demands; to give up superstition and polygamy.

Ozigbo (1988) also notes that apart from the image of Africa, the theological culture of the evangelicals is such that the Jewish biblical and patristic view of "idols" and "gods", and of "idolatry", had hardened into a rigid Christian dogma, long before the missionaries arrived Africa. Saturated and burdened with cultural borrowings from other people, the missionaries had developed a phobia against syncretism. The European missionaries seem to believe that by insisting on accommodating African peculiarities, they might be aiming a fatal blow at the universality of the Church where everyone of every culture should feel at home. Okere (2005) articulates the fear of the European missionaries in the following questions:

> Has there not been enough lamentation and wailing for instance at the loss of one universal language of the Church, especially in liturgical functions? Would further nibbling at the Church's external unity not lead ultimately to a fragmentation of what was a fine, solid piece? Would not the irrefragable truth and the very deposit of faith be compromised if each little minority tribe, each little pocket of humanity was to aim at refashioning the gospel according to its own image and likeness? (p. 48).

Thus, when one element after another was denounced as heathen, marriage, masquerade, medicine, music, dance, funerals, sculpture, and theology-it was a whole culture, a whole world that was being bulldozed out of existence, and the movement of a people's conversion became an insidious iconoclasm. (Okere, 2005).

The evangelicals also believed in the doctrine of extreme civil obedience; this view which believes that the Secular Empire cannot exist without inequality in person, that some be free and some in bondage, some masters and some subjects played a major role in the suppression of African patriotism by the European missionaries in Africa. This idea, according to Enwerem (1995) informed a racialist gradation of races. Baumer (1977) further describes the race gradation of the period as meaning that the best endowed obviously meant Homo Europeans, who were at that time carving out empires all over the world. Thus, it could be inferred that Christianity, the religion of the finest race (Europeans), was superior to 'paganism'. The evangelical's doctrine of obedience to the state represents inbuilt nationalistic and patriotic tendencies within Protestant theology. This nationalism and patriotism were equally strong among the European missionaries in Africa. However, they were disguised under the mantle of Christian evangelism among the 'heathens'.

British nationalism and patriotism were not only built into Protestant evangelical theology but were rampant in the British life and society. Stratford (cited by Kamuyu, 1988) observes that "since the middle of 18th century the spirit of nationalism and patriotism was on the increase in Britain and the Wesley's revival movement had kindled British patriotism and gave it a divine direction" (p. 160). He goes on to argue that the patriotism of many Englishmen in both the 18th and the 19th centuries was based on both the idea of spreading civilization to other parts of the world and upon the hatred of atheism.

The above discussion provides us with background information to show that before the missionaries left Europe they were committed not only to the preaching of the Christian gospel but also to the spreading of the European culture with its prevailing nationalism and patriotism.

The Period of Crisis

From the 1860's, European missionaries entering different parts of Africa were beginning to speak a language that their African colleagues had not been accustomed to hear in the time past. The European missionaries where beginning to see themselves as rulers, and the word 'native' was acquiring a new and sinister meaning. The earlier cooperation between the white and black missionaries in the founding of Christian Churches in Nigeria prior to 1860 was no longer fashionable. This change in the relation between the European and African missionaries from the 1860's had great effects both in the Church and elsewhere. The reasons for the change may be attributed to economic, political and social influences.

First, there is the moving story of the conflict within the missionary bodies, especially within the C.M.S of two irreconcilable views on the strategy for successful missionary enterprise amongst native peoples. One view of which Henry Venn, the secretary of the C.M.S., was the leading exponent, declared that the firm foundation of Christianity amongst native peoples was through the creation of local Churches which, while orthodox in doctrine would be capable of self-government, self-supporting and self-extension. With the first of these goals in mind, Venn had, from the start of C.M.S. activities in Africa, sought to provide for training Africans that are largely Christians-to fill the necessary positions. Moreover, owing to the point of view of Europeans, the shortness of missionary purse as well as the lesson from the sad failure of earlier Roman Catholic efforts, the solution to the above ideas was seen by its exponents as the settlement of the native Church upon the ecclesiastical basis of an indigenous Episcopate independent of foreign aid and superintendence. This view implies an impressive measure of confidence in the ability of the natives.

The missionaries in the field did not agree with Venn on this issue. Their opinion was that the African was good as an assistant to European missionaries. The chief exponent of this view was Henry Townsend of the Yoruba mission. Townsend had superiority complex believing erroneously that Europeans were born to rule and that Africans were devoid of both moral and spiritual characters and qualifications to be able to take over the administration of the Church. Olanisebe (2006) captures Townsend's notion about African agents thus; there were like babies yet to be weaned from breast feeding. On one occasion, when Henry Venn proposed that two more Africans should be ordained as clergymen in addition to Samuel Ajayi Crowther who had been the only African ordained clergy man before 1851, Townsend opposed the idea vehemently saying "I have a great doubt of African clergymen. They want years of experience to give stability to their characters; we would rather have them as schoolmasters and catechists" (Ajayi, 1965: 181). More so, Townsend believed the respect that the Negroes had accorded the white stemmed from the belief by the former that God had bestowed talent on the white which should be held in trust and used for the Negros's good. Shrinking this responsibility given to the white, to Townsend, was tantamount to sinning against God. The tussle between these points of view at first resulted in the temporary victory of Venn over Townsend, a victory which was made manifest in the consecration of

Samuel Crowther as the first African bishop. In 1873, however, Henry Venn died and with him disappeared the last remaining obstacle to the triumph of the other point of view. Unfortunately, Henry Venn's dream did not materialize. Venn's successors at the C.M.S headquarters in London thought differently about Africans. According to Gaiya (2001) "the successors of Henry Venn began to unwind his indigenization policy. They looked down on Africans and relegated them to the background, probably because of pigmentation of skin" (p. 5). Tasie (1978) gives a similar testimony as he notes that Henry Venn, Crowther's patron in C.M.S. and whose faith in the bishop and Africans in general was unlimited, was by this time already dead. By the mid 1870's the reasons for continuing the Niger mission as a field entirely manned by African agency no longer had strong support. Almost immediately Townsend's view, this time, got the upper hand under a regime of arrogant young men who claimed to be burning with the zeal of the Lord, but whose actions and policies would seem to have sprung from a racial arrogance clearly incompatible with the Christian ideal of equality of all before God, as well as from their subscription to contemporary pseudo-scientific anthropological speculations on the Negro's place in nature. Consequently, from the 1870's African agents of the missions within the historic Churches were condemned to subordinate status.

Secondly, medical facilities had since improved the European life span in most parts of West Africa. By 1877 Europeans had become convinced that the talk of the treachery of the African tropical climate was rubbish and they urged white missionaries to be ready to go to areas hitherto feared because of their deadliness. Incidentally, this was the period when there was the general belief among all classes of Europeans-missionaries, traders, explorers and administrators-that Africans were inherently incapable of comprehending the eternal principles of the Christian faith, or that it would be in the distant future before genuine Christian converts could be made. If it took Christianity centuries to find roots in Europe, it seemed to them, how could it be expected that Christianity would be implanted in primitive Africa in matter of years or decades? The implication of this was that the spiritual fitness of African agents of the missions who were spreading Christianity, not merely as auxiliaries but in many cases as pioneers, had been too much exaggerated; that by allowing African missionaries to disseminate Christianity without the physical supervision of white missionaries a grievous harm had been done to genuine Christianity in Nigeria. To correct

the 'regrettable mistake' that had been inadvertently made, it was absolutely necessary for the white missionaries to resume all control of existing mission establishments and pioneer all new openings. Ajayi (1965) adds that the missionaries as Europeans became like gods and tended to treat their parishioners as less than men. The dialogue was virtually suspended, for gods have no need to argue. The missionaries were able to exploit the prestige and the power of the white man already won by the colonial soldiers and administrators.

It was obvious that this generation of European missionaries adopted the early attitudes of Townsend, and in this circumstance was able to force acceptance of their racial ideas, translated in hierarchical term, though not without damaging the structure they sought to build. The early European ambivalence seen first in Townsend, had arisen over the role of Samuel Crowther, and it was in respect to his position that the abnormalities of the situation first became apparent. His rank helped to unify the opposition of the European missionaries to the African assumption of power and to extend their arguments from Crowther to the men who followed in his path.

From the economic point of view, missionary enterprise in Africa that had benefited from its close contact with trade and government was to be disadvantaged as they became increasingly Europeanized. This was the period of growing competition between European nations known as the scramble for Africa. Crampton (1978) notes that "Goldie, the principal British trader in Nigeria, desired to eliminate competition between the British firms and exclude foreign competitions; to accomplish this he used political as well as commercial intrigues" (p. 25). Although he was not a missionary, Goldie knew how to appear as philanthropist to the public in Britain and he gave the impression to the C.M.S authorities that he was sympathetic with their aims. Particularly he appeared as the champion of those opposed to the trade in spirits. Goldie however, disliked the C.M.S. mission agents from Sierra Leone, many of whom were closely connected with African middlemen who he desired to eliminate from trade (Flint, 1960). The African missionaries were naturally sympathetic to the native traders who were their relatives, friends and parishioners than to the remotely controlled European company of Goldie. It is little wonder that the Europeans desired to discredit the African missionaries. Some of them may be embarrassed by the presence of African representatives of the faith whose teachings many of them were not living up to. The European traders also resented the policy of Sunday observance maintained by African missionaries. They maintained that it was a peculiar invention of African missionaries unknown in European Christian countries. Walker (1931) who gives the semi-official C.M.S story says that:

> Traders and other Europeans brought stories of incapacity and even of moral failure. Probably some of these tales were untrue and others greatly exaggerated by white men who were unsympathetic or even hostile to the mission, but there were enough in them to cause Bishop Crowther and the C.M.S committee the gravest anxiety. (p. 153).

In the period under discussion the tension within the mission circle erupted into an open controversy and assumed a wider significance when educated lay Africans joined the issue on the side of the native agents of the missions. Both African clerics and laymen saw as their chief opponents to European missionaries who, so they charged, through fierce sectarianism but common contempt for African customs and institutions, were doing grave harm to Africans by creating new divisions among them and by destroying the wholesome base of African society. They argued that reform was necessary; and was to be brought about through the agency of an independent African Church movement. They regarded this as a thing ordained by God and the beginning of African Christianity.

African Response and the Emergence of African Church Movements

The history of African Church movement is largely the history of the reaction of the African people to the colonial tendencies of the European missionaries. Meanwhile, there was a large participation of the blacks in the founding of Christianity in Africa from the periods before 1860. In order words, early attempts to evangelize Africa involved the blacks already resident in Sierra Leone after the abolition of the infamous slave trade by the British government. However, despite serious participation of blacks in the founding of the Churches in Africa, a dramatic change in European relations with Africans came in the 1860s manifesting in the inhuman treatment of native agents and the relegation of the blacks to the background after Christianity had been planted in Africa. The change affected relations in the Churches as well as in other sections of public life. Shapperson (1968) notes that:

Africans reacted against over strict disciplining of native converts by European missionaries, showing the desire of some native separatist ministers to increase their personal power and status by administering Church property and money, the creation of native Churches in which due respected was to be paid to native customs, and the rejection of the colour bar in many European controlled Churches. (p. 251).

However, this reaction against colonial tendencies of the European missionaries can be seen in two broad forms.

First is the establishment of Ethiopian or African Churches. These Churches were established as separated groups from the historic Churches because the founders wanted their own indigenous leadership. They usually kept the doctrine and forms of worship of their "mother Churches". They are called Ethiopian or African Churches and they began at the end of the 19th century and flourished especially in the first decades of the 20th century. In Nigeria, the United Native African Church was constituted as early as 1888. The Native Baptist Church had broken away from the Baptist Church, in protest the unpleasant treatment of the first Nigerian Baptist pastor Moses Ladejo Jones. By 1901, the African Incorporated Church came into existence. The Church which called itself the United African Methodist (Eleja) Church was born and it used the fish as it symbol (Omoyajowo, 1995). They were in a sense, secessionists. They were referred to as Ethiopians probably because they derived their inspiration from the oldest Church in African, the Ethiopian Orthodox Church. These Churches are also called African Churches because most of them included "African" in their names as a way of expressing their Africanness or African consciousness.

Some of the schismatic sects in the independent Churches were inspired by Hebraic influences as well as by African traditions and beliefs. The willingness of the local Christians in Africa to assert their independence of foreign missionary bodies was practically demonstrated in their readiness to make financial contributions towards the maintenance of their own Churches. As early as 1869, indigenous Christians had begun to relieve the missions of the burden of funding education. In 1873, Nigerian Christians in Lagos formed the Society for the Promotion of Religion and Education. This act annoyed the European missionary bodies who saw it as a conspiracy to drive them out of Nigeria.

Except for the Catholic Church, many other missionary bodies began to have local protests within them. The African members felt uncomfortable and cheated. Some protested against the administrative setup in the Church, others complained of discrimination or obvious doctrinal issues. Ogungbile (2001) also notes the founding of the Ethiopian communion Church on October 1, 1919 by an Ibadan indigene, Adeniran Oke. The Church is still in existence presently but with a change of nomenclature, National Church of Christ *(IJo Orile-Ede Adulano Ti kristi)*. The Church incorporated certain African cultural elements into their liturgy, songs, and ritual practices. It is also important to note that Nigeria gained her independence the same date and month that the Church was founded.

These separatist movements were remarkably early manifestations of protest against white domination and the status of inferiority. Barrett (1968) sees these separatist movements as that geared towards the principle in which the individual congregation or Church is an autonomous and egalitarian society free from any external ecclesiastical control. Idowu (1965) sees it as a movement of the Church of God in Africa, which must know and live in the watchful consciousness that she is part as well as "presence" of One Holy Catholic and Apostolic Church. Onuwa (1991) sees it as the desire for autonomy and independence of African Churches, which was the genesis of the development that crystallized into what we know now as Nigerian nationalism as well as the struggle for political independence. There is also the natural and logical desire to found Christianity more firmly in African culture by the acceptance and encouragement of African clergy. Hence, Parrinder (cited by Okere, 2005) avers that the:

> Ethiopian Churches have arisen not because of different doctrinal opinion since there have really not been many formal African heresies. They are the expression of need for freedom and independence, at times in the face of dictatorial missionaries, at times against the alien, formalistic style that stifles the spirit. There is a general fear that African customs, laws, dance, families, marriages, languages, dress, foods, etiquette, proverbs and philosophy would disintegrate or be altogether destroyed. The new Churches have kept the Bible, the prayer books and the hymnals of their original missions but they have added their own colouring, playing the calabash instead of the dreary, boring harmonium. (p. 57).

Babalola (1988) supports that the Ethiopian or African Churches had little quarrel with the doctrine, practice or ritual of mission Christianity. Rather the Ethiopian or African Churches came into being only because they emphasized important Christian truth neglected by European missionaries or because they valued their independence too highly to accept colonial missionary status. Their main complaint was the monopolization of leadership by Europeans.

African Response and the Native Pastorate Question

While Ethiopianism in Africa aimed at secession from the mission established Churches to form independent African Churches under the control of Africans themselves, the native pastorate aimed at the advancement of the 'natives' to the highest ecclesiastical offices within the mission Churches. It was a struggle towards the actualization of the far-sighted vision of Henry Venn whose idea was a clear-cut distinction between the duties of a missionary and that of a local pastor. For Venn, in all questions relating to settlement of a native Church in any mission field, it is important to keep in view the distinction between the office of a missionary, who preaches to the heathen, and instructs inquirers or recent converts, and the office of a pastor, who ministers in holy things to a congregation of native Christians. While the work of a missionary may involve for a time the pastoral care of newly baptized converts, it is important that, as soon as settled congregations are formed, such pastoral care should be devolved upon native teachers (Shenk, 1983). Native teachers are to be regarded, after their ordination, as pastors of the native Churches, rather than as the agents of a foreign society, or of other independent parties.

The native converts assumed that the European missionaries would wittingly co-operate with them in their aspiration for the realization of the native pastorate scheme; the consecration of Samuel Crowther as bishop of the Niger territories and the complete Africanization of the Niger mission before 1870 excited the hopes of Africans. But in the eighties their hopes in the foreign missions began to wither away. According to Ajayi and Webster (1999):

> Beginning from the 1880s the ideas of racist who believed in the inherent inferiority of Africans, intellectually, morally and spiritually began to be popularized. This idea formed up the tide of the native pastorate principle. (p. 152).

60

The missionaries overtly sanctioned the imperial policy of the British government and the natives virtually lost their rights and became mere servants to the white people. The progressive policy of Henry Venn could no longer found favour with European missionaries who began to discredit native pastors as not possessing the requisite experience and moral standing to lead the congregations. Africans who felt that the time had come for them to stand on their own and make Christianity reflect the religious and political environment of Africa began to nurse the seedling ambition of the actualization of the native pastorate scheme. Some who were impatient with the European missionaries' imperialistic policies broke away to form the Ethiopian or African Churches. Others who believed in the consummation of the native pastorate principle remained in the mission Churches to pursue their aspirations.

They envisioned an African Christianity which would incorporate suitable aspects of African religion, adopt its own language, hymns and liturgy, and create a Christian nation because for them, the Church of England is not their own. They considered the native pastorate as an acceptable means to that goal. This nationalists' hope troubled both the European missionaries and the administrators; however, the native pastorate was established and grew. In Sierra Leone, committees were set up to collect contributions for the native pastorate scheme. Rieber (1977) also notes that "by 1889 all the Churches in Lagos but one had been absorbed into the native pastorate, and already in 1882 it had become a missionary body with stations outside of Lagos" (p. 269). On 29 April 1892, the Delta pastorate was created among the Igbo in the Onitsha district (Ayandele, 1966).

Some other missions seemed to profit from the C.M.S. experience. The Wesleyan mission conceded to the Lagos Circuit, organized in 1878, all authority in managing its affairs, including the payment of salaries. Self-government was complete by 1880. Also, by 1880 the Scottish Presbyterians among the Efik had a committee which controlled all finances. The American Southern Baptists had to learn in their way. Even though the mission had been kept alive by Blacks from 1863 to 1874 and the missionary sent in 1875 was sympathetic to African aspirations, W.J. David still felt that Africans must accept the leadership of white men; on the other hand, M.L. Stone had carried on too frequently and ably on his own as a Church leader to accept such a secondary role. When David sought to restrict stone's opportunities, violated Baptist constitutional procedures, and arbitrarily dismissed Stone from the mission, most members separated from the Church in Lagos and became the native Baptist Church in 1888. Consequently, European Baptist missionaries were withdrawn from Lagos until after 1914 and the independent Lagos Churches again returned to the mission fellowship with much greater strength as the native pastorate.

To make it indigenous the prayer book was revised to exclude prayers for the Queen of England and prayers for the native kings were substituted. Native names became acceptable for baptism and native airs were sung in the Church. Consequently, by the end of 19th century the prestige of the white missionaries had fallen sharply, and the days of the all-powerful, paternalistic and patronizing missionaries were clearly over. By 1889 James Johnson had concluded that African converts had vindicated their ability to administer and organize and that they were mature enough to be allowed by the British government to participate in the administration of their country by the election of representatives to the legislative chamber (Ayandele, 1970). A European missionary remarked in 1880 that:

> The native pastorates have done their best to bring about a root of revolting spirit in the Church. The cry the native, the native, is simply the worst you can do to them. They cannot bear it. This spirit of revolt against the white elements in the Church will it not go over to politics? (Ayandele, 1966: 102).

Conclusion

The years between 1860 and 1930 were ones of tensions between the Europeans, both as missionaries, traders and colonial masters on one hand, and the Africans as educated elite and Christian converts especially the ex-slaves from Sierra Leone who had returned to their fatherlands following the expansion of Christianity and European influence on the interiors of Africa, on the other. This study has shown how evangelical theology and political ideas prevalent in Europe in the 18th and 19th centuries influenced and affected the work of European missionaries in Africa and consequently strained their relationship with their African partners. It was discovered that the evangelical theology was selective, individualistic, pietistic, and often unreflective. Hence missionaries saw African religious and secular life as a reflection of the kingdom of Satan, and traditional religion simply as idolatry that must be fought with and destroyed. It was also discovered that British patriotism and nationalism of the 18th and 19th centuries were built into evangelical theology such that the missionaries were not only preoccupied with the desire to evangelize the un-evangelized Africa, but they were much more endued with the erroneous belief of the superiority of Europe over Africa.

Undoubtedly, the last quarter of the 19th century which saw the partition of Africa also saw a definite growth in Europe of the feeling that Europeans were a superior and the Africans an inferior race. The interest of the European power in Africa was rising. In place of the lonely missionary explorer largely dependent on African goodwill in the interior of Africa and therefore in a position to show respect and deference to Africans where this was due, there began to descend upon Africans a horde of European adventurers and explorers backed up powerfully by European government, often with an army of porters and mercenaries bearing deadly maxim guns. They had no need to show deference to Africans; it was unnecessary, impolitic and inexpedient.

Coming into Africa as contemporaries and landsmen of the rapacious vanguards of imperialism would not quite easily have endeared the bearers of the good news to the native population who had just been recovering from the ravages of the slave trade. The missionaries, zealous apostles, but still people of their time and place and race, entered Africa heavily loaded with prejudices and complexes. At this period too, the belief that European missionaries, by virtue of their society's long experience of Christianity, were the best instrument for the propagation of the gospel began to gain currency, correspondingly the view began to be strong that the evangelization of African peoples was no longer safe in the hands of educated Africans. As a spokesman declared openly in Exeter Hall in 1881:

> The romance of missions must be given up for the facts of missions. The unique experiment, which is of a completely African staff under an African bishop, was henceforth supposed to have failed. The Saro agents, 'foreign Africans', were now considered a curse rather than a blessing; their removal would be a blessing and not a regret; genuine Christianity could be propagated only by Europeans. (Ayandele, 1967: 56).

In the circumstances, the old theory of equality was being challenged not just by individual missionaries but by official general body of Europeans in Africa. Many missionaries would themselves have none of the scientific evolution or anthropology, but they gave consideration to the theory that Africans were the sons of Ham cursed by Noah to serve forever the children of Shem and Japheth, particularly Japheth, consequently, the type of aspersions cast by Henry Townsend on his African colleagues, which had been treated in C.M.S House in the 1850's as heresies, had by then become an everyday orthodoxy (Ajayi, 1961).

Real power was often in the hands of the Europeans on the spot and they often used it to retard the advancement of their African colleagues and to discourage the development of higher education for them locally or overseas claiming such education unfitted them for missionary work as it cut them off from their own people. In the circumstances, some Africans became frustrated and they began to revise their opinion of the intentions and the benevolence of the Europeans. One main result of this new development was that conflict became discernible in the ranks of the educated Africans. A small extremist group, finding the tutelage of European missionaries irksome and frustrating, began to question the whole basis of the partnership between the educated Africans and the missionaries. They therefore began to denounce the mental slavery which, they said, the missionaries were substituting for the old physical slavery in Africa and to urge the mental emancipation. Africans in the mission Churches, therefore began to pursue vigorously the realization of the Native Pastorate agenda on the conviction that there were equipped to run the affairs of their local Churches. Those who were not patient with the Native Pastorate agenda decided to pull away from the mission founded Churches to establish African Independent Churches. In either case, both the Native Pastorate agenda and the independent Churches did not only ensure African leadership of the Churches but African customs and practices acceptable by Christian ethics were accommodated in Christian life and liturgy thereby carving out a niche for a distinctive African Christianity in the global comity of Christians.

References

Ajayi, A. J.F. (1961). Nineteenth century origins of Nigerian nationalism. *Journal of Historical Society of Nigeria*, 11, 1, 196-210.

Ajayi, J. F.A. & Webster, J.B. (1999). The emergence of new elite in Africa. In J.C. Anene & G.

Brown (Eds.). *Africa in the nineteenth and twentieth centuries* (pp. 149-164). Ibadan: University of Ibadan.

Ajayi, J.F.A. (1965). *Christian missions in Nigeria, 1841-1991: The making of new elite*. London: Longman.

Ayandele, E.A. (1966). *The missionary impact on modern Nigeria, 1842-1914: A political and social analysis*. London: Longman.

Ayandele, E.A. (1970). *Holy Johnson: Pioneer of African nationalism, 1836-1917*. London: Frank Cass.

Ayandele, E.A. (1964). Traditional rulers and missionaries in pre-colonial African. *Tarikh* 3, 1, 21-46.

Barrett; D.B. (1970). *Schism and renewal in Africa: An analysis of six thousand contemporary religious movements*. London: Oxford University.

Bauner, F.H (1977). *Modern European thought: Continuity and change in ideas, 1600-1950: New* York: Macmillan.

Baur, J. (2005). *2000 years of Christianity in Africa: An African Church history*. Nairobi: Paulines.

Enwerem, I M. (1995). *A dangerous awakening: The politicization of religion in Nigeria*. Ibadan: IFRA.

Gaiya, M.A.B. (2001). *The Pentecostal revolution in Nigeria:* An occasional paper presented at a seminar at the centre of African Studies, University of Copenhagen.

Idowu, E.B. (1968). The predicament of Church in Africa. In C.G. Baeta (Ed.). *Christianity in tropical African* (pp. 417-440). London: Oxford University.

Okere, T. (2005). *Church, theology and society in Africa*. Enugu: Fourth Dimension.

Olanisebe, S. O, (2006). The role of the church in the development of nationalism in Nigeria: Past and present. In S.Akinrinde, D. Fashina & D. O. Ogungbile (Eds.).*The humanities, nationalism and democracy* (pp. 311-326). Ile-Ife: Cedar.

Omoyajowo, J.A. (1976). *The Church and society*. Ibadan: Baptist.

Onunwa, U. (1991). Missionary factor in African nationalism. *Indian Mssiological Review,* 30-38.

Ozigbo, I.R.A.. (1988). *Roman Catholicism in south eastern Nigeria, 1885-1931. A study in colonial evangelism*. Onitsha: Etukokwu.

Reiber, C. (1979). Christianity as an African religion. In N.S. Booth (Ed.). *African religions: A symposium* (pp. 225-274). New York: Nok.

Shepperson, G. (1968). Ethiopianism: Past and present. In C.G. Baeta (Ed.). Christianity in tropical Africa. London: Oxford University.

Tasie, G.O.M. (1978). *Christian missionary enterprise in the Niger Delta, 1864-1918*. Laiden: J. Brill.

Hans-Georg Gadamer's Praxis and the Ethics of Subjectivity

Chris TasieOsegenwune Ph. D

Department of Philosophy, University of Lagos, Akoka

Abstract

The problem of value in postmodern discourse has thrown up the fallacies and contradictions that were taken for granted in traditional presentation of ethical issues. The introduction of hermeneutics by Gadamer through postmodern perspective emphasizes the inevitability of praxis to guide moral behavior. Praxis according to Gadamer, is the realm of knowledge where non-positivistic, qualitative/interpretative inquiry finds its home. He sees praxis as a universal form of human life which embraces, yet goes beyond, the technical choice of the best means for a pre-given end. Praxis involves the making of responsible political and practical decisions about happiness, health, peace and freedom, and other stable factors of human being in nature. The application of philosophical hermeneutics by Gadamer has improved understanding the ontological under-current of taste and judgment which traditional and modern scholarship had rendered oblivion. He argues that the idea of a universal theory that will guide human actions is not only unrealistic but also untenable. For this reason, he recommended a sound approach for the study and interrogation of human affairs, through an ontological dimension to individual and group interests to reduce tension and instability.

Traditional ethics has operated from the point of view of seeing an object from a fixed angle. This approach has not taken into consideration the fluctuating nature of reality as fluid. That reality is fluid recognizes the position of diversity in our approach to understanding the complexity of human affairs. This paper examines the ontological dynamics in Gadamer's philosophical hermeneutics.

Key words: *Hermeneutics, Ontological, Praxis, Interpretative, Postmodern*

Introduction

This paper is an exposition of Gadamer's notion of philosophical praxis and its implications to ethical subjectivity. Praxis originally refers to action, doing, activity contrasted by Aristotle with poiesis and theoria. Ted Honderich, defines praxis as the process by which a theory, lesson, or skill is enacted, embodied, or realized. Praxis may also refer to the act of engaging, applying, exercising, realizing, or practicing ideas.[1] The foundation of praxis as a philosophical concept can be traced to the philosophies of Plato and Aristotle in the classical period and Immanuel Kant, Soren Kierkegaard, Karl Marx, Martin Heidegger including Hannah Arendt in the modern period. In Ancient Greek, the word praxis refers to activity engaged in by free men. In Aristotle's philosophy three dominant activities of man were mentioned. These are theoria, poiesis and praxis. Corresponding to these three mentioned activities are three types of knowledge namely; theoretical which had truth as its goal, poietical whose goal was production; and praxis whose goal was action. Aristotle

further divided practical knowledge into ethics, economics and politics distinguishing between "good praxis" and "bad praxis" or misfortune.[2] "Good praxis" as the name implies refers to actions whose goal is positively oriented while "bad praxis" are actions whose goal is negatively oriented.

In Kant, praxis is the application of a theory to cases encountered in experience, but is also ethically significant thought or practical reason, that is, reasoning about there should be as opposed to what there is. Kant's placing of the practical above the theoretical influenced subsequent thought in German idealism.[3] Kant appears to be influenced by the old philosophical controversy of giving practice due recognition over theory. This controversy between theory and practice should not have arisen in the first place as theory formulation provides the basis for practical activity. The emergence of Marxism made praxis central to the new philosophical ideal of transforming the world through revolutionary activity.[4] In Marx's view, the subordination of theory to practice is connected with the inability to resolve contradictions, which are instead removed by dialectical progress of history. Praxis for Marx therefore, connected with genuinely free, self-conscious, authentic activity as opposed to the alienated labor demanded under capitalism. For Marx furthermore and later Marxist, the free conscious, creative, essentially human activity alone is capable of generating knowledge which is new creating a better social order.[5] For Habermas, the concept of praxis is applicable to communicative interaction between people, which is governed by moral norms. Habermas contrasts praxis with instrumental action, example, in the production of commodities which is governed by technical rules.[6]The contributions so far have been able to dichotomize practical philosophy from theoretical philosophy. Theoretical philosophy tends to be dominated by contemplation which is one of the primary tasks of philosophy as a human activity while practical philosophy is action driven.

Gadamer's philosophy grounds the concept of praxis on hermeneutic phenomenology, an accretion from Heideggerianism. Hermeneutic phenomenology is purely interpretative depicting the fluidity of human experience. His philosophical thought began with Plato and Aristotle. For him, Plato and Aristotle provided the intellectual foundation for the interpretation of the Pre-Socratics where Western philosophical tradition took a cue. Gadamer has argued that without philosophy everything is historicism.[7]A strand of historicism very popular in modern scholarship, stresses the assumption that the course of history is governed by general laws. Knowledge of these makes it possible to predict the future of society and possibly of a civilization. Another strand of historicism stresses the uniqueness of individuals, events, cultural phenomena, etc. in opposition to what is seen as a distortingly abstract rationalist search for timeless truths about man and history. On the basis of this position, Gadamer sees philosophy as the highest supreme science. Science in this context is not the specialized sciences in search of reality but the synthesis of theory and practice.

Gadamer's notion of praxis encompasses understanding through a well-grounded knowledge for the consolidation not only of cultures but also human civilization. Understanding creates a platform for communication through a sustained dialogue to mitigate the crisis in human communities. Gadamer's philosophy of praxis lays a solid foundation for ethical subjectivity the central theme of this discourse stressing the view that we should not be slaves to methodology in ethical decision as each decision is unique in terms of situation and circumstance.

Gadamer's Epistemological Hermeneutics

Hermeneutics right from the beginning is structured to the tasks of interpreting life experiences and expressions that appear to be fixed. "Hermeneutics" is a term that covers many levels of reflection, as is frequently the case with Greek words that have become part of the terminology in our scholarly disciplines. "Hermeneutics" refers, first of all, to a practice, an art, that requires a special skill. ThIs points to a further Greek word, namely *techne*. Hermeneutics is the practical art, that is, a*techne*, involved in such things as preaching, interpreting other languages, explaining, and explicating texts, and, as the basis of all these, the art of understandingan art particularly required any time the meaning of something clear and unambiguous.[8]In Gadamer's view, the task of an interpreter is precisely that of translating something foreign or unintelligible into the language everybody speaks and understands. The business of translating therefore always has a certain "freedom." What hermeneutics accomplishes, then, is this bringing of something out of one world and into another, out of the world of the gods into that of humans or out of the world of a foreign language into the world of one's language.Hermeneutics is an art, a teaching or doctrine of a certain art, like the art of speaking, the art of writing or the art of calculating with numbers, and as an "art", it is a more practical ability to do something (a *techne*) than a "science." Gadamer made a distinction between the content of speech and the style of presentation. According to him, rhetoric which is a method of presentation of speech is concerned with the impact of speaking in all immediacy. Rhetoric is emotionally laden with the orator carrying away his audience because the convincing power of his arguments overwhelms his listeners. This is where the content of speech becomes important as the listeners are critical about what is being said.[9]The impact of rhetoric in speech making was made popular by the Sophists, a group of thinkers who raised critical questions on ethical and epistemological issues. They taught politicians and aspiring politicians how to make fantastic speech by playing with words. With the way these speeches were presented, people were carried away without considering the content of such speech. This brand of thinking in Gadamer's opinion is not philosophical in the true sense of the word. According to him, philosophy meant the whole of theoretical, and, therefore, scientific interest, and there is no doubt that it was the Greeks who instigated a world-historical decision with their own thinking and decided the path of modern civilization with the creation of science. What separates the Occident, Europe, the so-called 'Western world' from the great hieratic cultures of the Asian countries Gadamer observes is precisely this new awakening of the desire to know with Greek philosophy, Greek mathematics, Greek medicine and the whole of their theoretical curiosity and intellectual mastery.[10]This kind of philosophical thinking prepared the ground for the craftsman, the expert, the creator of new shapes and forms, the technites, the man who masters a technique and at the same time finds his proper place. Placing philosophy at the appropriate level requires the discovery of a free space for creative production that will be available to it in the middle of a pre-given nature, a wholeness of the world that orders itself in stages and forms. Philosophy is the actualization of thinking which leads to posing questions such as; what was in the beginning? What does it mean to say that something is? Is nothing something? The posing of these questions gave rise to the birth of philosophy.[11] Answers to these questions may not be forthcoming. Sometimes, instead of answers more questions are raised which provides a platform for conversation eliciting diverse interests.

Hermeneutics as Praxis

"Hermeneutics" as a concept is generally understood as the theory or art of explication, of interpretation. It is translated from a German word *kunstlehre* which translates to (a teaching about a technical skill or know-how). In its original Greek word, it means *techne*. The Greek word*techne* links hermeneutics with such arts as grammar, rhetoric and dialectic. Praxis as a concept in philosophical scholarship has a background in Aristotle's *philosophiapractica* (sivepolitica) or political philosophy. Practical philosophy otherwise known as praxis for Aristotle meant science, that is, knowledge using demonstration and generating doctrine.[12] The kind of science been talked about is not what the Greeks regarded as the model of theoretical knowledge, or episteme (mathematics) but a science of practical production notably the artistic creation. True philosophy is an art, and a genuine philosopher is a creative individual with inner vision and projection. A philosopher with a creative metaphysical temperament is a creative statesman bubbling with ideas for social and political transformation of society. Philosophy is a general nonmathematical science otherwise referred to as political philosophy. The task of this aspect of philosophy is the organization of the "polis" known as political society. Theoretical philosophy according to Aristotle comprises physics, mathematics and theology. Political Philosophy as conceived by Aristotle is in the realm of practical philosophy because it has to do with the conduct of men as creators of values in the allocation of resources and power distribution. This accounts for the tag of man as a political animal living in civil and political society. As a political animal man cannot avoid living together in societies, which through interaction, impose order and cooperation for the survival of society and for human progress.

Praxis, for Gadamer, means practice, a Greek word for pragma which is in the realm of practical philosophy. This takes us back to Aristotle's concept of *theoria* which refers to practical activity. Practice which refers to the basic character of being alive, stands between activity and situatedness. It is not confined to human beings, who alone are active on the basis of free choice. Praxis instead means the actuation of life, anything alive to which there is a correspondence to a life, a way of life, a life that is led in a certain way.[13]Gadamer's notion of praxis even though is scientific captures the ethical dimension of philosophy where acting is crucial to decision and responsibility in human affairs especially in conflict situations. For Gadamer practical philosophy is determined by the line drawn between the practical knowledge of the person who chooses freely and the acquired skill of the expert that Aristotle named *techne*. Practical philosophy, then, has to do not with the learnable crafts and skills, however essential this dimension of human ability is for the communal life of humanity; rather, it has to do with what is each individual's due as a citizen and what constitutes his arête or excellence.[14] What Gadamer is saying put in another way is that the essence of praxis as a dimension of philosophy is not the aspect we can learn and the skill associated with it but the ability of the individual to apply the rule for adjustment when the need arises. This requires praxis to take into consideration the fluctuating and temporal character of human reality. From here, one can distill Heidegger's phenomenology in relation to the nature of realty and how it can guide human action. The response to human actions and decisions is situation because of the complexity of reality.

To appreciate the complexity of human actions and the way decisions are taken, Gadamer leans on Aristotelian ethics by contrasting *techne* and praxis. While *techne* is anchored on technical skills and craftsmanship and can be learned, praxis is concerned with the knowledge of human beings, especially human action, and carries a moral dimension to it since individual action connect a researcher with other persons. According to Gadamer, we learn a *techne* and can also forget it. But we do not learn moral knowledge nor can we forget it.15To drive his point home, Gadamer maintains that a person who has learned a *techne* can be successful in producing something with his or her tools and equipment, while an individual simply cannot act without thinking of the consequence when dealing with others. This is why praxis, unlike *techne*, always involves a 'concern' for other beings, and thus underscores the need for moral judgment. By the adoption of Aristotle's ethics, Gadamer locates the human sciences in the realm of praxis; human sciences, for him, are inherently moral, and praxis is the domain of knowledge where non-positivistic, qualitative/interpretative inquiry finds its destination. For Gadamer, then, praxis is 'a universal form of human life which embraces, yet goes beyond, the technical choice of the best means for a pre-given end'.[16]Gadamer explains further that praxis involves the 'making of responsible political and practical decisions about happiness, health, peace, freedom, and other stable factors of human-being-in-nature'.[17] The underpinnings of Gadamer's praxis as reflected here is to show the realistic natural condition of human beings. Sometimes, we assume that we can predict human actions irrespective of these natural conditions of man. The natural sciences can make such predictions whose results can be exact. Gadamer's praxis takes care of the limitations arising from human actions and prepares us for taking responsible decisions capable of affecting the welfare of human beings. Our belief that the natural sciences are capable of solving our numerous problems is one of the greatest errors in the management of human affairs. What are the problems of the natural sciences? What are their limitations and the freedom of the individuals in a scientific society? This will take us to the next segment of the discourse.

Science and Freedom

In discussing the freedom of the individual, Gadamer maintains that 'no higher principle is thinkable than that of the freedom of all, and that we understand actual history from the perspective of this principle: as ever-to-be-renewed and the never-ending struggle for this freedom'.[18]For Gadamer, the intrusion of scientism in human life is "the" enemy of freedom; scientific domination alone is the "cause" of unfreedom'[19]. Gadamer's research, therefore, is a protest against the myth and the imperialism of science. Science has dominated

human affairs many centuries ago because of its achievement in various sectors of production. We cannot deny the successes made by science in all areas of human endeavor, but we cannot close our eyes to the destruction society has gone through with the imposition of the scientific culture. Gadamer's praxis has the responsibility of providing a platform for the defense of practical and political reason against the excesses of the domination of science and technology. Scientific methods according to Gadamer, is not only dehumanizing but, also, demean people without giving them the freedom of choice. He put the argument in this way;

> *Only by the demythologication of science… Can the mastery of*
>
> *knowledge and ability become self-mastery… Self-knowledge*
>
> *alone is capable of saving a freedom threatened not only by all*
>
> *rulers but much more by the domination and dependence that*
>
> *issue from everything we think we control* [20].

The point Gadamer is making here is that modern science sets out to identify stable, universal and lawful knowledge of human beings. What human scientists seek, sometimes differs from what they hope to find. Errors resulting from scientific predictions are quite understandable if we follow what Gadamer is saying. What follows from here is that the scientific method is only one way of knowing as there are other ways of knowing other than science. This is where he draws vital lessons from hermeneutic understanding to which we now turn.

Hermeneutic and Understanding

For Gadamer, one can associate understanding with an epistemological or cognitive process. To understand implies to grasp something, to see things clearer which were previously obscure or ambiguous. Gadamer's philosophical hermeneutics is centered on the process of understanding. According to him, the role of the interpreter becomes not to figure out how to make understanding happen, but rather, to explore the everyday happening of understanding that gives communication and human interaction their meaning. He observes again that understanding cannot escape the historicity of tradition because knowledge seems to arise from tradition. If knowledge arises from tradition and the discernment of truth answers to temporal positioning, it means that no correct or final understanding is possible. This accounts for the role of interpretation to alter a phenomenon.

The position Gadamer is canvassing is the view that understanding has an affiliation with tradition and colored with biases and prejudices. Prejudices are usually to be avoided because it distorts the truth. Incidentally, he sees prejudices as the basis of all understanding. Prejudice actually refers to 'prejudgment' which can be positive or negative. It means that for us to assume that all prejudices are illegitimate and misleading represents simply a 'prejudice against prejudice'.[21] The outcome of his position is that in order to gain understanding, every individual undergoes a process of projecting his or her prejudices. For Gadamer therefore, communicative understanding requires:

The suspension of ones prejudices, whether this involves another person

Through whom one learns one's own nature and limits, or an encounter

With a work of art, or a text; always something more is demanded than

To understand the other, that is to seek and acknowledge the immanence

Coherence contained within the meaning claim of the other.[22]

Understanding is not only a skillful and painstaking activity; it requires patience from the individual. In order to understand, one opens up oneself to other possibilities or prejudices. Being open in this regard does not mean starting from no prejudice or bias; rather one learns to differentiate productive prejudices from the unproductive or counter-productive ones. Explaining this position, Deetz,[23] points out that one who thinks that 'he is free from prejudices not only becomes unconsciously dominated by them but cuts himself or herself off from their positive insight'. The positive insight of prejudice arising from Gadamer, Deetz observes, is that other people become a means for us to evaluate and correct our understanding.[24] White's view in this regard is that Gadamer's hermeneutic perspective, instead of adopting an objective and neutral stance, calls for bracketing of all presumptions and biases and qualifying

them as such in order to understand other's perspectives compared to one's own prejudices.

The concept of bracketing goes back to the phenomenology of Edmund Husserl in his concept of "*epoche*". As the name implies, *epoche* simply means putting into abeyance or suspending our assumptions, prejudices, biases and presuppositions of all that we have known of an object of experience. Husserl used this approach to emphasize the possibility of describing an object without our pre-conceptual scheme. His position is that things can be described the way they are, what causes distortion is the way and manner we position ourselves in relation to the object of our investigation. *Epoche* therefore requires us to deliberately avoid all factors likely to affect our analysis. The equivalent of the *Husserlianepoche*for Heidegger is phenomenological reduction where we are expected to critically drop all those entanglements that distort our ability to carry out a rigorous analysis of our object of experience. I see a radical difference in Gadamer's use of prejudices to that of Husserl and Heidegger even though they belong to the phenomenological temperament. Gadamer sees prejudices as inherent in the culture and civilization of a people which also affects their tradition. Husserl and Heidegger tend to agree with this and suggested that we should jettison them if we want to make a radical analysis of the object of experience. The essence of understanding in Gadamer's hermeneutics is to foster effective communication through language as a tool. Communication through the deployment of dialogue is imperative to ensure stability in interpersonal relationship. This is where Gadamer's praxis enters the realm of ethical subjectivity to which we now turn.

Hermeneutics and Ethical Subjectivity

One salient issue raised by Gadamer in his hermeneutical philosophical thought concerns the way understanding affects human existential condition. In this regard, understanding is not a matter of trained, methodical, unprejudiced technique, but an encounter in the existentialist sense, a confrontation with something radically different from ourselves making understanding an engaging process between human beings.[25] To engage people involves the issue of value judgment through dialogue. Gadamer's philosophical hermeneutic underscores the necessity for a dialogical relationship. In Truth and Method, his seminal work, he adopted the Socratic model of dialogue. According to him, truth emerges only from a genuine dialogue between the text and the reader. He is of the view that by participating in a genuine dialogue, by constant questioning and answering will truth be removed. Language as an inevitable tool of communication makes the attainment of peace and stability through dialogue possible. Speaking about language he has this to say:

> *In all our knowledge of ourselves and in all knowledge of the world, we*
>
> *are always already encompassed by the language that is our own. In truth*
>
> *We are always already at home in language, just as much as we are in the*
>
> *World.*[26]

The use of language as a medium of expression shows its ontological status. Language constitutes more than a tool to accomplish one's purposes. Language also typifies the character of an individual, showing who he is and what will become of him. Heidegger had earlier declared that language is the house of being. Gadamer's recognition of language as an inevitable tool for meaning making and decision is fundamentally the Heideggerian philosophical influence on him. In this regard, he sees language as being central to all understanding. For him, the world springs from human language. He portrays the power of language in creating and recreating a different world from what it was. He says further:

> *Language is not limited to a stock of words and phrases, of concepts*
>
> *view-points, and opinions… language is not its elaborated conventionalism,*
>
> *not the burden of pre-schematization with which it loads us, but the*
>
> *generative and creative power to unceasingly make this whole*
>
> *again fluent.*[27]

The use of language to achieve dialogue and understanding enables us to appreciate the necessity of philosophical ethics by constructing a list of values that affect human interests. Gadamer relies on Aristotle's practical philosophy through the concept of virtue. According to him, we know virtue in order to be good. This proposition is his influence from the ethics of Socrates and Plato. For Socrates had maintained that virtue is knowledge but ignorance the root of moral evil. The transition to praxis is inherent here, because, knowledge is not an aggregate anonymous truth, but a human comportment. Even the *theoria* does not stand in absolute opposition to praxis but is itself the highest praxis, one of the highest modes of human being.[28]

The greatest outcome of dialogical relationship is to create a platform for human interaction because of the involvement of values. All genuine dialogue involves not simply understanding what the other is saying and how the other feels but coming to grips with one another. For Gadamer, this shared understanding means transcending to a higher universality that overcomes not only one's own peculiarity, but that of others as well. Gadamer's deployment of dialogue as a basis for human existential relationship comes close to the position expressed by Martin Buber on human relation through the instrumentality of dialogue. According to Martin Buber[29] to man, the world is twofold, in accordance to his twofold attitude. The attitude of man is twofold, in accordance with the twofold nature of the primary words which he speaks. The primary words are not isolated words, but combined words. The one primary is the combination of I-Thou. The other primary word is the combination I-It; wherein, without a change in the primary word, one the words He and She can replace it. Hence, the I of man is also twofold. For the I of the primary word I-Thou is a different I from that of the primary word I-It. He observers that primary words do not signify things rather, they intimate relations. Primary words do not describe something that might exist independently of them but being spoken they bring about existence. Primary words are spoken from being. If Thou is said, the I of the combination I-It is said along with it. The primary word I-Thou can only be spoken with the whole being. The primary word I-It can never be spoken with the whole being. There is no I taken in itself, but only the I of the primary word I-Thou and the I of the primary word I-It. The point Buber is making is that when a man says I he refers to one or the other of these. The I to which he refers is present when he says I. Further, when he says Thou or It, the I of the two primary words is present. The existence of I and the speaking of I are one and the same thing. When a primary word is spoken, the speaker enters the word and takes his stand in it. Buber is stressing the importance of dialogue to understanding, communication and cooperation. I and Thou demonstrate an indissoluble connection between persons in a relationship. In such a relationship, there is mutuality, communion and empathy.

Martin Buber's illustration of I and Thou shows the inevitability of understanding through cooperation between human beings. It shows that no man is an island because we need interaction at every level of social activity. This relationship is characterized by mutuality, openheartedness, directness, honesty, spontaneity, frankness, lack of pretense, non-manipulative intent, communion, intensity, and love in the sense of responsibility of one human for another.[30] Similarly, on I-It relationship, a person uses and experiences the other person as an object for his or her profit or self-interest. Gadamer and Buber are in accord in respecting the individual and given him the appreciation he deserves in all his or her uniqueness and is not treated as an object. This dialogic relationship helps humans attain their ontological completeness by understanding one another in a spirit of authenticity. The greatest error Gadamer's ethics of subjectivity strongly corrects is treating the individual with utmost disdain regarding him as an object. An object is predictable given its mechanical disposition. His ethics of subjectivity emphasizes values in a fluctuating and changing world.

Conclusion

Gadamers praxis is located within the matrix of the humanistic sciences using philosophical hermeneutics. First and foremost, he exhumed Platonic and the Aristotelian philosophical ethics to show the nature of values epistemologically and ethically. Plato's dialectics shaped his understanding of raising questions while looking for answers while Aristotle's ethics provided a platform for his understanding of practical and theoretical philosophy. The old question between theory and practice in the realm of the natural sciences and the humanistic sciences came to the fore.

As a study in the humanistic sciences, Gadamer adopted the position of not being a slave to a universal scientific methodology which will produce robots without the capacity to think and make adjustments necessary for human development. This position was made popular in his famous work Truth and Method where he undercut the basic assumptions of modern epistemology in terms of theory and practice. He argues that the Cartesian, Kantian and Lockian epistemology that values a universal, law-like theory is not only illusory but also unnecessary in the domain of the humanistic sciences. In the realm of human affairs, he recommended the ethics of Aristotle with the distinction between techne and praxis.

Praxis as a value category involves the making of responsible political and practical decisions about happiness, health, peace, freedom, and other stable factors of human being in nature. Praxis from this point of view does not subscribe for the imperialism of science, rather, a platform should be made available for the proliferation of activities in the natural and humanistic sciences. The natural sciences method constitutes one out of other methods in the pursuance of human knowledge and should not be imposed on any discipline as there are peculiar issues other branches of human knowledge are pursuing.

Gadamer's praxis and ethics of subjectivity restates the need for dialogue to communication practice among cultures of the world. Communication promotes good human relationship through the reduction of tension, instability and conflict. The major reason for the proliferation of crisis is lack of understanding, mutual suspicion and dishonesty. These factors could be mitigated by creating an enabling enhance environment for cooperation, tolerance and effective understanding.

Bibliography

Aristotle, *Nicomachean Ethics* translated with an introduction by Martin Ostwald, (New York: Macmillan Publishing Co. 1962).

Buber, M.*I and Thou,* trans by W. Kaufman, (New York: Charles Scribers and Sons, 1970)

Chen, K. H. *Beyond Truth and Method: On misreading Gadamer'spraxical hermeneutics. Quarterly Journal of Speech,* 1987

Deetz, S. *Conceptualizing human understanding: Gadamer's hermeneutics and American Communication Studies. Communication Quarterly,* 1978, 26

Gadamer, Hans-Georg*Hermeneutics and Social Science, Cultural Hermeneutics* 2, 1975

Gadamer, Hans-Georg*Hermeneutics, Religion and Ethics* trans. by Joel Weinsheimer (Yale: Yale University Press, 1999)

Gadamer, Hans-Georg*Philosophical Hermeneutics*, trans. and edited by David, E. Linge (Berkeley: University of California Press, 1976)

Gadamer, Hans-Georg *Reason in the Age of Science*. F.G. Lawrence trans. (Cambridge: The MIT Press, 1998)

Gadamer, Hans-Georg *The Beginning of Knowledge* trans. by Rod Coltman. New York: Continuum, 2002)

Gadamer, Hans-Georg*The problem of historical consciousness*. J.L Close trans. in P. Rainbow and W.M. Sullivan (eds.) *Interpretive Social Science: A second look.* (Berkeley: University of California Press, 1987)

Gadamer, Hans-Georg,*The Beginning of Philosophy* trans. by Rod Coltman(New York: Continuum, 2001) Gadamer, Hans-Georg,*The Gadamer Reader, A Bouquet of Later Writings* edited by Richard E. Palmer (Illinois: Northwestern University Press, 2007.

Gadamer, Hans-Georg,*The Gadamer Reader, A Bouquet of Later Writings* edited by Richard E. Palmer (Illinois: Northwestern University Press,2007)

Gadamer, Hans-Georg,*Truth and Method*, J. Weinsheimer and D.G. Marshall, trans. (New York: Crossroad, 1989)

Honderich, T. Praxis The Oxford Companion to Philosophy, (Oxford: Oxford University Press, 1995)

Johannesen, R.L. *The emerging concept of communication as dialogue Quarterly Journal of Speech* 5, 1971

Mautner, T. *The Penguin Dictionary of Philosophy* (London: Penguin Books, 2000)

Outhwaite, W. Hans-Georg Gadamer in *The Return of the Grand Theory in the human Sciences* edited by Quentin Skinner(Cambridge and New York: Cambridge University Press, 1985)

Praxiswww.philosophycs.com/praxis.htm retrieved 20th June, 2016.

White, K.W. Hans-Georg *Gadamer's Philosophy of Language: A constitutive-dialogic approach to interpersonal understanding*, in K. Carter and M. Presnell (eds.), *Interpretive Approaches to Interpersonal Communication.* (New York: State University of New York Press, 1994)

Logical Implications of Leibniz Theory of Knowledge on Social Relations, Religion and Ethics

T.V. Ogan PhD

Department of Philosophy, University of Port Harcourt
E-mail: tamunosikivictor@gmail.com

Abstract

Epistemology provides the major premises with which the knowledge of God, man, nature, society, ethics and science can be approached. If we know the basic assumptions about reality and the method of knowing it, we can deduce the criterion for determining right and wrong, man's relationship with the other, and the Supreme Being. Amongst the attempts to solve the problem of knowledge is the rationalist and empiricist schools of thought. Leibniz from the rationalist school of thought proposed his theory of monadology which is a simple, unextended; substantial, dynamic being of a physical nature that reflects and represents the whole universe within itself, spontaneously and consciously without direct interaction with any other being. Leibniz believed that the monad is the unit of life and cannot be changed by anything outside of it. This theory of Leibniz has implications in social relations, ethics and religion.

Keywords: Knowledge, Social Relations, Religion and Ethics

Introduction

The philosophers of the modern era were faced with the problem of knowledge. "The source of knowledge was initially taken to be psychological inquiries concerning the factual genesis of our concepts, judgments and thought in general" (Ogan 35). All modern philosophers wanted to prove the source of knowledge unlike the pre-Socratic philosophers. This struggle led to the separation of the thinkers into two groups, the rationalist and empiricist groups.

The rationalists held that knowledge is gotten through the activity of the brain. For the rationalists, the human mind is not a "tabular Rasa" on which experience writes. Knowledge for the rationalists is possible through the activity of the soul through logico-mathematical reasoning. They believed in the principle of 'innatism'.

The empiricists on the other hand, held that knowledge comes entirely through sense experience. For them, the subject must be gotten through experience. The object must be perceived and bathed in light. In other words, for anyone to say he or she is knowledgeable, the object must be touched, felt, seen and tested. Among those who belonged to the rationalist school of thought is Leibniz, a rationalist of the 17th century. To duly understand Leibniz's thought about knowledge, his purpose of philosophising must be put into consideration.

Leibniz wanted to reconcile various beliefs. In religion, he wanted to harmonize Protestantism and Catholicism. According to him, he was interested in a universal religion based on Christian principles. Therefore, he spoke of a City of God which tolerates no theological differences, in which men of good will find divine grace and salvation. Leibniz also wanted to reconcile science and theology. He tried to find a middle ground between the theory that only universals are real and the opposite theory that only particular things have objective existence (Mayer 154).

It is against this background that this paper shall try to examine what Leibniz says about knowledge and the implication of his theory of knowledge on religion, ethics and social relations.

Leibniz Theory of Knowledge

Leibniz divided knowledge into two types, namely: knowledge which is concerned with eternal truths, and knowledge which is based on sense observation, which he calls contingent truth of facts. According to Leibniz, eternal truths are "important for logic and mathematics because eternal truths cannot give certain knowledge about phenomenal things that can be applied only tentatively to the realm of existence' (Mayer 155). The contingent truths on the other hand, are guided by the law of sufficient reason, and this law of sufficient reason demands the why of things.

The system of the law of sufficient reason is important because it establishes regularity and order in the world, if not the world would be in a chaotic state. Truth for Leibniz is not discovered from without, but it exists within us. Just as in metaphysics, he believed that what characterises every human being is force, activity and energy. This energy is not determined by anything outside; it is autonomous and constitutes an entelechy (Russell 565).

For Leibniz, there are no breaks in the universe and no sharp distinctions. This explains his concept of continuity. In his universal world only, monads are real and are also the centre of spiritual forces (Mayer 160). The universe of Leibniz therefore, is made up of an infinite number of Monads.

Leibniz was not satisfied with the way Descartes and Spinoza described the nature of substances which he feels distorted our understanding of human nature, freedom, and the nature of God. Hence, he came up with his theory of Monads, to explain the reality of knowledge in man.

Meaning of Monad and Leibniz's Theory of Monads

Monad is from the Greek word "monas" meaning a unit or individual entity. "It is a simple, substantial and dynamic being of a physical nature that reflects and represents the whole universe within itself, spontaneously and more or less consciously without direct interaction with any other being." This concept dates back to the philosophy of Plato who sought an original unit from which to derive the many or pluralistic beings in the universe (Berger 735).

Leibniz for whom the monad became a principle of panpsychism (the doctrine or belief that everything material, however, small, has an element of individual consciousness) began by seeking to improve on the notion of substance as developed by Rene Descartes. For Descartes, monads are points or psychical centres of force and the substantial elements of which the universe is composed, that is, the ultimate individual substances of which reality is made (Mason 576). Leibniz theory of monads is a recapitulation and ultimate extension of the formula of Benedict Spinoza: *Deussivenatura* (God or nature). However, he relates all monads to the first and principal monad- God:

Thus, there remains only my hypothesis, that is, the way of pre-established harmony, according to which God has made each of the two substances from the beginning in such a way that, though each follows only its own law which it has received within its being, each agrees throughout with the other, entirely as if they are mutually influenced or if God where always putting forth his hand beyond his general occurrence (Leibniz 152-153).

His theory is essentially different from Spinoza's (Berger 736). Leibniz believed that the monad is the unit of life and cannot be changed by anything outside of it. He held that in every created substance, there exists a principle of change, an identity that produces changing states while still preserving its own unity. He opines that these monads are unextended, immaterial and simple, without size, shape or quantity and are indivisible. In the words of Omoregbe, "it is a self-contained and windowless entity which develops on its own from within according to its inner principle of activity." Monads are spiritual souls, which constitutes the smallest units, or the basic elements of which everything in the universe is made. By implication, Leibniz means that the universe is made up of spiritual souls, therefore denying the existence of matter (Omoregbe 34-36).

Leibniz thereby affirms the idealistic doctrine that the whole universe in the last analysis is not made of matter but of spiritual immaterial elements. Though he maintained that each is windowless and preserves its own unity and principle of change, Leibniz holds that each monad reflects the inner principle of change of other monads from their individual stand points. By this, he implies that every essential attribute in the cosmos must be discoverable in even Monad. In other words, all monads must be different embodiments of a single reality. Furthermore, Leibniz uses his concept to explain the complex substance of every human experience. He saw individual lives as a harmonized grouping of simple monads around a core soul or directing monad which can finalize the whole. He holds that all monads are spiritual and that the material which we see, is only a complex arrangement of monads finalized to form an extension. The human mind, he believes is the core monad of the human person (Jones 229-234).

Logical Implication of Leibniz Theory of Monad to Social Relation

Monads for Leibniz are unextended, without shape or size. Each monad is independent of other monads, and they do not have any casual relation to each other. They are not only independent and different; they also contain the source of their activities within themselves. The rest of the universe does not affect their behaviour, they are windowless. They do not communicate to each other. They live in their own world and there is a kind of demarcation between each monad.

The above shows that there is a problem between monad and its environment. If monads are self-enclosed, independent, unextended and windowless that have no causal relation to each other, questions arise: How can monads' societies grow? And how can monad itself grow and improve?

The human society has been formed to be a community of human beings sprung from the same source. From the onset, the Supreme Being created man and made him to look after all that he created and to improve the world with his intellect. God actually wanted a society where people could relate and be creative. This reflected when he created Adam and said it was not good for him to be alone, then God fashioned out of Adam, a woman. The purpose therefore, which God created the world has to be fulfilled – a society where people live together in a community, to relate and share ideas together- symbiotic and harmonious relation.

A further question would be: If monads are self-enclosed, how can monads create a better society? If they do not communicate, are in their own world and do not know what is going on, how can it be developed? Man has to use his intellect to create his society and make it a better one. For instance, civilisation and globalisation are results of man's contribution to the society. If man has been self-enclosed, not exercising his talent, the discoveries of computer, internet, and all technological attempts and innovations would not be made.

Based on Leibniz theory, happenings in the universe can only be explained with the supposition that every event emerges from the depth of each individual monads. For instance, a teacher does not need to teach a student since every individual has sufficient knowledge innate in themselves and do not need to receive knowledge from others. Leibniz also asserted that monads mirror the principle of change in other monads, such that what happens in one monad can be reflected in another monad. For instance, when the dead batteries of a clock are replaced, it does not need anyone to reset the correct time. The clock is by Leibniz theory, supposed to mirror the change in other clocks and reset itself.

Leibniz theory of pre-established harmony holds that "God first created the soul or some real unity in such a way that everything would evolve from its own depth with perfect spontaneity in respect to itself but nevertheless in perfect conformity with the things outside itself" (Jones 229). He believed that this pre-established harmony is God's plan to create a finite world that would best express his infinite perfection (Gilson and Langman 157-161).

Leibniz thus, reduces human relationship to automatic pre-planned workings as in a puppet world or as in the famous comparison of the working of individual clocks which keep perfect time because their maker constructed them in such a way that they each keep perfect time independently and harmoniously, without affecting each other in any way (Marias 241).

Logical Implication of Leibniz Theory of Monad to Ethics

In Leibniz theodicy, he declares the absolute goodness of God but affirms the presence of evil in the world created by God. Leibniz attributes the presence of this evil, be it moral, physical or metaphysical evil, to man. This attribution of evil to man comes after declaring that everything that occurs is previously included in the monad. This seems a contradiction of the asserted goodness of God. What it implies is that, God infused evil tendencies in man at creation and that man in his evil or immoral state is only exhibiting what a faultless creator infused in him. However, if God has no negation or contradiction then he cannot infuse in another what he does not possess.

To justify the presence of evil in the world, Leibniz therefore explained the causes of different evil tendencies in the world. According to Leibniz:

> Metaphysical evil derives from the impossibility of the world being infinite like its creator; physical evil has its justification in that it gives rise to higher values... moral evil which is what constitutes the most serious problem is actually a deficiency (which God permits)

because it is a condition for other greater good (Marias243).

From Leibniz argument, we can deduce that man should not be blamed for his immoral actions since he is not responsible for what he does. Secondly, it implies that actions should not be adjudged good or bad since every action is ordered towards a higher good. Unfortunately, this line of argument does not agree with ethical theories, which hold that man is responsible for his moral actions and that depending on the effects of his actions on the other person; his actions can be judged as morally right or wrong.

Leibniz theory also implies that humans cannot learn ethical codes from the society or be influenced by the behaviour of others. Neither can cultural values nor morals be transmitted or taught to others. Leibniz theory of monad then contradicts ethics.

Logical Implication of Leibniz Theory of Monad to Religion

Leibniz monadology proposes the view that God is the highest monad. This Leibniz proves through the principle of continuity, principle of sufficient reason, and the law of pre-established harmony. The principle of continuity demands a highest monad at the end of the series of forces. The principle of sufficient reason states that for everything that is real or true, there must be a sufficient reason why it is real or true. And the order and harmony in the universe calls for a harmonizer. The monads were created by God and He alone can destroy them. They depend on Him for their existence and essence.

However, the essence of rational soul or spirit is much more than that of the simple soul. It is only a mirror of the universe of creatures, but also an image of the Divinity (Smith and Greene 327). And since God is the most lovable of substances, His love consists in the perfection and happiness of the loved object. Hence, man is compelled to love God as he ought, but man cannot perfectly love God because of an imperfect knowledge of God. However, man possesses some qualities and attributes of God in a certain degree and has a longing for God (Thilly 392-393).

Moreover, man's love for God makes him enjoy a foretaste of future felicity. It constitutes our greatest good and interest for it gives us perfect confidence in the goodness of our Author and Master, producing a true tranquillity of mind. Hence, this participation supposes the immortality of the rational soul, not only in its substantial nature, but also in its entire personality, including memory and acquired knowledge. Minds are called to a special union of knowledge and love with God, considered as Lord and Father. However, this supreme felicity can never be full, because since God is infinite, he cannot be wholly known.

Religion is an integrative force in society; it establishes codes and patterns of morality and principles for its adherents to follow. Religion also unites people of different tribes, culture and language together. Religion enables us to interact, share and acquire more knowledge about God the Supreme Being. Since Leibniz theory holds that monads do not interact with each other, the practice of religion through belief in God will contradict his theory. It will mean those who do not believe in God do not need to come together to learn about God or hear sermons since they would have the knowledge of God already innate in each of them.

Evaluation and Conclusion

Leibniz monad shows him as a pluralist as against Spinoza's monism. In an attempt to create a harmonious universe out of the multiplicity of existence, and to posit the priority of reason over experience, he posited subjectivity. Hence, the supposed parallelism or concomitance which exists between the soul and the body is only idealistic. It destroys the unity of the human person. And the immortality of the rational soul with its memory and knowledge is a materialistic conception of religious issues. The world of the monads upholds the rationalist's view of the primacy of reason over experience but stifles social communication and relations.

Reading through Leibniz theory, it is clear it is not an abstract theory but has practical effects on man and to the development of his society at large. However, Leibniz line of arguments in his theory of monads is far from solving satisfactorily, the problem of knowledge. The theory rather created further problems on the explanation of human existence and interaction. In other words, his theory is a contradiction of the day to day experience of human living. This goes without saying that the problem of knowledge is not one that can be easily solved by mere postulation of theories but one which needs an alternative observation and attention to the realities and experiences that are present in human situations. The various evidences from the theories of philosophers who existed before Leibniz, and from Leibniz himself show that the reality of human existence and the knowledge about the entire universe is beyond the total comprehension of rational man. Consequently, it can be claimed that the problem of knowledge is not one that can be solved at a particular instance but one which will continue to be deliberated upon by rational and evolving humanity.

Works Cited

Collins, Anthony. *History of Modern European Philosophy*. Milwaukee: The Bruce Publishing Co.1954.

Berger, Hirsch. "Monad" *New Catholic Encyclopaedia*. New York: Jack Heraty and Associates, 1967

Jones, WilliamTyson. (1969) *A History of Western Philosophy: Hobbes to Hume*. New York: Harcourt, Bruce and World Inc.

Leibniz, GottfriedWilhelms "Philosophical Letter and Paper." Flew (ed.) *Body, Mind and Death*. New York: MacMillan, 1994

Marias, Julians. *History of Philosophy*. New York: Dover Publication, 1967

Mason, W.J. "Monad" Halsey, D.W. *Colliers Encyclopaedia*. New York: Macmillan Educational, 1974

Mayer, Frank. *A History of Modern Philosophy*. California: American Book, 1951

Ogan, Tamunosiki. "Divisions of Philosophy" Udoidem S.I. (ed.) *Foundations of Philosophy and Logic*. Lagos: African Heritage, 2002

Omoregbe, Joseph. *A Simplified History of Western Philosophy*. Lagos: Joja Press, 2001

Russell, Bertrand *A History of Western Philosophy*. London: George Allen and Unwin,1979 Smith, T.U. and Greene, M. *From Descartes to Locke*. Chicago: University of Chicago Press, 1970

Thilly, Frank. *A History of Philosophy*. New York: Henry Holt and Co, 1951

International Journal of Integrative Humanism Vol 9. No 1. June 2018. ISSN: 2026 – 6286

Diaspora and the Fluidity of Identity: Perspectives from Tess Onwueme's *The Missing Face*

Adie Edward Ugbada PhD

Department of Theatre, Film and Carnival Studies, University of Calabar

Yusuf Ninzim SHAMAGANA

Department of Theatre and Performing Arts, Ahmadu Bello University Zaria

Adie Margaret Funmilayo

Unical International Demonstration Secondary School, Calabar

E-mail Address: yusufshamagana232382@gmail.com

Abstract

The concept of identity has over the centuries being a subject of critical discourse, especially in the diasporic context. Some scholars have attempted to ascribe identity to the handiwork of nature or biology, while others have argued, that identity is purely a product of social construction. Within the diasporic space, the issue of identity is usually articulated against the backdrop of power relations among the various peoples that make up the population. Hence, concepts such as ethnicity, racism and racialization often come up to encapsulate the nature of identity politics that play out in the diasporic space. This paper examines the fluidity of the concept of identity within various diasporic entities, especially, the black diaspora. Benedict Anderson's concept of 'imagined communities' is utilized as the theoretical anchor for the study because it reiterates the point that most identities are socially constructed, not biologically determined. Tess Onwueme's The Missing Face is discussed here to illustrate how the politics of identityhas impacted on the lives of black diaspora.

Introduction

The concept of identity pertains to cultural descriptions of persons with which we emotionally identify and which concern sameness and difference, the personal and social. Chris Barker (2004:93) avers that identity is a cultural construction because the discursive resources that form the material for identity formation are cultural in character. He further asserts that we are constituted as individuals in a social process that is commonly understood as acculturation without which we would not be persons. This implies that the very notion of what it is to be a person is a cultural question, and without language the very concept of identity would be unintelligible to us. Within cultural studies, identities are understood to be discursive-performative. That is, identity is best described as a discursive practice that enacts or produces that which it names through citation and reiteration of norms or conventions. The concept of identity is further deployed in order to link the emotional 'inside' of persons with the discursive 'outside'. That is,

identity represents the processes by which discursively constructed subject positions are taken up (or otherwise) by concrete persons' fantasy identifications and emotional 'investments'. The argument that identity is not a universal entity but a culturally specific discursive construction grounded in an anti-representationalist account of language whereby discourse defines, constructs and produces objects of knowledge. Consequently, what we can say about the identity characteristics of, for example, men, is culturally circumscribed.

The popular cultural repertoire of the Western world holds that we have a true-self, an identity which we possess and which can become known to us. Here, identity is thought to be a universal and timeless core, an 'essence' of the self that is expressed as representations that are recognizable by ourselves and by others. That is, identity is an essence signified through sign of taste, beliefs, attitudes and lifestyles. However, cultural studies writers question the assumption that identity is a fixed 'thing' that we possess.

Identity, it is argued, is not best understood as an entity but as an emotionally charged description. Rather than being a timeless essence, what it is to be a person is said to be fluid, plastic and changeable, being specific to particular social and cultural conjectures.

This argument points to the political nature of identity as a 'production' and to the possibility of multiple, shifting and fragmented identities that can be articulated together in a variety of ways. It is the very fluidity of identity that makes it politically significant since contestation over the meanings of identity categories concerns the very kinds of people we are becoming. No single identity acts as an overarching, organizing identity, rather, identities shift according to how subjects are addressed or represented. Thus, we are constituted by fractured multiple identities. Premised on the foregoing, this paper examines the fluidity of identity within the context of diaspora, with particular focus on the effects of identity politics in the lives of black diaspora. Tess Onwueme's *The Missing Face* is used to illustrate how ethnic and racial identities inform power relations between white and blacks in America.

Conceptual Framework

This study is anchored on Benedict Anderson's concept of imagined communities, which provides a strong foundation for understanding the invented nature of social identities (Anderson, 1983:04). Imagined communities are socially constructed communities of people who cognitively see themselves as a part of a larger group. These communities are imagined in the sense that the shared identities of members are not intrinsic, they are socially constructed and are given meaning through a complex web of human interactions. Thus, the critical marker between identity groups is that members of distinct groups view themselves and non-group members differently.

The construction of both racial and ethnic identity, as will be seen in the case study text, is a multi-faceted process that is shaped by social, political, economic and historical factors. These factors combine to determine the general well-being of various diasporic entities, specifically the black diaspora. Hence, Anderson's concept of imagined communities reiterates that ethnic identities are created through boundary work of individuals and groups; collective establishment of meaning and reification of a certain way of life, particular ways of thinking, and unique cultural products.

Ethnic Identity

Traditionally, the concept of ethnicity has emphasized the sharing of norms, beliefs, cultural symbols and practices. The formation of "ethnic groups" relies on common cultural signifiers which have developed under specific historical, social, and political contexts and which encourage a sense of belonging based, at least in part, on common mythological ancestry. This view is corroborated by Hall who reveals that "the term ethnicity acknowledges the place of history, language and culture in the construction of subjectivity and identity, as well as the fact that all discourse is placed, positioned, situated, and all knowledge is contextual" (Hall, 1996:446). However, ethnicity is not based on primordial ties or universal cultural characteristics possessed by a specific group, for identities are unpredictable productions of specific history and culture. What this implies is that a person is social and cultural construction all the way down. That is, what it means to be Hausa, Yoruba, Igbo, Ebira etc, changes over time, and from place to place. It also means that ethnicity is formed by the way we speak about group identities and identify with the signs and symbols that constitute ethnicity for us.

Barth (1969:73) opines that Ethnicity is a relational concept concerned with categories of self-identification and social ascription. What we think as our identity is dependent on what we think we are not. For example, the Yorubas are not Igbos, who are not Nupe. Consequently, ethnicity is best understood as a process of boundary formation constructed and maintained under specific socio-historical conditions.

Furthermore, ethnicity is constituted through power relations between groups. It signals relations of marginality, of the centre and the periphery, in the context of changing historical forms and circumstances. Here, the centre and the margin are to be grasped through the politics of representation, for as Brah argues "it is necessary for it to become axiomatic that what is represented as the 'margin' is not marginal at all but is a constitutive effect of the representation itself. The 'centre' is no more a centre than is the 'margin'" (Brah, 1996:226).

In Nigeria, ethnic identity has an inextricable link with one's citizenship, which in turn determines the extent to which one accesses basic means of livelihoods. Citing Nnoli (1978: 191), Okwori (2005:09) opines that:

Perhaps the greatest threat to citizenship in Nigeria lies in the concept of foreigner. In Nigeria, whether you were born in a state or had lived and worked there all your life, as long as it is not your state of origin, you are still a stranger, non-indigene who is not entitled to the status and benefits enjoyed by those who are "bona fide" owners of the State. Even when you have a job with the state, such a job is on contract basis. The northernization policy defined in 1957 by the Public Service Commission of the Northern Region as a hiring system, illustrates this phenomenon vividly: "if a qualified northerner is available, he is given priority in recruitment; if no northerner is available, an expatriate may be recruited or a non-northerner on contract terms"

Okwori further argues that it is only if the establishment is a federal one that you can have tenure appointment but even then, the tendency nowadays is that the states insist that certain positions within the federal establishments in their states be reserved exclusively for their people, even if there are better qualified Nigerians from other states. It is no wonder therefore that ethnic identity articulation becomes a matter of necessity in Nigerian cities and one that drives a very strong wedge between being a Nigerian and being a member of an ethnic group.

Discourse of ethnic centrality and marginality are commonly articulated with those of nationality. History is replete with examples of how one ethnic group has been defined as central and superior to a marginal 'Other'. Nazi Germany, apartheid South Africa, ethnic cleansing in Bosnia, Gikuyu versus Luo ethnic groups political struggles in Kenya, and Rwandan Genocide (Hutu versus Tutsis) are among the most clear-cut examples of this phenomenon. However, the metaphor of superiority is also applicable to contemporary Nigeria, America, Britain and Australia. Thus, ethnicity has been closely allied to nationalisms that conceive of the 'nation' as sharing a culture and requiring that ethnic boundaries should not cut across political ones (Though they often do).

Another perspective from which we can view ethnicity is discussed in Omi and Winant's seminal work *Racial Formation in the United States: From the 1960s-1980s* (1986). They discuss the concept of ethnicity as an element of social discourse that emerged as a new way to discuss race through a focus on culture as opposed to biology.

Hence, they argue that culture is crucial to the idea of ethnic identity and it is the primacy of culture that separates ethnic identity and racial identity.

Citing Hall (1996), Chris Barker (2005: 268) opines that ethnic identity is not a fixed universal essence, but an ordered way of speaking about persons. Ethnicity is always already constituted by representations formed through regulatory discourses of power. It is important to note that the regulatory aspects of discourse involve an element of identification or emotional investment that partially stitch together discourses and psychic forces. Identification is also understood as an affiliation or emotional tie with an idealized and fantasized object. Further, identification constitutes an exclusionary matrix by which identification with one form of identity frequently involves the repudiation of another. Example, I am Hausa, therefore, I can never be Igbo. Nevertheless, emotional identification with any given form of identity is only ever partial. Hence, ethnicity remains an achievement of language users, not a crude reflection of one-dimensional discursive subject positions.

Also, identifications can be multiple and need not involve the repudiation of all other positions. People are composed of not one, but several, sometimes contradictory identities, enabling subjects to assume a variety of shifting identities at different times and places. For instance, ethnic identities are articulated with those of class, gender, nation and age. Hence, subjects cannot legitimately be reduced to ethnicity, nor can ethnicity be represented in a pure form, set apart from other facets of our acculturated selves.

Race, Racialization and Power Relations.

The concept of race can be said to have traces of its origins in the biological discourses of Social Darwinism that emphasize 'lines of descent' and 'types of people'. Here, the concept of race refers to alleged biological and physical characteristics, the most obvious of which is skin pigmentation. These attributes, frequently linked to 'intelligence' and 'capabilities', are used to rank 'racialized' groups in a hierarchy of social and material superiority and subordination. These racial classifications, constituted by and constitutive of power, are at the root of racism.

As a discursive construct, the meanings of 'race' change and are struggled over. Thus, different groups are differentially racialized and subject to different forms of racism. For example, British Asians have historically been subject to different forms of stereotyping and have occupied a different place in the social and racial hierarchy from British Afro-Caribbeans. While British Asians may be second-class citizens, black Britons are on the third rung of the ladder. British Asians are stereotyped as doctors and shopkeepers while young Afro-Caribbean men are cast in the role of criminals.

The idea of racialization, or 'race formation' is founded on the argument that race is a social construction and not a universal or essential category of biology. Races, it is argued by Hall (1990, 1996, 1997), do not exist outside representation. Rather, they are formed in and by symbolization in a process of social and political power struggle. Thus, observable characteristics are transformed into signifiers of race. This includes the spurious appeal to essential biological and cultural difference.

In Britain, America and Australia, the historical formation of 'race' is one of power and subordination. That is, people of colour have occupied structurally subordinate positions in relation to every dimension of 'life chances'. For instance, British Afro-Caribbean, African Americans and Australian Aboriginal peoples have been disadvantaged in the labour market, the housing market, the educational system, the media and other forms of cultural representation. In this context, race formation (racialization) has been inherently racist for it involves forms of social, economic and political subordination that are lived through the categories and discourses of race. Hence, Miles submits that the "concept of racialization refers to those instances where social relations between people have been structured by the signification of human biological characteristics in such a way as to define and construct differentiated social collectivities".

Diaspora: a cultural tapestry.

A diaspora is scattered population whose origins lies in a separate geographic locale. In particular, diaspora has come to refer to involuntary mass dispersions of populations from its indigenous territories most notably, the illegal dispersion of Africans through Trans-Atlantic slave trade, the southern Chinese or Indians during the coolie trade, and the Irish during and after Irish Famine. Other examples include the expulsion of Jews from Judea and fleeing of Greeks after the fall of Constantinople. Recently, scholars have distinguished between different kinds of diaspora, based on its causes such as imperialism, trade or labour migrations,

or by the kind of social coherence within the diaspora community and its ties to the ancestral lands. Some diaspora communities maintain strong political ties with their home land. Other qualities that may be typical of many Diasporas are thoughts of return, relationships with other communities in the diaspora and lack of full integration into the host community.

According to Chris Barker (2005:255), a diaspora can be understood as a dispersed network of ethnically related peoples. This notion focuses our attention on travels, 'where, when, how and under what circumstances'. Thus, 'diasporic identities are at once local and global (i.e. glocal). They are networks of transnational identifications encompassing 'imagined' and 'encountered'communities (Brah, 1996:196). This automatically makes diaspora a cultural tapestry of some sort where different identities are weaved together within a common diasporic space, and social context. Diaspora is a relational concept referring to configurations of power that differentiate diasporas internally as well as situate them in relation to one another. As Brah (1996:183) succinctly puts it:

> Diaspora space as a conceptual category is inhibited not only by those who have migrated and their descendants, but also by those who are constructed and represented as indigenous. In other words, the concept of diaspora space includes the entanglement, the intertwining of the genealogies of dispersion with those "staying put". The diaspora space is the site where the native is as much a diasporian as the diasporian is a native.

Globalization provides the context for an increased interest in the study of diaspora in recent years. In particular, patterns of population movement and settlement instituted during colonialism and its aftermath established diaspora populations at the heart of Western cultures and nation states.

The strength of the concept of diaspora according to Barker (2004) lies in its encouragement to think about identities in terms of contingency, indeterminacy and conflict of identity in motion rather than of absolutes of nature and culture. Gilroy (1997) describes this process as involving routes rather than roots; a 'changing same' of the diaspora that involves hybridized cultural forms. His prime example is encapsulated in the concept of 'Black Atlantic'. Here, cultural exchange within the black diaspora produces hybrid identities and cultural forms of similarity and difference within and between its various locales. The physical meeting and mixing of peoples across the globe that is exemplified by diaspora throws the whole notion of pure national or ethnic cultures into doubt. For example, in a Caribbean context, the idea of 'Creole Continuum' has continued to gain significance. That is, a series of overlapping language uses and code-switching that deploys not only the specific modes of other languages, say English and French, but invents forms peculiar to itself. In this case therefore, neither colonial, nor colonized cultures or languages are best understood as 'pure' forms separated from each other but rather as elements in the construction of new hybrid cultural forms.

By and large, diasporic space can be understood as a space punctuated by hybrid cultural identities. The issue of ethnic centrality and marginality as influenced by race is a key feature of diaspora. That is, race determines 'who gets what, when and how'. This implies that the so-called coloured or black in diaspora occupy a social position that is different from their white counterparts. They are often disadvantaged in almost all spheres of human endeavours. Hence, the hope of return to their ancestral home, or maintaining ties with their home countries has become a major characteristic of some black diaspora. This situation is graphically illustrated in Tess Onwueme's The Missing Face.

Tess Onwueme's *The Missing Face* and the Experience of Black Diaspora in the United States.

Tess Onwueme was born in Nigeria and has established a significant reputation as the leading African female playwright, with international distinction in Africa, North America, and Europe. After her BA and MA degrees from the University of Ife, Nigeria, she earned her PhD in Literature from the University of Benin, Nigeria. In both the year, 2000 and 2001, she was awarded substantial grants for her creative writing and production by the Ford Foundation. In 1994, she joined the University of Wisconsin Eau Claire, Wisconsin as the first Distinguished Professor of Cultural Diversity, and Professor of English. Other international institutions she has taught include: Vassar College, Poughkeepsie, New York, Montclair State University, Montclair, New Jersey, Wayne State University, Detroit, Michigan, the University of Ife, Federal University of Technology, Owerri, and Imo State University, Nigeria.

The Missing Face dramatizes the conflicts involved with personal and collective survival and renewal. Like the archetypal Sankofa bird (which strain her neck to reach back and retrieve the egg left behind), Ida Bee, an African American woman, takes her teenage son, Amaechi on a very tedious journey, back to their ancestral roots in the African kingdom of Idu. Their primary quest is to find Amaechi's father, Momah, who had abandoned them in Milwaukee after his studies in the USA to return to his African homeland. Having "lived from pay-check to pay-check", with insecure, run down inner city neighbourhood, where the black men are increasingly being incarcerated in prisons that are often fed by crime, unemployment, racial, gender, and class crises. Ida Bee decides to find her son's father so that he too, does not end up like other kids from broken families in Milwaukee. Above all, she wants to provide a strong family base to secure her son's sense of manhood, identity and pride.

On this mythical journey, Ida Bee and Amaechi carry with them the heavy burden of the split "Ikenga". The "Ikenga" signifies the Igbo ancestral symbol of manhood and personal achievement. This split "Ikenga" had been passed down from previous generations of her family in the diaspora, with the injunction that she must "find the missing half of the face". On arrival, Ida Bee meets Odozi, a 76-year-old uncle of Momah, and other villagers at the grotto. The occasion is the celebration of New Yam Festival, and also the rite of passage of Momah to manhood. Ida Bee reveals their mission to Odozi and the villagers, reiterating they belong in Idu. The villagers vehemently kick against Ida Bee's claim. The conversation below captures how Ida Bee and Amaechi are interrogated on their arrival in Idu:

ODOZI: …No one knows you here. And I certainly don't know you. Do you know who I am?

IDA BEE & AMAECHI: No.

ODOZI: Well, if you say you are one of us, you must know me. I am the Diokpa, the oldest man in Idu. And I think I have borne witness to the birth of everyone here…the birth of so many seasons that I should know who my own people are. Strangers, this is Idu, our homeland. Where do you say you come from?

IDA BEE: We come from America, but our ancestors are from here.

ODOZI: But what lineage do you belong?

IDA BEE: Idu…

ODOZI: Yes, Idu. But no one comes just from Idu. Idu is a whole kingdom, made up of nine clans. Everyone belongs to a particular clan and lineage. And if you say you are from here you must have a lineage so which lineage do you belong? (P9-10)

IDA BEE: I can only say what I know.

ODOZI: And what is it? Now tell us. What is it that you, mere children could know that an old man like me who has been an elder , a titled chief who has been in this land for all my life got to teach me about my own lineage? Strangers, tell us what you know.

IDA BEE: Our ancestors came from here. My father came from Idu. That is all that my father could tell me.

ODOZI: Your father?

AMAECHI: And my father too…

ODOZI: Hmm… Came from Idu?

IDA BEE & AMAECHI: Yes!

ODOZI: Wonders shall never cease! (Turning to Villagers) I have said it time and time again. I have growntoo old. Age is truly a burden… Before your eyes, one day I shall be lingering here where white albino will come to this land and claim that my seed had fathered him…. Strangers, you stretch our patience. How can you come from…from "Amilika" and say that your father comes from our land? How? How can that be? How does this happen? (P 12-13)

The above conversation encapsulates the rigorous interrogation Ida Bee and her son have to be subjected to in the process of negotiating their identity. In this case, ethnic identity does not occur by mere profession or verbal confession, but by locating your position in the larger matrix of people's signifying practices. As such, for one to really belong in Idu, one must have come from a particular lineage and clan. In this lies the dilemma of black diaspora who nurse the hope of returning to their ancestral home one day. The question that continues to lingeris: will they ever be welcomed in their "imagined" ancestral home any better than their "encountered" home?

In the case of Ida Bee, through the mechanism of flashback, she reveals how she was impregnated by Momah seventeen years back in the U.S when he was a student of Urban Development in the University of Wisconsin, Milwaukee. Through the help of the Griot (native Historian dubbed 'The Eye has Seen it All'), Odozi confirms the authenticity of Ida Bee's story, as Momah also admits it. Through a symbolic display, Amaechi is 'circumcised' again and his umbilical cord burried in the land of Idu. Nebe, Momah's mother and wife to Odozi finally welcomes Ida Bee to their fold by symbolically 'cutting her neck' with a palm leaf. In what seems like a dramatic twist, Momah, although admits that Amaechi is his son, he refuses to have Ida Bee as his wife. He instead banishes her into the evil forest. It is in the evil forest that Ida Bee undergoes what seems to be an excruciating journey of purging herself of every iota of European identity in her. As a result of her experience in the evil forest, Ida Bee begins to exhibit symptoms of insanity as she sings and talks to herself. At the end of the play, Ida Bee emerges from the forest looking tattered and unkempt. It is at this time that she brings out the split Ikenga and begin to brandish it. Nebe recognizes it and asks her whose image is it. Ida Bee replies that it is the image of her father Meme:

IDA BEE: Meme, my own father. Kidnapped, snatched, robbed of manhood and snatched by strange hands on the night of initiation to manhood. In the struggle that ensued, Daddy's symbol was split-one half lost but the other he carried with him which he handed to me as LE-GA-CY.

With this revelation, Nebe discovers that Ida Bee is her step-daughter, while Momah embraces her as he calls her sister! In Idu, Ida Bee finds the other half of the Ikenga which is the 'missing face'. This, metaphorically means the final reconstruction of her identity. By finding the missing face, Ida Bee has been able to successfully unearth her root in the African soil as a black diaspora. Also, the text gives us some useful insights into the socio-economic condition of black diaspora in the United States, and further contributes in crystalizing the concepts of race, ethnicity and identity of ethnicity which are discussed below.

From the text, there seems to be two categories of black diasporic entities in the United States: the so-called native African Americans and the immigrants. Whereas the natives are indigenes, who are ordinarily supposed to be entitled to all the rights and privileges that U.S citizens enjoy, the immigrants are entitled to all of them. Ironically however, the natives are constantly faced with the question of their identity due to the excruciating effects of trans-Atlantic slave history. Although no longer in the slave era, the spirit of that era has continued to inform the manner African Americans are treated by their white counterparts. This has led many African Americans to despise their American citizenship and fantasize Africa, where they believe is their ancestral roots. The immigrants on the other hand seem to be eager to acquire the white identity to the detriment of their own native identity. This scenario plays out in the text during Ida Bee's first encounter with her husband Momah, who was a young black student of the University of Wisconsin. Momah has just introduced himself to Ida Bee as Jack.

IDA BEE: I've never heard of an African named Jack.

MOMAH: Well, that's what I'm called, Jack.

IDA BEE: Most African names have meaning. What's the meaning of Jack?

MOMAH: Hmm… Well, I don't know. Don't know really…em… it's just a name. A name has no meaning. What should I care about the meaning of a name anyway?

IDA BEE: It matters! It does! To me…to us… who are here without. It has to do with essential African Quality. If you had been addressed as boy and called "Hey Boy! Come here!" as if you werea dog or something, you would have understood that you had a name. A name which meant so much to you and your world. A man who knows the meaning of his name answers to the ancestral rhythm and knows where he is going, Brother! If people attached any meaning to your name, they won't call you "Boy" at 50. What does your mother call you?

MOMAH: Momah… Momahnjo.

IDA BEE: Meaning?

MOMAH:"Don't think evil."

IDA BEE: You see! "Don't think evil!" it has profound meaning! It reveals a value system, a way of life, of peace, unity,

justice. Not one like ours, here in these states where the colour of a man's skin classifies him as evil, and certain people, exploiting class, exploiting race, feed on nothing but evil. (P25-26).

From the excerpt above, we are exposed to the existential realities of the two kinds of black diaspora in the U.S. wherethe issue of name connotes identity and dignity. This fact doesn't seem to settle well in the hearts of young black immigrants as represented in the character of Momah. Ida Bee, on the other hand leads us into salient issues of dehumanization African Americans are subjected to, such as the use of the word "Boy" to address a grown man of about 50 years. Today, despite the inhuman treatment blacks are subjected to in the U.S, there are many 'Momahs' out there who still sacrifice their African roots and identity in order to gain acceptance in the white society. This is one of the realities of diasporic space.

Another reality of the black diaspora as encapsulated in the text is the problem of structural injustice. By structural injustice, we mean the use of institutional apparatus against the blacks in almost all spheres of human endeavours. It could also mean a sort of injustice against the blacks in the U.S which the state seems to permit and accommodate. This is another issue Onwueme's *The Missing Face* brings to the fore. Injustice can be seen as an unfair treatment of a person or group of persons, which can be manifested in refusal to give them what they duly deserve. For example, denying a worker his pay-off package when his services are no longer required in an organization or industry. In the American society, injustice is largely influenced by race. Ida Bee's father is one of the victims of structural injustice in the American society. According to Ida Bee "Daddy was a labourer who had been laid off his job without compensation. He felt demolished because he could not support us. He left one day in search of work and never returned" (P 24).

The consequences of such injustices are manifested in the fractured lives of blacks in America.This arguably encapsulates the experience of black diaspora, especially African Americans in the U.S, and by extension in other western countries. The first level of fracturing could be said to have occurred during trans-Atlantic slave trade where black people from Africa were forcefully whisked away from their ancestral roots. This marked the beginning of loss of identity, unity, wholeness and communal brotherhood that characterize the African society. The process of fracturing the lives of blacks subsequently continued after the slave era, and still continues today. This is made possible through systematic manipulation of institutions of state by the white supremacists against the blacks as discussed above. The resultant effect on many African Americans has been loss of hope, frustration, violence, prostitution, alcoholism among other social vices. In a nutshell, living an unfulfilled life tantamount to living a fractured life. Ida Bee paints a vivid picture of this experience thus:

> All we got in Milwaukee is a bunch of fractured lives. Uncle Henry is an alcoholic. His wife and children livin' up in Kenosha with Uncle Ron, whose little Oshkosh job can hardly feed himself, let alone some extra mouths. And Uncle Charlie? Well, you know Uncle Charlie. So, slick he can't keep himself out of jail. And Aunt Gloria is alone. She's got seven children and she's alone and doesn't even know it. Alone with no place in the world. And Uncle Mikey, the baby in the family, who carried so much promise for us, went off to college, got himself a big time corporate job and forgot all about us when he hit the Big Apple. (P4).

Furthermore, it is important for us to note that Onwueme's *The Missing Face* graphically projects the flexibility of the concept of ethnicity. That is, the meaning of ethnic ties or identity in a given social context could be different in an entirely different social context. For example, Ida Bee claims ethnic ties with Momah immediately she meets him, before even inquiring where came from in Africa. She calls him 'Brother', and also takes it upon herself to re-educate him on the importance of maintaining and upholding African identity (Name). At this moment, what binds them together is the common acceptance of Africa as their ancestral roots. However, when Ida Bee finally arrives in Idu Kingdom, the concept of ethnicity changes to something more than mere declaration and skin pigmentation. For her to be accepted into the fold of Idu ethnic group, she must identify the lineage she came from, and the clan she belongs to. This becomes very necessary for her because she and her son have hybrid identity which requires verification by the people Idu. Hybridized identity is an important and common feature of the diasporic space.

The concept of hybridity highlights cultural mixing and the emergence of new forms of identity. According to Barker (2004: 2558), the concept of hybridity remains problematic so far as it assumes or implies the meeting or mixing of completely separate and homogeneous cultural spheres. For example, to think of British Asian or Mexican American hybrid forms as the mixing of two separate traditions is problematic because neither British, Asian, Mexican nor American cultures are bounded and homogeneous. Each category is always already hybrid form that is also divided along the lines of religion, class, gender, age, nationality, and so forth. Thus, hybridization is the mixing of that which is already a hybrid. Nevertheless, the concept of hybridity has enabled us to recognize the production of new identities and cultural forms. In the text, Ida Bee and her son Amaechi personify hybridized identity. They are a product of contact between African culture and American one, to the extent that Odozi refers to them as 'albino' and 'oyibo' (whites). This is how Odozi tries to make sense of their hybridized identity:

> …the bat's place is split between two worlds. Only the bat cannot be placed fully as an animal that lives on air. Nor can you place it fully as an animal that lives on land. But you are not bats. You are human. I can see resemblance. You look like us. You claim to be one of us. And yet you do not speak our tongue. You do not understand us, we do not understand you. Why? Because you speak Oyibo…the white men's tongue. You talk like them, not like us… not like anyone in our world. And if anyone were to ask me, I would tell them you are Oyibo. You belong to the white world, where you come from. And now that you insist you are from here and yet cannot tell where you belong. I am confused… I cannot understand… your mission brings us confusion. (P 11)

Racial discrimination and violence against blacks is another experience of the black diaspora that is anchored on the question of race and ethnic identity. Whites naturally feel superior to the blacks, as such they discriminate against them in almost all areas of human endeavour. This often manifest in forms of physical violence against the blacks. In the playtext, Ida Bee recounts a similar episode thus:

> In the beginning, a fire raged on North Avenue, Milwaukee, a fire set by angry white men that swept through my home, trapping mother inside

with flames. Nothing was left of her besides her charred body amidst the debris. The fire had snuffed out my sense of hope… (P24).

Finally, blacks in diaspora seem to nurse undying hope of returning home to Africa to reconstruct their identity and reclaim their lost dignity. This hope is so strong that in the wake of decolonization of many African countries, it inspired negroe movements that rooted for the repatriation of blacks from America back to Africa in the mid-20th century. One of the prominent advocate of Negroe repatriation was Marcus Garvey. This hope is what inspires Ida Bee to undergo a tedious journey back to Africa with her son Amaechi. In Africa, Ida Bee hopes to find her "place in the world" where life is more meaningful, and not about paying bills. When Amaechi, who represents the younger generation protest the excruciating journey his mother is subjecting him to, she responds thus:

> What do you know about getting' anyplace? I'm the one who works from paycheck to paycheck in an empty job goin' nowhere. Nike shoes and video games bills keep piling up before I even earn the money. Hate to see the mailman comin'. There's got to be more to life than payin' bills. That's why we must find our place in the world. A place where we can be whole… a place that can fill the emptiness with kinship and the spirit of our ancestors" (P 3-4).

The above excerpt captures the hope of many black diaspora. Although they live in an 'encountered' community, they usually fantasize their 'imagined community'. A community where their dignity will be restored, identity reclaimed and standard of living improved. This in summary is the story of many diasporic entities, especially the black diaspora.

Implications of Identity Politics to the Lives of Black Diaspora

Based on the exploration of the dilemmas and existential challenges confronting African Americansin the study text, it can be inferred that in a typical American society, the blacks re by default expected to occupy the lowest social ladder in the society. This is despite their level of contribution to the country. The larger implication of this is that their efforts towards national development are seldom given due recognition and reward.

Racial and ethnic politics can also be understood through the process of racial profiling. For instance, casting young blacks as criminals, or people who have natural inclination to commit crime has had serious implications to the lives of African Americans. They are often viewed with suspicion by the corporate establishment, and subjected to extra scrutiny during business transactions. This is capable of dissuading many ambitious blacks from pursuing success in the corporate world, although there are few dogged ones who have made their marks despite these impediments. Hence, it can be argued that in American society, the colour of your skin and ethnic identity are more important than individual capabilities. This has partly been responsible for the structural injustice against the blacks.

Furthermore, there seems to be another manifestation of oppression of blacks by Europeans in the home countries of the former. In recent times, there have been cases of expatriates who, motivated by the spirit of racism, molest and dehumanize blacks in their home country. The paradox of this situation is that, whether at home or in diaspora, the black man remains a constant object of dehumanization in the context of diaspora.

Also, it is important to note that since race and ethnic identities are products of social construction, there are no rigid and universally recognized definition of these concepts, both theory and in practice. The implication of this to the lives of black diaspora is that, whereas they may always identify themselves with their brothers in Africa as members of the same ethnic group, they can hardly fit into the African ethnic identity due to their exposure to the western culture. This is graphically illustrated in the case of Ida Bee and her son Amaechi whose claim of sharing same ethnic identity with people of Idu is vehemently kicked against by the indigenous people. In other words, Amaechi and Ida Bee's understanding of the concept of ethnicity is different from that of the people of Idu.

Lastly, the question of ethnic identity has arguably been responsible for bitter ethnic politics that characterize many nascent democracies in the developing world. In Nigeria for example, ethnic affiliation is a major factor in determining 'who gets what' in relation to national wealth and resources. Ethnicity plays out in the process appointments to government agencies, admissions to institutions of learning and even federal allocations to the states of the federation.

Conclusion

This study has interrogated the fluidity of identity in diasporic space.; a fluidity that is informed by identity politics where ethnicity and race are key determinants of 'who gets what, when and how'. The study, through a critical examination of Tess Onwueme's *The Missing Face* has also given us insights on the possible identity crisis that can confront black diaspora at any given time, unless this is effectively negotiated. By and large, we submit that the issue of identity within diasporic space, is also a process of social and cultural construction, and thus, subject to changes. Lastly, the process of identity creation is political, while the representation and projection of identity is also a political endeavour.

References

Anderson, B. (1993) *Imagined Communities: Reflections on the Origins and Spread of Nationalism*. London: Verso.

Barker, C. (2000) *Cultural Studies*, London: Sage Publication.

---------------- (2004) *The SAGE Dictionary of Cultural Studies*. London: Sage Publication.

---------------- (2005) *Cultural Studies: Theory and Practice*. London: Sage Publication.

Barth, F. (1969) *Ethnic Groups and Boundaries*. London: Allen & Unwin.

Brah, A. (1996) *Cartographies of Diaspora*. London: Routledge.

David, M.& Kuan, H. (1996) *Critical Dialogues in Cultural Studies*. London & New York: Routledge.

Gillespie, M. (1995) *Television, Ethnicity and Cultural Change*. London and New York: Routledge.

Gilroy, P. (1987) *There Ain't No Black in the Union Jack*. London: Unwin Hyman.

------------ (1993) *The Black Atlantic*. London: Verso.

------------ (1997) 'Diaspora and Detours of Identity' in K. Woodward (ed.) *Identity and Difference*. London and Thousand Oaks, C.A: Sage Publication.

Hartley, J. (2002) *Communication, Cultural Media and Studies: The Key Concepts*. London: Routledge.

Okwori, J.Z (2005) 'The Patchwork that is Nigeria: Implications and Impact on Citizenship, Participation and Accountability' in O.S Abah (ed.) *Geographies of Citizenship in Nigeria*. Zaria: Tamaza.

Onwueme, T. (2012) *The Missing Face*. Ibadan: Heritage Press.

Community Media as Strategic Tool in The Economic Development of Nigeria's Pluralistic Society

ADESEYE, Bifatife Olufemi (Ph. D)
Department of Theatre and Media Arts, Federal University, Oye, Ekiti State, Nigeria
Email: bifatife.adeseye@fuoye.edu.ng, touchbfatfe@gmail.com

LAMIDI, Ishola Kamorudeen
Department of Mass Communication, Adekunle Ajasin University, Akungba – Akoko, Ondo State, Nigeria.
Email: isholalamidi@yahoo.com

Abstract

The question of the role of community media in economic development has always been in the middle of contending discourse in media economics as community media have always been attached to play key roles in mainly democratic participation. This paper, through economic development models and development media theory, captures the interrelationship that exists between community media and economic development. Our study uses explorative and development communication theoretical frameworks to identify the strategic roles of community media in the economic development of Nigeria. We play close attention to the proximity between community media and members of the rural community within which they operate. Community media feeds on the community for sustenance and therefore maintains a symbiotic relationship with the host. Our paper interrogates the relevance of the various ownership systems operating in Nigeria. We also relate the cliché that says, "who pays the piper dictates the tune" from the perspective of joint ownership structure.

Introduction

The concept of community media has been one that has been defined from diverse perspectives according to different schools of thought. The   in the term has made different scholars to focus on certain characteristics such as ownership, locations, and   in defining a community media, leaving out other core identity of an ideal community media or what community media is all about. In justifying this stand, Carpentier, Lie and Servaes (2003) posit that "this theoretical problem necessitates the use of different approaches towards the definition of CM, which will allow for a complementary emphasis on different aspects of the identity of CM" In classifying these approaches used by scholars when discussing Community media, there are approaches often used: (i.) serving the community, an alternative to mainstream, part of civil society, and rhizome (Carpentier, Lie and Servaes, 2003). Hence, Community Media will be defined alone with these approaches.

Approach One: Serving the Community

From this viewpoint, community media is defined as media platform solely set out to achieve the goals of the community. Community media, in this case, is meant to serve the community. The emphasis is on the community. Community media can be referred to as any form of media that are created and controlled by a community, either a geographic community or community of identity or interest. Community media are media designed, developed and operated to serve the needs of rural areas or of a particular locality/community within a rural, sub-urban, or urban setting (Folarin, 1997, cited in Lamidi, 2011; Mojaye and Lamidi, 2015). In this definition, the locality of the community media is given more prominence than the duties of the media to the general welfare.

However, community in this case could be a geographical entity or a community of interests of people with shared interests. Community media in the case of geographical entity is meant to service the people within a geographical entity. In addition, it dwells predominantly on the concepts of community and ethnicity as the frameworks for collective identity and aspiration. Carpenter, Lie and Servaes (2003, p.243) posit that "the audience is not defined as an aggregate of individuals who only share socio-demographic or economic characteristics, but as a collective of people holding a series of identifying group relations." On the other hand, community media in the area of community of interest cuts across a specific geographical location. The core factor in this conceptualisation is that community media seeks to service people across various geographical locations with similar interests. Lindolf (1988) conceptualises this form of community media as "interpretative community", while Cohen (1989) conceptualises it as "community of meaning."

Approach Two: Community Media as an Alternative to Mainstream Media

Another approach often taken by community media scholars is alternative to mainstream media. Community media in this sense is referred to as an alternative media which seeks to supplements or complements the activities of the mainstream media. Also, community media seeks to replicate what is being produced by mainstream media to its local audience. This means that community media is expected to provide the local audience with whatever they might have missed on the mainstream media.Carpenter, Lie and Servaes (2003, p.243) mention that community media as alternative media are;

> small-scaled and oriented towards specific communities, possibly disadvantaged groups, respecting their diversity; independent from state and market; horizontally structured, allowing for the facilitation of audience access and participation within the frame of democratisation and multiplicity; and carriers of non-dominant (possibly counter-hegemonic) discourses and representations, stressing the importance of (sic)the self.

Approach Three: Linking Community Media to the Civil Society

Servaes (1999, p.260) defines community media as a third voice between state media and private. Benedetta (2015) also captures this as "civil society based media, with the aim to provide an alternative to national broadcast system - which are often under government control- and to private commercial media, which are run for profit and not for social benefit." The evolution of community media as a tool for the civil society started with the formation of social movements which are created with the goal of fostering political change, economic development and even political participation. In this sense, community media are viewed as a mouth-piece for suitable growth and development in the society. Also, the aim of community media as a civil society is to foster development and social change, not necessarily to service the interests of members of a society. On the other hand, civil societies are a group of intermediate organisations, which are different from the privately-owned organisations whose goals are to make profit and are also distinct from state-owned or quasi-state organisations.

Towards linking community media to the civil society, a number of international bodies have been carrying out some projects. One of such is UNESCO's project tagged"International Programme for the Development of Communication" (IPDC), which is directed at promoting pluralism, freedom of expression, and development (UNESCO, 2001). Similarly, UNESCO recognised community media as a "third media sector" at its conference in Namibia in 2001 where it adopted the African Charter on Broadcasting.

Approach Four: Community Media as Rhizome

Literally, a rhizome refers to "the thick stem of some plants, such as iris and mint, that grow along or under the ground and haveroots and stems growing from them. The rhizome approach combines both civil society approach and alternative media approach in defining what a community media is; pointing out the relationist elements that can be found in the two approaches. This approach is better captured by the Deleuze and Guattari theory of the rhizome which is based on the comparison of rhizomatic and arbolic thinking (Deleuze and Guattari, 1987; www.thoughtleader.co.za accessed June 21, 2018). The arbolic is linear, hierarchic and sedentary, and could be represented as the tree-like structure of genealogy, branches that continue to subdivide into smaller and lesser categories (Wray, 1983). On the other hand, Deleuze and Guattari (1987) posit that the rhizomatic is "non-linear, anarchic and nomadic unlike trees or their roots, the rhizome connects any point to any other point…"

Relating this theory to community media, it is the duty of community media to build linkages or connections between civil society, the state, community and even the market. Just like how Carpentier, Lie and Servaes (2003, p.261) put it thus; "these connections apply not only to the pivotal role that community media (can) play in civil society, but also to the linkages (and other civil organisations) that can be established with (segments of) the state and the market, without losing their proper identity."

Having considered the four approaches to community media, hence community media can be defined as a non-profit media outlet in form of radio, television, newspaper or other forms of mass media, saddled with the responsible of fostering political development, economic development, social change and political change, thereby servicing the interest of the community it was established for and serving as an alternative media to more-development media platforms. Similarly, AMARC-Europe (1994, p.4) defines community radio station which is a subset of community media as "a 'non-profit' station, currently broadcasting, which offers a service to the community in which it is located, or to which it broadcasts, while promoting the participation of this community in the radio".

Pluralistic Society

The concept of pluralistic society is derived from the concept of pluralism which has its origin in the ancient Greek politics where Democritus and Epicurus posited a "polarity of worlds" (in the cosmology of Democritus – www.astro.bas.bg> issues > 11_EDanezis) while Herodotus and Xenophon emphasized the cultural differences between Greeks, Egyptians and Persians. Pluralism suggests existence of many groups of people with diverse religious, political, ethnic, or tribal backgrounds. In addition, it is a political philosophy which supports peaceful co-existence among people of different interests, convictions, and lifestyles. This depicts that a pluralistic society is made of people with diverse background in form of politics, religion, ethnicity and tribe.

Development Theory

This paper is anchored on the development media theory which is meant to explain the normative role or behaviour of mass media in developing countries. The mass media in this sense are expected to foster or champion development and social change through its activities. Folarin (2006) identifies the following as characteristics of developing countries "absence or inadequate supply of requisite communication infrastructure; relatively limited supply of requisite professional skills; relative lack of cultural production resources; relatively limited availability of media-literate audiences; and dependence on the developed world for technology, skill and cultural products."

In tracing the history of development media theory, Okunna (1999) posits that the theory was postulated as a result of the emerging gap in terms of information flow between developing and developed countries. This gap became obvious as the four normative of the press postulated by Siebert, Peterson and Schramm (1956) were not encompassing enough to accommodate for the needs and aspirations of developing countries. In view of this, Denis McQuial (2005) proposes the development theory to correct the imbalance in information flow which has resulted in digital divide over the years. Hamelink (1997) also argues that developing countries should focus more on using indigenous media which are local to the people and canvass for the total departure from the use of foreign technologies. McQuail (2005) summarises the following as the tenets of development media theory;

> Media must accept and carry out positive development tasks in line with nationally established policy; freedom of the media should be open to economic priorities and development needs of the society; media should give priority in their content to the national culture and language(s); media should give priority in news and information to links with other developing countries, which are close geographically, culturally or politically; journalists and other media workers have responsibilities as well as freedom in their information gathering and dissemination tasks; in the interest of development ends, the state has a right to intervene in, or restrict, media operation; and devices of censorship, subsidy and direct control can be justified.

In sum, development theory supports the channelling of the mass media for national development, socio-political autonomy, socio-political autonomy and cultural identity of any developing country, for a participatory communication model and to foster economic development and nation-building (Ese, 2012).

Economic Development

Economic development is a multivariate concept having no all-encompassing definition as scholars have defined from various points of views over the years. In simple terms, economic development can be viewed as the process in which low income countries transform into modern industrial economies, driven by advancement in science and technology. From Kindleberger andHerrick's (1958) perspectives, economic development is geared towards "improvements in material welfare especially for persons with the lowest incomes, the eradication of mass poverty with its correlates of illiteracy, disease and early death, changes in the composition of inputs and output that generally include shifts in the underlying structure of production away from agricultural towards industrial activities…" Also, Meier (1964) also defines economic development the "process whereby an economy's real national income increases over a long period of time."

From the social factors point of view, McGranahan (1972) views social factors such as education, health, housing and other social components as prerequisites for economic growth. The neglect of these social factors could have adverse effects of economic development. Singer and Ansari (1977) from another point of view posit that economic development refer to decrease in poverty level. They mention that "by economic development is meant not simply an increase in the GNP of a country but rather a decrease in poverty at an individual level. Probably the best indicators of poverty are low food consumption and higher unemployment." If the problems of poverty and low food consumption are effectively dealt with, this will amount to economic development (Singer and Ansari, 1977). From the perspectives of developing countries, economic development will have to do more with poverty alleviation, increase in GDP, and increased employment rate.

Overtime, four models or approaches have been developed in explaining the concept of economic development; (1) the linear-stages of growth model, (2) theories and patterns of structural change, (3) the international-dependence revolution, and (4) the neoclassical, free-market counterrevolution. Since the early 1950's and 1960's, scholars have linked development to economic growth. Development in this case is viewed as a series of economic progresses a country must attain before it can attain the developmental stage. Factors such as GDP, Investment, savings, and exportation were considered as part of

determinants for development, leaving other factors such as political participation and governance.

Community Media in the Economic Development of Nigeria's Pluralistic Society

Community media, no doubt, have been identified as key players in the development of any nation, especially a pluralistic nation like Nigeria. Historically, the first instance where the connection between media and economic development was identified was in the issue of how media was used to overcome public choice problem in connection to the prevention of famine (Sen, 1984). Similarly, the ground for economic development of a country through the roles of the community media has been justified by the rapid economic growth of countries such as Estonia, Hungary, Czech Republic and Singapore, paying close attention to the roles community media played in this regard (Coyne and Leeson, 2004; in *The Plight of Underdeveloped Countries* pdf downloadedJune 21, 2018).

One of the way in which community media can contribute effectively to economic development is by providing economic players with accurate and factual information about local production and agriculture among the local populace or community within which they operate. Community media have been found to be at the closest level to farmers who contribute majorly to the Gross Domestic Products of Nigeria. Despite the abundance of oil in Nigeria's GDP, the impact of local production can be overlooked. The role community media are expected to play in this regard is to provide government economic experts with information about local level of production. In a paper entitled "Read All About It! Understand the Role of Media in Economic Development" by Coyne and Leeson (2004), they analysed the role of media in attaining economic development and used Poland and Hungary as part of the examples. They discovered that "not only has the media played a role in transforming situations of conflict into coordination, but also access to information has allowed politicians and the populace to coordinate on good conjectures leading to economic progress."

Using the case of Nigeria as an example, the media, particularly community media, because of their grassroots nature, can help to foster economic development by helping governmental economic players with factual information about production at the local level. For instance, community media could be of help by informing government players of statistics of farmers in need of fertilisers and mechanised equipment which will help boost agricultural production.

Closely tied to the role of providing information to economic players, another way in which community media are very instrumental to economic development is providing local product producers like farmers, traders and artisans with relevant productivity-enhancement information. This is crucial because local products are major contributors to the Gross Domestic Products (GDP) of any country which invariably lead to economic growth. This could be achieved by organising specific radio programmes for community radios and specific columns or features for community newspapers which could be about how farmers can improve or increase their farm products.

Community media are also keep players in playing the role of an interface or intermediary between government and people at the local level. Community media could perform this by providing programmes in languages that are peculiar to the people considering the multilingual nature of a country like Nigeria. By this, community media are expected to act as voice to the minority populace at the local level. However, it should be stressed that community programmes should be provided in languages and dialectics which are peculiar to the immediate community from which they operate.

Conclusion

The task of economic advancement of a nation, using Hungary, Singapore and Czech Republic as examples, does not lie solely in the hands of government or governmental economic experts. It is a joint task involving efforts from government, individuals, societal organisations and the mass media, especially community media. Community media play a key role in this regard because of their closeness to people at the grassroots level who also contribute significantly to GDP. Hence community media are referred to as grassroots media. The main theme of community media is to encourage participation, democratic involvement and bridge between local populace and government.

Recommendation

Community Media has the potential to contribute effectively to the economic development of any nation by providing economic players with accurate and factual information about local production especially relevant information about agriculture among the local populace or

community within which they operate. Community media have been found to be at the closest level to farmers who contribute majorly to the Gross Domestic Products of Nigeria. it is therefore recommended that more community media be established to bring media programmes nearer to the grassroot

References

AMARC-Europe (1994) *One Europe – many voices. Democracy and access to communication.*
Conference report AMARC-Europe Pan-European conference of community radio broadcasters, Ljubljana, Slovenia, 15-18 September 1994, Sheffield: AMARC.

Carpentier, N., Lie, R. and Servaes, J. (2003). Is there a role and place for community media in the remit? In G.F. Lowe & T. Hujanen (eds) *Broadcasting and Convergence: New Articulations of the Public Remit*, pp. 239-254, Göteborg: Nordicom

Coyne, C and Leeson, T. (2004). Real all about it! Understanding the role of media in economic development. *KYKLOS*, 57 (1), 21-44

Deleuze, G. & Guattari, F. (1987). *A thousand plateaus. Capitalism and schizophrenia.*
Minneapolis: University of Minnisota Press.

Ese, U. (2012). A case for community radio in the development of Okuama, Eku and Jeddo communities in Delta central senatorial district. A research project submitted to the Department of Mass Communication, University of Nigeria, Nsukka.

Folarin, B. (2006). *Theories of Mass Communication: An Introductory Text* (3rd edition). Ibadan: Bakinfol Publications.

Hamelink, C. J. (1997). World communication: business as usual? In Bailie, M & Winseck, D. (eds). *Democratizing communication? Comparative perspectives on information and power.* New Jersey: Hampton.

Kindleberger, C. and Herrick, B. (1958). *Economic development.* New York: McGrawHill.

Lamidi, I.K. (2011) "Mainstreaming Rural Broadcasting for the Attainment of Millennium Development Goals in Nigeria." *Akungba Journal of*

English and Communication.   Vol.1, No 11, pp
101-122

McQuail, D. (1983). *Mass communication theory: an introduction.* London: SAGE   Publications.

McQuail, D. (2005). *Mass communication theory.* (5th ed.) London: Sage Publications.

Mojaiye, E. and Lamidi, I. (2015). The role of community media in building democratic values   in Nigeria. *European Journal of Research and Reflection in Arts and Humanities,* 3 (1),   pp. 63-72.

Okunna, C. S. (1999). *Introduction to mass communication.* (2nd ed.). Enugu: New Generation   Books.

Sen, A. (1984). *Poverty and famines.* Oxford: Oxford University Press.

Servaes, J. (1999). *Communication for development. One world, multiple cultures.* Cresskill,   New   Jersey: Hampton Press.

Singer, H. and Ansari, A. (1977). *Rich and poor countries.* Baltimore: Johns Hopkins University   Press.

Wray, S. (1998) Rhizomes, Nomads, and Resistant Internet Use. Retrieved October 7, 2016,   from http://www.nyu.edu/projects/wray/RhizNom.html

International Journal of Integrative Humanism Vol 9. No 1. June 2018. ISSN: 2026 – 6286

A Critical Study of Inculturation And Evangelization of African Culture

Prof. John A. Onimhawo

Department of Religious Management and Cultural Studies, Ambrose Alli University, Ekpoma, Edo State, Nigeria

Dr. Peter O. O. Ottuh

Department of Religious Studies and Philosophy, Delta State University, Abraka, Delta State, Nigeria
Email: pottuh@delsu.edu.ng; ottuhpeter@gmail.com

Abstract

Culture and religion are two societal phenomena that cannot be separated from each other. Every religion has a coloration of the culture where it is founded, hence, culture propels religion vive visa. The process whereby religion localizes its activities in order for it to be closer and more understood by a particular people is termed inculturation. This paper therefore; argues that inculturation can promote Christian evangelism among African people. Using the descriptive and evaluative methods, the paper reveals that inculturation is a practical theistic response by the church in the midst of cultures, to reawaken the soteriological consciousness of the African people. The paper concludes that African Christianity and, indeed, African themselves must endeavor to understand their culture and embrace enculturation in order to achieve an authentic inculturation.

Key Words: Inculturation, Evangelization and Cultures

Introduction

Sincerely speaking, inculturaton and evangelization are independent variables, but play complementary roles. For decades, religious missionaries and revivalists seemed to have spoken strange languages to the evangelized, a sort of monological approach to the dissemination and preaching of their "Good news". But the spirit of post Vatican II has yearned and is still yearning for a more genuine approach to conversion of the people who do not belong to our own faith through inculturation, that is, through the mutual sharing of our positive values, and indeed through genuine cultural interaction (Echekwube, 1999). Culture itself cannot be separated from religion (Alao, 2005). This is why most religions are rooted in the cultures of their original founding places.

Therefore, it becomes obviously clear that inculturation is an indispensable preparation for effective evangelization. It is on this note that we shall do some unbiased examination of the roles of inculturation and evangelization of cultures especially in our African setting. The best place to start this discussion is to give an explanatory note on each of the operative words in our title. These are inculturation, evangelization and cultures.

Clarification of Terms

The term, "inculturation" either as a process or a concept is very difficult to define. For this reason, many definitions and explanations have been advanced. Most times some scholars have employed such terms as adaptation, Africanization, accommodation, indigenization, incarnation, acculturation, contextualization, etc., to connote the term, "inculturation" (Kurgat, 2009). In the logical sense of it, none of the above terms can alternate inculturation.

For some, inculturation is God's self-revelation from a people's cultural perspective, tradition and life and the same people responding from the same perspective (Ndiokwere, 1994). Others define inculturation as the activity of the church, at a particular place in time, to present and live the Christian message faithfully in languages, signs, and symbols and actions which speak to the people in so convincing way that they naturally and readily identify with it and whole heartedly participate in it and contribute to it (Ndiokwere, 1994; Ottuh, *et al,* 2016). A more acceptable definition of inculturation may be cited from the work of Crollius (cited in Ndiokwere, 1994). According to him, inculturation is:

> .... The integration of the Christian experience of a local church into the culture of its people in such a way that this experience not only expresses itself in elements of this culture so as to create a new unity and communion, not only within the culture in question but also as an enrichment of the church universal (31).

The anthropological and theological elements in the above definition of inculturation give way for its wide acceptance.

Our next operative word is "Evangelization". The term is rooted in the English word, "Evangelism" which in fact, is a transliteration and not merely a translation of the Greek word *"euangelion"* for "gospel". The close identification of the English word evangelism with the Greek word for gospel may account for a common definition of evangelism as the proclamation of the gospel (Miles, 1983). Besides, some Christians insist that evangelism is simply the proclamation of the gospel. They do that on the basis of the etymology of the words: evangelism, evangelize (evangelization), and evangelist (cf. Gurreth, 2005). Their conception is also rooted in the way the Bible uses the above clusters of Greek terms.

Our last operative word is "culture". Culture refers to all the things which human beings do but which have no biological bearing (Ikenga-Metuh and Ojoade, 1990). This means that all non-biological actions and behaviors of man are products of his culture. Generally speaking culture is a unique way in which a community lives and does things. For Echekwube (1999), culture is a functional system in which all activities are organically coherent. Scholars in various fields of endeavor, especially sociologists, have also defined culture, as a broad concept, and anthropologist who analyze it from various angles even though their definitions connote the same meaning. Categorically, culture can be termed material and immaterial, normative and cognitive. Culture therefore, is an all-embracing concept. It influences all the aspects of human life. Hence Adelakun (cited in Ikenga-Metuh and Ojoade, 1990) refers to it as the "finer things of life" (p.5).

The Problem Areas

The problematic nature of inculturation is a known phenomenon. The mycological concept of inculturation can be said to have burst upon the missiological landscape with a tremendous force. It is still gathering momentum and outshines in its premise such rival ideas as adaptation, accommodation, incarnation, contextualization and indigenization. The term promises to resolve all missiological issues. Both groups and individuals from the ecclesiastical conferences, missiologists and the native clergy, everyone is snapping up inculturation as the "open sesame" of the new science of missiology, the conceptual framework in terms of which a comprehensive system of missiological analysis can be constructed (Ndiokwere, 1994).

The non-acceptance of the people's cultures constitutes a hindrance to evangelization and missionization of the people (Dei and Emeagwali, 2014). Hence, the first and best starting point towards inculturation is the comprehensive knowledge of the people's cultures, the system of symbols and meanings through systematic, scientific and sustainable effort at research into the elements of the people's cultures.

The problem is that earliest missionaries had presented the African culture as barbaric, fetish and superstitious. These missionaries saw nothing good in the African culture; they portrayed Africa as "good for nothing". This is why at the time the Africans were deprived of ecclesiastical leadership positions even though they had the same qualifications and abilities with their European counterparts. However, today, inculturation is an on-going process and also in dire need of revival. Expatriate missionaries have taken most of the initiatives at inculturation, but a through work to be done, Africans themselves must be involved in the process of inculturation.

Another problematic area revolves around the misconceptions about inculturation even by the African themselves. This trend has led to a confused situation whereby inculturation has either become an unwelcome development or even dismissed out rightly. This is because, inculturation is seen as a destructive development, which is set out to either destroy or corrupt the Christian religion. To many critics, inculturation is the "mixture of the old and new wine together. They see inculturation as the mixture of African traditions with Christianity. To them, these are susceptible to adulteration and therefore unacceptable.

Other problems identified include language barrier, syncretism, skepticism, un-patriotism and selfishness. Unless all these problems are resolved there can never be a result –oriented inculturation and evangelization of cultures.

What Inculturation Is Not

Those who criticize inculturation do so probably because of their lack of understanding of the subject. They also do so because of their lack of knowledge about their culture. Gcichure (cited in Nnamani, 2006) is probably right, when he opined that:

> Our biggest problem is that we do know which our culture is. Is it what our forefathers and mothers used to do or what we are doing now? Is it what we feel to be good now or advantageous to out situation that we are going to accept as our culture or is there something more constant that need to be respected? Due to lack of enculturation, Africa has become the tomb of all cultures… A culture must be lived so as to have a meaningful inculturation (.350).

What the above statement implies is that enculturation (knowing one's culture) is a stepping stone towards understanding and practicing of inculturation.

Inculturation is neither doctrination nor indoctrination. It is not all about traditions or the adulteration of Christianity with "black arts". Inculturation is not idolatry. Besides, it is neither skepticism nor syncretism. Inculturation is collaboration through culture. Culture itself is not evil. It is dynamic, socialization and progressive. This is why culture itself is an instrument of evangelization.

Significance of Culture

Culture as a life system can only be understood and appreciated when its importance and relevance are known. The importance of culture is found in its functions.

Culture through the various institutions and normative patterns simplifies and guides behavior, provides rules, defines relationships and exerts social controls over members of society. Culture serves as the "stamp" that distinguishes one society or people from another. Hence,

culture is an "indicator". It gives identity to people. People are easily known by their culture. Besides, culture serves an instrument of integration and development. It systematizes, and interprets the values, institutions, and norms of a society or people.

Culture furnishes society with the basis for social unity and solidarity. Cultural unity normally inspires loyalty, patriotism and devotion. Moreover, culture guides and coordinates the activities of society and people. Also, culture is the architect and molder of personality. Above all, culture can create wealth if it is wisely annexed, and thus, improve the peoples' economic standards.

Culture provides rules that govern individuals in adjusting to their environment. In any society, there are norms and values which individuals must observe in order to fit into that social group or society. For instance, respect for the worth of others is an attribute which individual must cultivate in order to fit into a democratic society. Another importance of culture it its role in the differentiation of functions or responsibilities of the individuals in a society. From the foregoing, it will be agreed that the importance of culture cannot be underestimated. When it is carefully analyzed, it would be crystal clear that the functions of religion (or the church) and that of culture are complementary. Both are geared towards the common good of the society or people.

The Importance of Inculturation and Evangelization of Culture

One most important point to be established first is the fact that the personality of a particular people is tied down to this and it gives peculiarity to each culture. The collective conscience of a people is expressed in their culture. By the process of self –defense, each culture conserves its specific identity, security and patrimony of values through the process of inculturation. One thing that will encourage inculturation is the fact that most African culture is religious cultures. African cultural heritage is embedded in that fact.

Inculturation will make people to experience the dynamism of culture and to learn to engage ourselves in a Christian evangelism that would meet with success. Inculturation will be an exercise aimed at creating awareness and the spirit of nationalism among people. In this way, inculturation makes for the emergence of a new identity in every Christ –culture contact, and identity compatible both with the demands of the gospel and with the positive qualities of a people's culture. Inculturation may assume the role of liberation theology whereby the present is emphasized more than the past. Inculturation also addresses socio-cultural as well as socio –political and economic issues.

Inculturation will enhance evangelization. This is because African culture such as hospitality, generosity and brotherhood tally with the gospel message of love for one another and God. The Council Fathers through the Vatican II document were equally vocal in the matters of inculturation. This is why the document declares inculturation as not merely a temporary option but as a lasting imperative (Ndiokwere, 1994). The importance of inculturaton is also acknowledged when the pastoral constitution of the Church in the modern world recognizes the constancy of the inculturation factor throughout the history of the church and sees it as an outgoing process; a kind of adaptation and preaching of the gospel which must ever be the law of all evangelization (Ndiokwere, 1994).

The importance of inculturation in evangelization was recognized and emphasized when in 1982, Pope John Paul II voiced out another encouraging pronouncement on inculturation. According to him, every important aspect of evangelization is the total dimension of the inculturation of the gospel into the lives of the people (Ndiokwere, 1994).

Inculturation makes the gospel message of Christ meaningful to the people.

The Basis of Inculturation

Historically the term, "inculturation" was first used as a missiological concept or term in the 1960s and later authenticated by the Synod of Bishops in 1977 (Ndiokwere, 1994). Afterward, it has gained much ground in the church evangelical missions. But we can assert however, that inculturation as a concept was dated back to the apostolic times in the Bible. For instance, the stage was set for inculturation when the Apostles at the Council of Jerusalem declared the non-imposition of Jewish culture on non-Jewish Christians (Acts 15:1-30). This paradigm suggests a basis for enculturation and inculturation. This simply suggests that the new Christian converts were allowed to live and practice their own culture.

Incarnation in another basis for inculturation, just as the word of God become flesh in us, more also, the inculturation of the Gospel takes on all authentic human values, thus, purifying them from sinfulness and restoring them to their original meaning. From the foregoing, the concept of incarnation is best expressed in the doctrine of inculturation. The historical Jesus Christ authentically set the standard for inculturation. Christ's status as a universal Christ also sets the pace for inculturation. This is the more reason t he inculturation model of Jesus Christ must become the guiding principles for effective and authentic inculturation.

Worth noting is the fact, that, even before the encouragement given by Pope John II in 1982, the address by Pope Paul VI delivered at the Cathedral of Kampala, Uganda on 31st July 1969 formed a basis for the church's involvement in inculturation. His declaration in clear terms set the pace for inculturation. He advocated a full adaptation of the Christian life in Africa in the fields of pastoral, ritual, didactic and in spiritual activities. The Pope made it clear that African must have an "African Christianity". Actually, what we advocate in this research is incarnational and not adaptational inculturation.

Taking into cognizance the richness of African culture, the successful implantation of Christianity in African begs for inculturation. This is why; the church from time truly respects African culture. The church on her own part recognizes the rich cultural values of the African people. This she does through the power of the Gospel and takes into Christian worship, certain elements of a people's culture. In her task, the church is the Gospel conveyer, conveying the Gospel to the people through the people's way of life. The attitude of the church in this regard suggests evidence of enculturation and inculturation.

Towards Inculturation and Evangelization of African Cultures

The absence of authentic inculturation has in the recent past contributed to the poor success recorded by the early Christian church in African in the area of evangelization. It is a fact that the early Christian missionaries were ignorant of African languages and cultures (Ndiokwere, 1994). Theirs was a Gospel presented in foreign terms, and could not have influenced the African without "marrying" the people's culture. Lack of inculturation will continue to constitute a stiff challenge to the growth and existence of Christianity in Africa. Lack of inculturation will continue to undermine the evangelizing mission of the church in contemporary Africa.

Scholars are unanimous in one thing, namely, that the historical contacts with forces from outside Africa have combined to uproot Africans from evolving culture identity. This is dangerous to Christian evangelization. Thus, the reaction to the neglect of African cultures has given African theologians a vice in the wider church. Hence, inculturation has become a potent theological vocabulary that specifies the current orientation of evangelization throughout the world. The present clamour for inculturation and culture evangelization is a bid to authentically develop a truly African Christianity, meaning, an African expression of the Christian faith within its original milieu (Mbefo, 1996).

The Popes, Paul VI and John Paul II in their visit to Africa towed this line when they encouraged the full integration of African cultures into the Christian enterprise. That is to:

> Formulate Catholicism in terms that are completely suited to your culture and to offer the Catholic Church the precious and original contribution of 'negritude' of which it has particular need at his point in history (cited in Mbefo, 1996 p.27).

To this end, African culture on the one hand and the Christian gospel on the other hand "inter-marrying" will result in an authentic African Christianity. For Christianity in Africa to become a faith that is truly accepted, practiced and lived, it must therefore become culture. This is why, John Paul II (1982) envisaged what he called "a symbiosis of faith and cultural values" (p.197).

In fact, the evangelization of culture is truly evident in God revealing himself to the Jews, the chosen people. The implication is that, he used a particular people or culture. Jesus Christ himself did the same, when through his human inculturation has also become a cultural inculturation.

As earlier said, the Christian mission has come to recognize the importance of African cultural values in the evangelization of African. The 1990 Lineamenta on the Synod of Bishops for Africa has recognized that, for effective Christian missionisation, the church must have recourse without undue hesitation to her philosophy, the wisdom of the people, that is, to their customs, their sense of life and their social order (Ndiokwere, 1994). This should be done both for a better comprehension of the gospel message as well as for an evaluation of their cultural values.

The rich African arts, music, dancing, drumming, can exert infections attraction on Christianity. In terms of music and dancing, one of the authors had a practical experience of this when he was a parish priest of St. Anne's Parish, Ososo, Edo State, Nigeria between 1983 and 1993. These and other cultural areas can be explored, and incarnated into the Christian religion. This means that African rich cultural heritage can be explored, purified and incarnated into the various aspects of public worship. This too, is a way towards achieving African Christianity. The church's task in evangelizing must take into consideration the necessity not only to adapt, but also to integrate, indigenize inculturate and make the Gospel message meaningful to the African. It is when this is done that the Africans can understand what Christianity is truly is.

For Christianity to be truly African, true inculturation must take place. For instance, the use of African names and languages in all aspects of liturgical practices must take place. The use of meaningless foreign names, elements and materials must be critically scrutinized. As suggested by some advocates of inculturation, African objects, such as yams, cassava, coco-yams, palm-wine, kola –nuts and other well refined African wines etc., should be used in the Eucharist instead of the usual foreign elements. These are just few examples. Other areas of inculturation which can bring the faith nearer of the Africans are the observance of the sacraments with the associated rituals and rites. These include sacraments of marriage, Reconciliation, Baptism, etc. When John Onimhawo did some research into the impact of Catholicism of Etsako Traditional Marriage, he suggested the retention of the filing of the teeth which was more meaningful to the Etsako people.

In language, the scriptures and other liturgical writings should be written in vernacular or the language of the Africans as has been in some of African major languages. This will make the scriptures to be better understood by the Africans. This is why the Nigerian Bible Society (NBS) must be commended for her role in the indigenization of the Bible Language which identifies a people more than other traits, including customs and traditions. Thus, couching the Gospel message in the original language of the people is an unmistakable ingredient of inculturation. As Ndiokwere (1994) noted that, "language plays the most leading role in the entire effort to bring Christianity much closer to the Africans" (p.41).

African Bishops, priests, pastors and other ministry workers, in fact, all missionaries should be trained to preach the gospel to the people in their local languages. In fact, they should be allowed to serve in their native land. To achieve an authentic inculturation, there should be the need to liberate our minds from alienation. This means, that things about Africa and Africans should not be looked upon as inferior or fetish. It is when all these obstacles are removed that an authentic inculturation which is an instrument of evangelization can take place.

What to Do

In order to achieve effective inculturation, any missionary or evangelizer should put certain things into serious considerations. The missionary should never confuse culture with religion. It is true that culture and religion are inseparable. In fact, while culture covers the whole of a people's scheme of life, religion gives direction and complexion to that scheme. It is such misunderstanding that led the early missionaries to brand certain cultural practices as religious practices. A missionary should shun particularism in approaching peoples of different cultures. A particularistic see nothing good in other people's culture and religion. The missionary should appreciate the Pauline approach to evangelism in his work among the Greeks, the Corinthians and the Galatians. Here we can recall the Athenian encounter when he confronted the Athenians on the inscription "To An Unknown God".

Conclusion

From the foregoing, this paper has pointed out adequately, the reason, importance and need for inculturation and evangelization of the Africa cultures. It is our candid opinion that Christianity must be brought much closer to the people, and that, the instrument for this, is inculturation.

To this end, Christianity must dialogue with this traditional self-understanding if its hopes rooted on the African 'world'. This means, that for the people to be evangelized, their culture and values must be evangelized first. More also, to achieve a truly African Christianity, the African themselves must understand their culture and embrace enculturation in order to achieve an authentic inculturation.

References

Alao, F.O (2005). Misconceptions about African Culture and Civilization. In: Ajayi, S.A (Ed.), *African Culture and Civilization* (pp.12-21). Ibadan: Atlantis Books

Dei, G. S and Emeagwali, G (2014). *African Indigenous Knowledge and the Discipline: Anti-Colonial Educational Perspectives for Transformative Change.* Netherland: Sense Publishers

Echekwube, A.O (1999). *African Philosophy and Cultural Transformation in Nigeria.* Lagos: Spero Books

Gurreth, W (2005). Some Challenges to Evangelization in Africa. *African Eccesial Review*, 2 (3), 311-321

Ikenga-Metuh, I and Ojoade, O (1990). *Nigerian Cultural Heritage.* Onitsha: Imico Publishing Company

Kurgat, S. G (2009). The Theology of Inculturation and the African Church. *International Journal of Sociology and Anthropology,* 1(5), 90-108. Retrieved 15 July, 2017 from: http://www.academicjournals.org/ijsa

Mbefo, I.N (1996). *Christian Theology and African Heritage.* Onitsha: Spiritan Publications

Miles, D (1983). *Introduction to Evangelism.* Nashville: Broadman Press

Ndiokwere, N.I (1994). *The African Church Today and Tomorrow Vol. 1. Prospects and Challenges.* Onitsha: Effective Key Publishers

Ndiokwere, N.I (1994). *The African Church Today and Tomorrow, Vol.II. Inculturation in Practice.* Enugu: Shaap Press

Nnamani, A.G (2006). What is an Inculturating Church? In: Obinwa, I.M.C (Ed.), *Collaborative Ministry in the Context of Inculturation.* (Pp. 350- 351). Onitsha: African First Publisher

Ottuh, P.O.O, *et al* (2016). Inculturating the Christian Eucharist in the Nigerian Context. *Abraka Humanities Review: A Journal of the Faculty of Arts,* 7(1), 167-188

Pope, P. VI (1982). African Terrae. In: Hickey, I (Ed.), *Modern* Missionary *Document and Africa.* (p.197). Dublin: n.p

International Journal of Integrative Humanism Vol 9. No 1. June 2018. ISSN: 2026 – 6286

Historical-Drama and Society, the Factual and the Artistic Ingenious: Appraisal of Femi Osofisan's *Women of Owu*

Joseph Agofure IDOGHO
Dept of Theatre and Media Arts, Federal University, Oye Ekiti, Ekiti State, Nigeria
Email: agofurei@gmail.com, agofure4u@yahoo.co.uk

Abstract

Drama and theatre has been extensively applauded as a tool for mirroring society hence the relationship between drama and society; reflecting the complex struggle of life, which, ever has its roots in the depth of human nature and social environment, and hence is, to that extent universal cannot be discounted. Thus, while drama entertains it also teaches reprimands, admonishes and informs. This powerful attribute of drama has been employed by playwrights over the ages; even sometimes resorting to history to make constructive commentaries on the happenings in society as it or would affect man and his environment. This paper attempts an analysis of Femi Osofisan Women of Owu; **an African retelling of Euripides, that re-enacts the bitter and gory historical experiences of the people of the then Owu Kingdom which happened sometimes around 1821.** *The thematic preoccupation of Femi Osofisan in* Women of Owu *is that; war is unspeakably horrible and that it could easily be averted if human excesses are checkmated. The playwright attempted in the various scenes of this tragedy to depict the suffering that war causes even for those innocents who do not fight in it, innocents such as women, children, and the elderly. The Playwright thus focuses on dissuading warfare, circumventing conflict and admonishing the populace of the aftermath consequences of hostility through dramaturgy.*

Keywords: Historical-Drama, Society, Factual and Artistic Ingenious

Introduction

Femi Osofisan has been adjudged as one of the leading Playwrights among the Nigerian second generation playwrights. Born in 1946 in Erunwon village in Ogun state, Nigeria, Femi Osofisan is a prolific critic, poet, novelist, and playwright, whose work mainly attacks political corruption, injustice and ethical issues. He was educated at the universities of Ibadan, Dakar, and Paris. A professor of Drama since 1985 at the University of Ibadan where he has spent most of his adult career, Osofisan was an erstwhile General Manager and Chief Executive of the National Theatre Lagos. He has won prizes from the Association of Nigerian Authors (ANA) for both drama (1980) and poetry (1989) and in 2004 he was awarded the Nigerian National Order of Merit (NNOM), the highest academic prize in Nigeria.

Femi Osofisan is among the second generation of Nigerian playwrights who has shown fidelity to historical materials in his dramaturgy like his first-generation Nigerian playwrights. Of all his plays to date, quite good numbers of his work are historical plays. They include: *The Chattering...*, *Once upon a Four Rubber*, *Tegonni; an African Antigone*; *Who is Afraid of Solarin* and *Women of Owu;* an African re-reading of Euripides' classic, *The Trojan Women*. This paper thus investigates the consciousness that has engenders the aforementioned artefacts and how they have affected society with particular emphasis on the play *Women of Owu* chosen as a case study for this paper.

Fundamentally, Historical fiction also known as Historical Drama or play is a literary genre in which the plot takes place in a setting located in the past. Historical fiction can be an ambiguous term: frequently it is used as a synonym for describing the historical novel or plays; similarly, the term can be applied to works in other narrative formats, such as those in the performing and visual arts like theatre, opera, cinema, television, comics, and graphic novels.

An essential element of historical fiction is that "it is set in the past and pays attention to the manners, social conditions and other details of the period depicted" (Samuel, 1960:1). Authors also frequently choose to explore notable historical figures in these settings, allowing readers to better understand how these individuals might have responded to their environments. Femi Shaka (2001) attempts an enunciation of the various consciousnesses that informed historical drama thus:

> There are a number of reasons why playwrights have, at one time or the other, restored history in their creative endeavour. Foremost among these, is the desire to use history to comment on contemporary issues of their times. Apart from these overriding factors, there have been instances when playwrights have had to approach historical sources for their creative materials because they felt the need to affirm aspects of their culture and history which have long been the subjects of derogation and misrepresentation. At other times the overriding factor has been the desire to popularize aspects of their history which were not sufficiently known to their people in order to push such aspects into their people's consciousness. Apart from instances already cited, there have equally been times when playwright's movement into history had been dictated by the desire to correct existing versions of history. (195)

Subsequently, dramaturgies like every other work of art-literature; human beings are afforded the opportunity to learn from the past to improve the present so as to better the future. According to
Babatunde Omobowale (2001):

> Two things at least are indispensable to the creation of a veritable work of art. The first is that it is a representation of life whose creation is propelled by a host of other factors; secondly, it is created to serve a pragmatic purpose, which is usually didactic in nature. (3)

One may therefore be right then to say that drama serves as a means through which the links between the past, the present, and the future are highlighted as a way of facilitating a positivist oriented growth of society. According to Chinua Achebe (1988):

> Literature, whether handed down by word of mouth or in print, gives us a second handle on reality. Achebe believes that literature has social and

political importance. It is much more than a creative ornament. It provides a necessary critical perspective on everyday experience educates us on the meaning of our actions and offers us greater control over our social and personal lives. According to Achebe, literature works by enabling us to encounter in the safe, manageable dimensions of make-believe the very same threats to integrity that may assail the psyche in real life; and at the same time providing through the self-discovery which it imparts a veritable weapon for coping with these threats whether they are found within our problematic and incoherent selves or in the world around us. (17)

Implicationally, this definition views literature; which drama is embedded as a multi-faceted field of research whose dynamic nature derives from the fact that drama, as an imitation of life, actually reflects life. In the words of Omobowale (2001); "literary creativity confers on the writer the ability to undertake a jumble exploration of different spheres of human endeavor in order to bring life into existence from multiplicity of angles" (3). Thus, drama as a reflection or refraction of society confers on the creative writer the roles of a chronicler, a social critic, and visionary. Thus, in the present reality, drama is being restored to its pristine position as a central cognitive recourse in society, as well as it's most faithful and comprehensive interpreter. Therefore, making the quadruple functions of drama; entertain, educate, enlighten and inform a reality in modern society.

Statement of the Problem

A cursory look at Nigeria society today reveals silent conflicts looming in every nook and corner; without the agitators or aggrieved considering the aftermath effect of confrontation on societies. Whereas such conflicts and warfare had at one time or the other occurred in our society, but human will not learn from history. Juxtaposing this predicament with the gadfly role of the dramatists in the society; to reprimand, admonish, and teach society: *Women of Owu* undoubtedly preaches against warfare, especially when mutual dialogue and negotiation could yield the same fruit. Perhaps, Modern Drama, as all historical drama, mirrors the complex struggle of life, the struggle which, whatever it's individual or topical expression, ever has its roots in the depth of human nature and social environment, and hence is, to that extent, universal. Such drama is at once the reflex and the inspiration of mankind in its eternal seeking for things higher and better. Accordingly, those who learn the great truths of the social travail in the school of life do not need the message of the drama. But the other individuals who have never tasted it are those, for whom these messages are indispensable. Thus, this article focuses on analyses of Femi Osofisan *Women of Owu* as Conflict circumvention homily for Nigerian populace and at the other hand evaluating the nonfictional merit of the work and artsy-crafty of the playwright.

Women of Owu: The Synopsis

The play comprises five pertained scenes. Like almost all dramas, it has a beginning, middle and an end, though a fragment of flashbacks is used through a recount of some incidents that occurred before others.

It opens with an aftermath of a tragic war that ravages a city-state called Owu with two aggrieved women sent to fetch water by the conquering Allied Forces of Ijebu, Ife and Oyo. The forces claim to have come for a rescue mission of the people of Owu from the bondage in the hands of their king, whom they refer to as a despot, and for the Maye, the leader of the Allied Forces, to re-claim his wife who was taken formerly as a captive along with others by the Owu soldiers after sacking the army of Ife in one of their previous battles. This second "reason" is in fact what causes the war.

The two women meet Anlugbua, a deified god and the former Owu leader. After showing his ignorance to what happened to the village, the two women accuse him, as well as other so-called gods whose responsibility is to safeguard the village, of laxity, carelessness and lack of concern towards their affairs.

Erelu, one of the women, and a royal queen of the former king of Owu, recounts her ordeal in the second scene. She and other distressed women lengthily lament their experiences and sing dirges. Then another deified goddess, Lawumi, who is Anlugbua's mother, comes onstage. She and Erelu, firstly, discuss how the village is ruined; Anlugbua later joins them. The two parties (of gods and humans) point accusing fingers at one another. The gods maintain that Owus err against a "higher" god, Sango (the Yoruba god of thunder), and hence they (the gods – Anglugbua and Lawumi) forewarn them of the war. The peoples' arrogance and defiance become their *hamartia*.

Gesinde, an officer and a herald of the Allied Forces, is sent by the generals to the women to tell them to prepare, as they would be shared among the senior military officers. The daughters of the royal house are the first; Orisaye is particularly chosen by Kusa, a top officer, while one other is murdered. She (Orisaye) tries to resist; further saying that she will smite the prospective husband if taken to him. Many take her as mad, and think that she can do no harm to him more especially since he is revered and regarded as a warrior by all and sundry.

In the midst of this, all eyes turn to Erelu; the women and particularly Adumaadan, her daughter-in-law, blame her for all the destruction of the city and the hardship they are in. Dejumo, the slain prince, her son, is destined, as cautioned by the gods, the oracles, since birth as an ominous baby to bring misfortune to the city if not killed. Dejumo was not killed in infancy, but lived to destroy his village for the sake of his hateful marriage with Iyunloye, the wife of Maye, the leader of Ijebu. It is in trying to take revenge after that the war is waged on Owu, which lasted for seven years, and, which, as a result of, the whole village is torn to shreds and rubbles; the king killed, his people massacred, and their women shared like war spoils and assigned to servitude under the Allied Forces. Even the life of the last heir to the throne of Owu is not spared.

Iyunloye, looked at by all as the secondary cause of the war, is severely accused and condemned. She is called all names. When the Maye expresses his desire to take her back, Erelu cautions him to be wary of her deception, or best, not to take her in his entourage. Before he makes up his mind, a story reached them that their town is being attacked. So they abruptly leave.

The summoning of the god, Anlugbua, by Erelu results to her death, an honourable death to save the future from eternal damnation. It is, again, an act like self-sacrifice as she cannot withstand the predicament. This seems the ultimate resolution reached in the play, which is somewhat uncommon of a tragic drama. The misery of the people does not end by her "honourable" death; the death, simply, uplifts her stature, and shrinks that of the gods.

As in the original play by Euripides, the reader is "lost in a forest of ambiguities" (Sewall, 1959: 83). If the gods are as useless as shown, then what is the essence of them being revered by the people? What is the fate of the women? Is Iyunloye taken by the Maye, left or killed?

Women of Owu, the Owu War: the Facts and Osofisan's Artistic Ingenuity

Drama over the years has been an essential platform for reflecting socio-political, cultural and economic struggles among other things. This creative art called drama is a source of dialogue, debate, exchange and innovation. A form of creativity which enhances transfer of culture and knowledge those are useful for coping with societal tasks. In other words, it paints life with a view to share human experiences, feelings, imaginations, observations, findings, predictions and suggestions for prevailing social realities. However, as open and flexible drama is, practitioners; writers and critics alike are advised to desist from arbitrariness. We conceive drama as something more than art for art sake not because such stance is wrong but because drama has other potent roles to play in human society.

The Yoruba Nation Prior to Nigeria Independence: Prior to Nigeria Independence in 1960, the Yoruba nation constitutes kingdoms and each tribal unit constituted itself an independent state: "the Ife's in the east and the Ijebu's in the south formed an alliance against the Owus to the south-west of the former and northwest of the latter" (Samuel, 1960: 206). The Owus (although now domiciled with the Egbas) are a family quite distinct from the Egbas or Oyos. "However, history had it that hardihood, stubbornness, immorality, and haughtiness are marked traits in their character, so much so that it has passed into a proverb "A bi omo I'owu, o ni ako tabi abo ni, ewo ni ko se omo nibe ?" "A child is born at Owu, and you ask male or female: which will be a proper child?"" (Samuel, 1960: 206). Either sex when roused by passion would sooner die than not take dire revenge. Their manners were totally different from those of the Oyos, but from the days of Sango they have been very loyal to the Alafin of Oyo (Samuel, 1960: 206).

History also had it that as warriors, the Owus were hardy, brave and courageous; they had no guns, their weapons consisting of the Agedengbe (a long heavy cutlass) with bows and arrows. Coming to close quarters with cutlass in hand was the mode of fighting characteristic of these brave people (Oladipo, 2014: 3).

The cause of the Owu war: According to Samuel Johnson (1960); during the reign of King Abiodun, express orders were sent from Oyo to the Ooni of Ife, and the Olowu to prevent Oyos being kidnapped and sold at Apomu, the great market town where the interior and the coast people met for trade. Now, since the commencement of the revolution, and the disorganized state of the kingdom, the practice was revived (206). The rebellion has rendered the Central Authority powerless, but there were still some men of considerable power and influence in the land. "A message similar to that sent by King Abiodun was now sent by the Onikoyi and the Kakanfo conjointly to the Olowu, and he in carrying out his orders had to chastise several towns; hence Ikoyi Igbo, Apomu, Ikire, Irkn, He Olupami, Itahakun, Iseyin Odo, Iwata, Akinboto, Gbongan, Isope, Iwara, and Jagun, were destroyed by war, all in Ife territory" (Samuel, 1960: 208).

According to Samuel Johnson version of the history: The Ooni of Ife was highly incensed at this and declared war against Owu. The Ifes thought they would make an easy conquest of Owu for they themselves are a brave people. "The Owus on the other hand received the news that war was declared against them with great indignation. They considered themselves the power in these southern regions, and what infatuation has led the Ifes to this presumption?" (Samuel, 1960: 209). Unanimously, they immediately marched out to meet them at this great distance. The engagement was a hand to hand fight in which the Ifes were completely routed; "their army was all but totally annihilated, only about 200 escaped to tell the tale of their dire misfortune!" (Samuel, 1960: 209).

The King of Iwo, in whose territory this disaster took place did not admit the survivors into his town for fear of incurring the displeasure of his formidable neighbours the Owus, whom he dreaded and of whom he was jealous, but he so far sympathized with them that he advised that they should not undergo the humiliation of returning home, and he allowed them to rendezvous in a place called Adunbieiye: "for the purpose of recruiting their army and to try another chance, secretly hoping that fortune may favour them next time, and being ill at ease with such a formidable neighbour as the Owus" (Samuel 211). This small army remained in this place for about five years, unable to return home from shame, and yet could not obtain re-enforcement adequate for the great enterprise. Just as this crisis was on:

The Owus and the Ijebu traders had a serious complication at the Apomu market. The dispute arose from the sale of alligator pepper, and it resulted in the rash expedition against Apomu by the haughty Owus; the town was destroyed, and many Ijebu traders and residents lost their lives or their stall" (Oladipo, 2014: 3).

The king of Iwo thereupon advised the Ifes to form an alliance with the Ijebus, who, like them, have now a grievance against Owu. When this was done, the men at home were now willing to re-enforce their wrecked army for a conjoint attack upon Owu. The Ijebus now declared war against Owu, and crossing the Osun River, encamped at the farm of one Oso (Oladipo, 2014: 3).

The Ijebus were better armed than either their allies or their foes, and indeed, than any of the interior tribes, for, being nearest to the coast, they had the advantage of obtaining guns and gun- powder from Europeans in exchange for slaves (Samuel, 1960: 211). "They were remarkable marksmen. The older men with their cloths tied round their waists, and the ends left flowing behind, constituted the regular fighting column: being too old or too heavy to run away, they were obliged to be courageous" (Samuel, 1960: 211).

The Owus were mad with rage at the receipt of the news that anyone, such as the Ijebus, had presumed to declare war against them who (as they considered themselves) were the first power in these parts (southern Yoruba) (Samuel, 1960: 211). They rushed out to check the progress of the Ijebus as they did that of the Ifes, and attacked them furiously cutlass in hand. But they were compelled to fall back from the steady fire of the Ijebus which did great havoc amongst them (Samuel, 1960: 211). Summoning courage, the Owus offered another obstinate battle, but they were again repulsed with a heavy slaughter, having lost in the first and second engagements about forty of their leaders. This was the first check to their pride (Samuel, 1960: 211).

They rallied, however, and retreated to a short distance, and then again ventured upon another attack, the Ijebus advancing as they were retreating: they finally met, and once more fortune was against the Owus, and they fled precipitately to fortify their city against the expected siege (Samuel, 1960: 211).

Woman: Yesterday, old man!
  For seven years we had held them off.

These invaders from Ijebu and Ife, together
With mercenaries from Oyo fleeing south from the

Fulani forces....
So for seven years they camped
Outside our walls, but were unable to enter...
(Osofisan, 2006: 2)

Woman: Seven years without rain they were, seven years
  Of failed harvest. All those terrible years
  Where were you Anlugbua?...

Woman: After three years, the city
  Began to starve of food and fruit,
  And the streets stank of disease and death, ...
(Osofisan, 2006: 2)

Perhaps the Owu War which Femi Osofisan used as a raw material in his dramaturgy actually existed; and the playwright has remained faithful in his treatment of this historical material, even up to the accuracy of dates. According to history; the Owu War actually happened around "1821 or there about and was said to have lasted for seven years..." The cause of the war on the other hand was also accurately captured by Osofisan:

Anlugbua: It had to be you, mother! That such
  A disaster would happen here, and I not know
  About it. But why did you do it.

Lawumi: They had to be punished.

Anlugbua: For what offence? What could they have done
  So unforgivable as to this merit?

Lawumi: Arrogance that was their sin! An insufferable display
  Of arrogance towards me, towards Ile-Ife, where
  We all come from! Yes, it's true
  That your father founded Owu, but it was only
  With the help and blessings of Ife
  It was because of a ----- married a princess
  Of Ife –me!-that my father agreed to give him a crown
  And make Owu one of the seven kingdoms
  Of Yorubaland. Is that a lie?

Anlugbua: No, but-

Lawumi: Owu forgot its history, forgot its origins!

Your people became drunk with prosperity!

And in their giddiness, they dared to send their army

Against Ife! Imagine it!

The razed the town down and reduced it to dust!

Anlugbua: But are you forgetting, mother? It was

The Ifes who first attacked Owu, at

The market of Apomu-

Lawumi: Because the Owus were selling

Other Yoruba into slavery! It was a law, wasn't it,

Laid down by our royal uncle and my son Sango

That no Yoruba should ever sell other Yoruba

Into slavery! But the Owus would not listen!

Flagrantly at Apomu, they broke the law, and

The only way to stop them was by force!

Anlugbua: This amount of force, mother? After all

Ife could have tried other means of persuasion. Besides,

Common sense advises that you don't send out your soldiers

Against an army far superior to yours!

Lawumi: Good, let the Owus eat that superiority now!

They sacked the Ife army, and took back

The Apomu market. But that was their undoing,

Because I led them on. I made them attack

Ijebu traders at the market too.

Yes, I made sure of that! Recklessly

They looted the stalls of the Ijebu, killed many

And sold the others into slavery! And of course

As I expected, the Ijebu rose in response

And send their dreaded army up against the city.

That was the beginning of the story

Whose consequences you see now before you!

(Osofisan, 2006:18-20)

The Ijebus with their allies the Ifes encamped to the west of the city of Owu, under a large tree called the Ogilngun, east of the town of Oje. We may here remark that although the Egba towns of Ofa and Oje were about a mile and two miles respectively from Owu, yet so bitter was the animosity between them that not only did these towns refuse their aid to Owu, but rather rejoiced at its misfortunes! (Samuel 1960: 210).

The Owus fought with their accustomed bravery and in one furious assault, routed the allies, and pursued them to Oje, Ofa, and Ibadan. "The first two places were deserted in the general confusion and panic, and all sought refuge at Ibadan. Here the allies received reinforcements from the Egbas, and from the Oyo refugees from the north whose homes had been devastated by the Fulanis and who were now scattered about the provinces homeless, and without occupation" (Samuel, 1960: 211). Glad to find some occupation in arms, these refugees flocked to the standard of the allies in numbers; and thus strengthened, the war was renewed. The siege lasted about five years (usually reckoned as seven years). The city was obstinately defended by the brave inhabitants from the walls, and from the forts built on the walls of the city.

Erelu: Oh you Ijebu beasts!

And the animals from Ife who are your allies!

You Oyo mercenaries who have been made homeless by

The Fulani, and so must make others homeless too!

All of you men over there preparing to return home

After destroying our city! My curse upon you!

May you never again know the soil of your motherlands! (Osofisan, 2006:12)

For all the famine within, the besiegers could neither scale the walls, nor force the gates open, until Akinjobi the Olowu opened a gate, and escaped to Erunmu, one of the principal towns in his territory. The chief of this place was one Oluroko who was nearly related to the Owoni of Ife. Oluroko protected his over- lord (Samuel, 1960: 211). The allies pursued the Olowu to this place, but Oluroko when called upon to answer for his conduct, submitted himself, and asked for pardon, showing that he could not have acted otherwise and be blameless. The allies reasoned with him, and pardon was accordingly granted him (Samuel, 1960: 211).

Woman: Not one was spared! Not a single male left now

In Owu, except those who escaped the night before

With our king. Oba Akinjobi. (Osofisan 3)

Gesinde: It was the Balogun, *Ayaba*. He warned his colleague

  Very strongly that their future would not be safe after this

  If they went away from here, and left a single heir

  To the throne alive. So it's no use resisting.

  Give him to me. ...

Adumaadan: And kill him?

Gesinde: Perhaps I should let you know-in case some of you

  Are nurturing some stupid hopes in that direction-your king-

  Your husband, Erelu-we caught him in the night, and

  He has already paid the price of his folly. You

  Must have heard someone screaming for a long time, begging

  For death. That was him, in the hands of the Generals.

  But luckily, it's over now for the poor man. ...

(Osofisan, 2006: 43-44)

According to Samuel Johnson (1960);

  Owu was thenceforth placed under an interdict, never to be rebuilt; and it was resolved that in future, however great might be the population of Oje the nearest town to it, the town walls should not extend as far as the Ogungun tree, where the camp was pitched: consequently, to this day although the land may be cultivated yet no one is allowed to build a house on it. (209)

Worthy of note in this section is that Osofisan is faithful to history and as well craftily drives home his messages dramatically via the same historical material. "The Owu war marked a definite period in Yoruba history. It was here for the first-time gunpowder was used in war in this country, and it was followed by the devastation of the Egba townships and the foundation of modern Abeokuta and Ibadan, to be related in due course" (Samuel, 1960: 210).

Woman: How we needed you all the time!

  It was a war, such as we had never known before:

  The Allied Forces came with weapons they call guns

  Guns, Anlugbua! Deadly sticks

  Which explode, and turn a whole battalion

Into corpses. Rags upon rags of bleeding flesh!

Woman: Among us

  Not one man had ever seen a weapon like that!

  But the Ijebu troops brought them in abundance!

  They got them, we learnt,

  From their trade with the white men on the coast!

Woman: Against these terrifying guns, Anlugbua,

  Your people had only their blades and incantations

  Where were you?

(Osofisan, 2006: 8)

However, Femi Osofisan invents a second cause of the Owu War (woman) to highlight the human foible which he intends to emphasize and drive home his message. Basically, three things are identified as to cause the downfall of man: Woman, Money and Power. In this case Femi Osofisan chooses Woman and Power-might which resulted to pride on the part of the Owus as dominant metaphors:

Woman: The very one! But when his favourite wife,

  Iyunloye, was captured and brought here, and given as

  Wife to one of our princes, Okunade became bitter, and

  Swore to get her back. Shamed and disgraced,

  He abandoned his tools and took to arms. And so fierce

  Was his passion for killing, that he rose rapidly?

  Through the ranks, and soon became the Maye!

  An Artist? He's a butcher now!

(Osofisan, 2006: 6)

This second invention is what we may refer to as artistic creation towards the realization of historical facts. In Samuel Johnson's version of the history of the Owu war, there is no mention of Iyunloye been forcefully taken from Okunaye. But Osofisan invents this in the play buttress his points of the attitudes of the Owu people and humanity in general. This also goes a long way to describe the relationship that exist between male and female in the society and that if not carefully handled could cause the down fall of a man and even of an entire nation.

Again, it takes a measure of ingenuity to transmute a fifth century long Greek play into the 19th century Pre-Nigeria socio-political atmosphere, at the dawn of imperialism. Osofisan has a peculiar conception of form, stylistic innovations and manner of organizing his plays that intrigues the reader. In his words, "I am always experimenting with form. I am discovering forms, some of which are already in use…. I pay great attention to form, to manner… these have been my guiding principles in all my works" (Awodiya, 1995:201).

In his treatment of *Women of Owu*, the playwright brings to bear on the form of *Women of Owu*, his principle of reconstructing history and mythology, using to the fullest the African dramatic mode of Song and Dance, not by any less costuming. At all events, the structure of Osofisan's plays manifests his artistic goals and the desired effect on the audience. And in this particular instance, (that of the *Women of Owu*) his goal is a adaptation /re-invention of history and myth of the Greek The Trojan Women by Euripides; in order to re-examine the issue of human pride and its effects; human foibles; and in particular, the pains of war in human society; at the end of which he expects an improved conscious renewal of the individual and the society as a whole.

Thus, *Women of Owu* has not failed in eliciting that profound catharsis. Osofisan uses a historical fact through retelling a Greek history to present ideas on war-mongering, and expose human predicament caused by another fellow human. It further clearly deals with topics such as the difference between a just and an unjustified war, the treatment of war victims, the principle of revenge, the fate of the defeated and, finally, the concept of sacrifice.

Notably the play *Women of Owu*, is a faithful adaptation of Euripides's *Trojan Women* by the Nigerian playwright Femi Osofisan. Though the play is set outside the burning city, not of Troy, but of Owu in Yorubaland, part of what is now Nigeria. It tells about the sufferings imposed by war: indeed, Owu is in ruins, and its former inhabitants are constantly threatened by rape, displacement, slavery, degradation, and death. Its main mode is empathy and pity for the victims of war, especially the women and all the issues raised in the play are all related to the blend of 5th century Greek, 19th century Yoruba, and contemporary European/American and, indeed, African elements: its presentation of an aggressive war and its consequences; its emphasis on communality rather than individuality; its treatment of gender; and its form and tone.

Conclusion

From the foregoing, it is apparent that Osofisan's ingenious dramaturgy has not just Africanized / reinvents the 5th century Greek history. In reconstructing the history of the Owu war, he serves as a pacifist and an antiviolence crusader who had seen wars: …, as I pondered over this adaptation of Euripides play, in the season of the Iraq War… (Osofisan, 2006: vii) and also forecast the possibilities of conflicts in the 21st century Nigerian /African environment and thus forewarns through drama. What with his rather ingenious use of dramatic devices; especially those of the African traditional theatre and the Brechtian epic theatre, both of which share a lot of things in common, to help the audience see the play in its proper perspective.

Perhaps, African drama is essentially representational. It is a body of work through which one can understand the twists and turns in African development. It is always eager to present the vivid picture of the African condition in a socio-political terrain. Furthermore, apart from revealing the lines and contradictions in the present African societies, the modem African drama is a potent means of recording African experiences in its numerous dimensions. Therefore, it has always been a realistic medium of expression of the different developmental stages of the African social consciousness. Thus, this article attempts to decode Femi Osofisan's *Women of Owu* with a view to make bare the representations of a society in an art work. In other words, we demonstrate the relationships between drama and Society, using fiction and nonfiction as our theoretical back-up. The paper concludes that drama is a functional weapon for social criticism which will bring about sustainable developments in various human societies.

Anlugbua: Poor human beings! War is what will destroy you!

As it destroys the gods. But I am moved, and I promised:

Owu will rise again! Not here,
Not as a single city again-Mother will not permit that,

I know-but in little communities elsewhere,
Within other cities of Yorubaland. Those now going

Into slavery shall start new kingdoms in those places,

It's the only atonement a god can make for you
Against your ceaseless volition for self-destruction.

You human beings, always thirsty for blood,
Always eager to devour one another! I hope
History will teach you. I hope you will learn. Farewell.

(*The Women's dirge begins to rise now*.) End of Play (Osofisan, 2006: 67)

The play is, more than obvious, about war; and the character ascribed to gods in it states that the making and ending of war is like any other decision, solely man's responsibility. Divine powers indeed exist, as part of the mystery of the universe; but the only one of them that man claim to know is his chance, which, unfortunately, is unreliable, elusive. The final conclusion reached is: trust no god, blame no god; look only at yourself and watch your actions.

Reference

Achebe, C. (1988). "What Has Literature Got to do with it" *Hopes and Impediment: Selected Essays.* Oxford: Heinemann Educational.

Awodiya, M. P. (1995)*The Drama of Femi Osofisan: A critical Perspective*. Ibadan: Kraft Books.

Johnson, L. Sarah. (2005). *Historical Fiction: A Guide to the Genre*. Westport, CT: Libraries Unlimited.

Oladipo, Y. (2014). "*Owu People*," Available: https://owulakoda.wordpress.com/owu-people/, Accessed, 15/12/2015.

Omobowale E. B. (2001). "Literature and Medicine: A Study of Selected Creative Works of Nigerian Physicians" Unpublished PhD Dissertation, Department of English, University of Ibadan.

Osofisan, F. (2006). *Women of Owu*. Ibadan: University Press PLC.

Samuel. J. (1960). *The History of the Yorubas: From the Earliest Times to the Beginning of the British Protectorate.* Lagos: CMS Books. Available: https://archive.org/details/historyofyorubas00john. 12/12/2015.

Sewall, R. B. (1959). *The Vision of Tragedy*. New Haven and London: Yale University Press.

Shaka, F. (2001). "History and The Historical Play: A Radical Study of Ola Rotimi's *Kurunmi, Ovoramwen Nogbaisi*, and *Hopes of the Living Dead*" (ed) Asagba, O. Austin. *Cross Current in African Theatre*. Benin City: Osasu Publishers, 1(95-215).

An Assessment of Communication Channels for The Prevention of Mother-To-Child Transmission of HIV In Rural Communities of Abuja

Dennis A. Mordi

International Centre of Excellence on Development Communication, Department of Theatre and Performing Arts, Ahmadu Bello University, Zaria, Nigeria.

Email- damordi@yahoo.com

Abstract

Mother-to-Child Transmission of HIV (MTCT) has remained a public health concern in Nigeria because local channels of communication that many rural communities relate to and associate with are scarcely deployed to build consensus and capacities of the people to tackle MTCT. As a result, community awareness about the benefits of Prevention of Mother-to-Child Transmission of HIV (PMTCT) intervention and uptake of the services remain poor. This study reports on the communication platforms and tools to bolster the prevention of new HIV infection among women and children in rural communities of IddoPada, Ushafa and Old Kutunku in the Federal Capital Territory of Abuja. Significantly, two of these communities are located within the two local government areas slated alongside 32 others (out of the 774 local government areas in Nigeria) for HIV epidemic control by US President Emergency Plan for AIDS Relief (PEPFAR). This paper focuses on the communication platforms for PMTCT awareness and their effectiveness in the aforementioned communities; and the barriers preventing women from accessing PMTCT services. Quantitative and qualitative methods of study were deployed to identify the communication platforms deployed by development agencies such as the Institute of Human Virology Nigeria (IHVN) to create awareness about prevention of mother-to-child transmission of HIV and find out the barriers militating against the communities' acceptance of IHVN's campaign on PMTCT. Consequently, this study found that the village heads using endogenous communication strategies such as word of mouth through town criers and their youths and children in school rather than the dominant technology-driven exogenouscommunication channels, are better positioned to share useful information about PMTCT to community members. Village heads in these communities have become pivotal resource persons as well as gatekeepers that development agenciesshould involve in designing and implementing PMTCT strategies for the prevention new HIV infection amongst children.

Keywords: *prevention of mother-to-child transmission of HIV, village heads, town criers, communication platforms.*

Introduction

One of the public health concerns in Nigeria is Mother-to-child transmission of HIV (MTCT), which has made the country home to more HIV infected children than any other country in the world. This is because local channels of communication that many rural communities relate to and associate with are scarcely deployed to build consensus and capacities of the people to tackle MTCT. As a result, community awareness about the benefits and components of prevention of mother-to-child transmission of HIV (PMTCT) intervention and uptake of the services remain poor in rural areas where most women and children live.

This paper aims at recognizing the communication platforms and tools to bridge this gap and bolster the prevention of new HIV infection among women and children in rural communities of IddoPada, Ushafa and Old Kutunku in the Federal Capital Territory of Abuja (FCT).FCT has an HIV prevalence rate of 7.5%, the fifth highest in the country after the states of Rivers, 15.2%; Taraba, 10.5%; Kaduna, 9.2%; and Nasarawa, 8.1% (PCRP, 2013 -2015). Two of the area councils: Bwari and Abuja Municipal are amongst the 32 out of the 774 local government areas in Nigeria with high HIV burden slated for HIV epidemic control by US President Emergency Plan for AIDS Relief (PEPFAR) under Joint United Nations Programme on HIV and AIDS (UNAIDS)'s 90-90-90 HIV strategy – an ambitious treatment target to help end HIV by 2030.

The progress report on the global plan towards the elimination of new HIV infection among children and keeping their mothers alive also reports that 60,000 Nigerian children were infected with HIV in 2012 (UNAIDS, 2013). Again, according to the National AIDS and STI's Control Programme (2016, p.65), "an estimated 380,000 children were living with HIV by the end of 2014 – making Nigeria home of over 30% of the global burden of HIV infected children." This situation has not changed.

Therefore, the need for channels of communication to preventMTCT in rural communities of Abuja has become a serious public health issue in recent times. This is because the ones in use in the urban centres are similar to the ones in use in rural areas without adequate consideration of the great differences between these two climes. While the urban towns can rely on conventional media such as radio, television, print media and billboard, the rural communities cannot benefit immensely from such channels because of the disparity in thelevels of education, culture, income and population. That perhaps has been the reason why there is much to be desired in the uptake of the prevention of mother-to-child transmission of HIV services in the rural communities, where local communication platforms and channels are scarcely used.

Although the number of people who die as a result of complications caused by HIV has dropped since the emergence of antiretroviral treatments in 1990s(ScienceDaily, 2018),this has not completely curbed the transmission of the virus from HIV-infected mothers to their children in Nigeria. Women infected with HIV need to know about their status through testing and counseling and those who have tested positive to the virus need to access HIV medications so that the virus will not be transmitted to their children. It is in the hands of the development agencies and government to commune with communities about this and the benefits of PMTCT services and where the services are available. Without this engagement withcommunity members in creating and disseminating information necessary for behaviour change that will eliminate HIV amongst women and children, no intervention can be successfully achieved. At the moment not many community members in rural areas of Abuja, Nigeria are involved in PMTCT programmes.

Part of the issues that can be attributed to this is thelow male involvement in PMTCT and stigmatization of People Living with HIV(PLHIV), which are affecting the uptake of PMTCT services. Also contributory to this is lack of awareness informationabout the components and benefits of PMTCT services, especially in the rural areas where resources are lean. These problems have been linked to communication platforms and channels deployed by development agencies and government, which informs the assertion ofAdedokun et.al (2010) that to position rural people to have necessary information for decision making and the relevant skills to improve their lives, communication must happen and be engaging and interactive between community members and information providers.

It is against this backdrop that this paper examined the communication channels or platforms that are effective in reaching out to rural women of child-bearing age and HIV positive pregnant women. This research attempts to identify the dominant communication platforms and channels that development agencies deploy to create awareness about PMTCT inUshafa, Old Kutunku and IddoPada in theFederal Capital Territory, Abuja.The effectiveness of these platformsvis-à-vis thebarriers militating against the communities' acceptance of the campaigns on PMTCT, and their implications was looked at to find out the measures that development agencies can adopt to achieve better result in their campaigns to prevent mother-to-child transmission of HIV.

Theoretical Framework

This paper takes on the Social Learning Theory as the theoretical framework to understand the mix between learning about PMTCT and participation in the uptake of PMTCT services so that women of child-bearing age can learn about PMTCT from mentor-mothers living with HIV and participate in the acceptance of services. This will guide programme interventions. Social Learning Theory is a psychological model of behaviour that posits that people learn new behaviour by watching the actions of others including the consequences of those actions. The exponent of this theory is Albert Bandura, who postulated that most human behaviour is learned in a social context and through observation, imitation and modeling. The theory is relevant to this study because the essence of strategic communication in health care delivery is to educate people to learn and subscribe to behaviour change necessary for the prevention of mother-to-child transmission of HIV. Since the process of learning is education and education has been referred to as a social vaccine against HIV/AIDS (Patrick, 2010), it helps to know what behaviours to avoid and what attitude to adopt to prevent new HIV infection amongst women and children.

Methodology

To achieve the above, the study was carried out in Ushafa village in Bwari Area Council; Old Kutunku village in Gwagwalada Area Council; and IddoPada village in Abuja Municipal Area Council, which are in FCT. Apart from the high HIV burden in the area councils, which necessitated the listing of two of the area councils for HIV epidemic control, the villages were also chosen because of their location within the three local councils of FCT dubbed as top sex spots by NACA, (Standard Telegraph, 2015).

To examine the communication channels that are effective in reaching out to rural women of child-bearing age and HIV positive pregnant women, qualitative and quantitative approaches to gather and analyze information were carried out in the villages, in addition to a few key informant interviews. To this end, 2377 copies of the questionnaire were administered in Ushafa, Old Kutunku and Iddo Pada in the Federal Capital Territory of Abuja – 792 copies in each of the communities. Two focus group discussions were also held in each of the villages to gather information about the local communication platforms and tools for PMTCT. However, the presentation of data shows 2278 questionnaire were returned.

The quantitative data analysis for this study was done with a free software tool called Epi Info 7.2.2.1 developed by the United State of American's Centers for Disease Control and Prevention (CDC) for public health practitioners and researchers. The frequencies and distribution of participants' baseline characteristics and other responses were computed and presented in tables. Other data gathering methods used include Focus Group Discussion (FGD) and Key Informant Interviews (KII) with select community leaders. The experiences of conducting the FGD and the survey are related because of the common characteristics of these communities. The three communities are located within the Federal Capital Territory, Abuja; they are inhabited by people of the same tribe who are mainly farmers, petty traders and potters. The data gathered for presentation are in the narratives, percentages, graphs and tables as shown subsequently:

Findings

The socio demographic characteristics of respondents in Ushafa, Old Kutunku and IddoPada villages, where this research was carried out are common. For example, the communities are located in the Federal Capital Territory, Abuja; and people of the areas understand each other, whether they speak Gbagyi or Gbari languages. The members of the communities are mainly farmers, petty traders and potters. The ages of the women of child-bearing age under this study were between 15 and 49 years old. Majority of them were 52.6% married and 27.9% single with 29.4% of them into petty trading and 27.9% into farming. The percentage of missing data was very negligible (<0.5%) as shown in Table 1, which is the true reflection of data obtained:

Table 1: Socio demographic characteristics of respondents (N = 2278)

Characteristics	n	%
Age (years)		
15 - 24 years	503	22.1
25 - 35 years	579	25.4
36 - 45 years	550	24.1
46 - 49 years	577	25.3
No response	65	2.9
Missing	4	0.2
Marital status		
Single	635	27.9
Married	1198	52.6
Divorced	118	5.2
Widowed	197	8.6
No response	125	5.5
Missing	5	0.2
Occupation		
Nothing	273	12.0
Petty trading	670	29.4
Farming	636	27.9
Pottery making	124	5.4
Civil servant	236	10.4
Others	221	9.7
No response	110	4.8
Missing	8	0.4

Source: Researcher's Field Survey, 2018

Existing knowledge-base of community members about MTCT of HIV

In the FGD conducted, the respondents show that they are aware of HIV/AIDS and how the virus can be prevented and the availability of medications for HIV. They have also heard about prevention of mother-to-child transmission and that HIV positive women can give birth to HIV negative babies if they go for early ANC at the Primary Health Care (PHC) nearest to them. However, the respondents have inadequate knowledge of the mode of paediatrictransmission of HIV. This can be adduced from these comments:

> Those who get infected, when a woman gives birth, when she does not take her medicine the child must get infected, but when she takes her medicine, when she gives birth she should not breastfeed, when she breastfeeds the child must get infected.

– YakubuGami, during FGD inUshafa Village, Bwari, Nigeria

> I got this information from school, my teacher during adult education classes mention that after delivery a woman living with HIV should not breastfeed the child because the baby is at risk of contracting the virus through breast milk, but if she does not breastfeed the baby, the baby will not be infected. This is because the breast

milk is from the mother's body which is connected to her blood and that also goes straight to the baby's body.

– Stephen Bawa, during FGD in Old Kutunku, Gwagwalada – Nigeria.

Figure 2 below shows the levels of this understanding and knowledge of HIV and PMTCT. The average score of the respondents' knowledge of HIV was 60.2%:

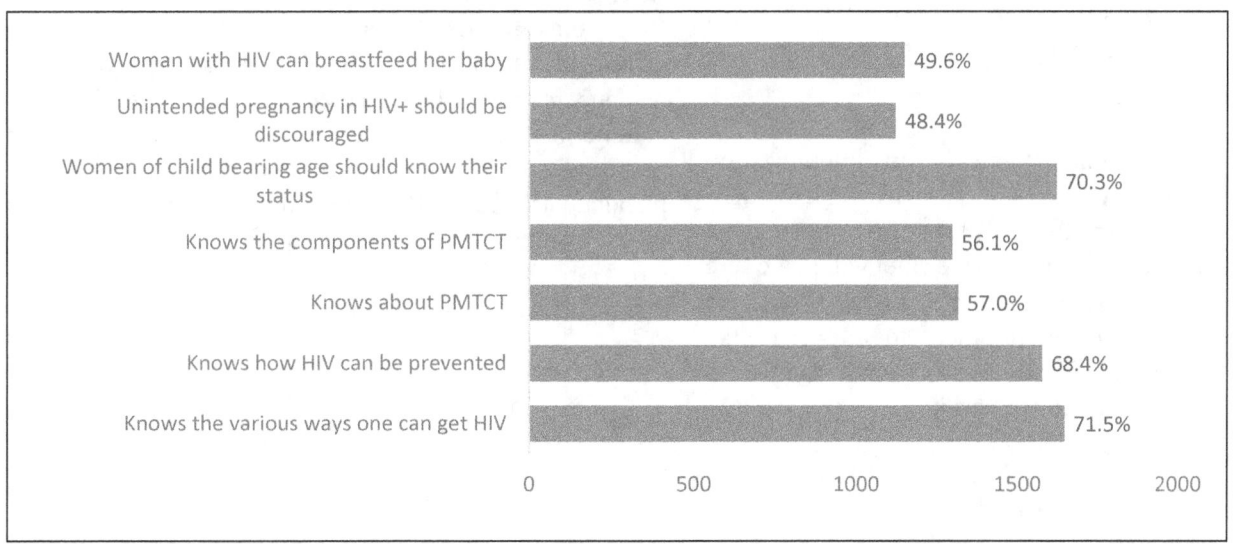

Figure 2: Knowledge of HIV and PMTCT (N = 2278), *Source: Researcher's Field Survey (2018)*

Crier, everyone must surely listen to hear the message (Bussa, 2018). Figure 5 below illustrates this:

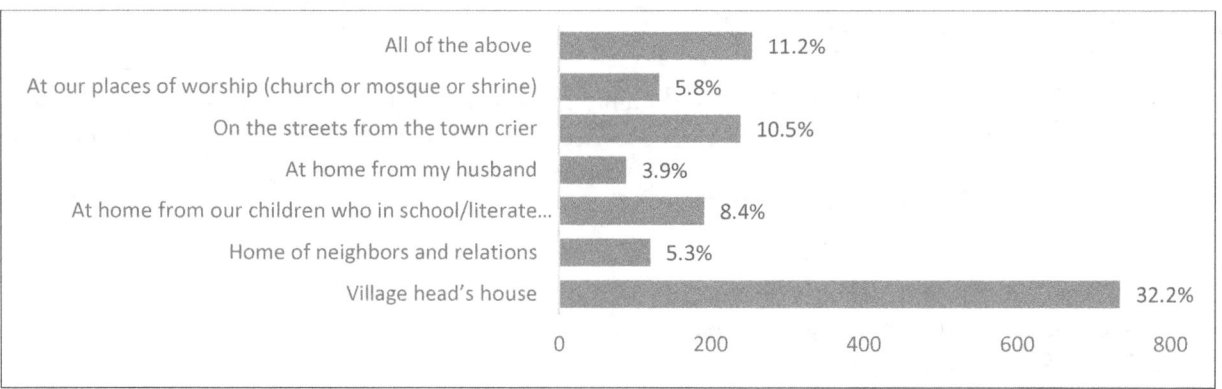

Figure 5: Where respondents receive health information apart from health facilities (N = 2278), *Source: Researcher's Field Survey, 2018*

The communication platforms for HIV awareness and effectiveness as seen above can also be alluded to from these comments during the FGDs conducted:

> Drums are usually beaten from an area to another and when people inquire for the reason behind the beating of the drum, the message can be passed to them that the chief wants to see the community people in relation to a health issue.

> – *HajaraGarba, during FGD in Old Kutunku, Gwagwalada – Nigeria.*

> Like when there is an immunization exercise to be carried out, their representative will come from the hospital to tell the chief and the chief will make sure the information is passed across to everyone telling them to all go to the hospital for drugs and what age grade should go to the hospital.

> – *Moses Pada, during FGD in IddoPada, Abuja – Nigeria.*

The researcher found that major development agency providing HIV intervention in the Federal Capital Territory, IHVN, uses different channels to communicate with the people of the villages about HIV/PMTCT services that it provides. According to Ukpabi (2018), the Institute's prevention, treatment and support messages are disseminated through radio jingles and announcements, sharing of pamphlets, posters, doctors and nurses at the PHC and through other interpersonal communication efforts as represented in the following graph, where the respondents reported that the 36.5% of Institute's communication to them come through the doctors and nurses at the PHCs in these villages. But 4.0% of the respondents said the Institute communicates to them using all the channels listed in Figure 6:

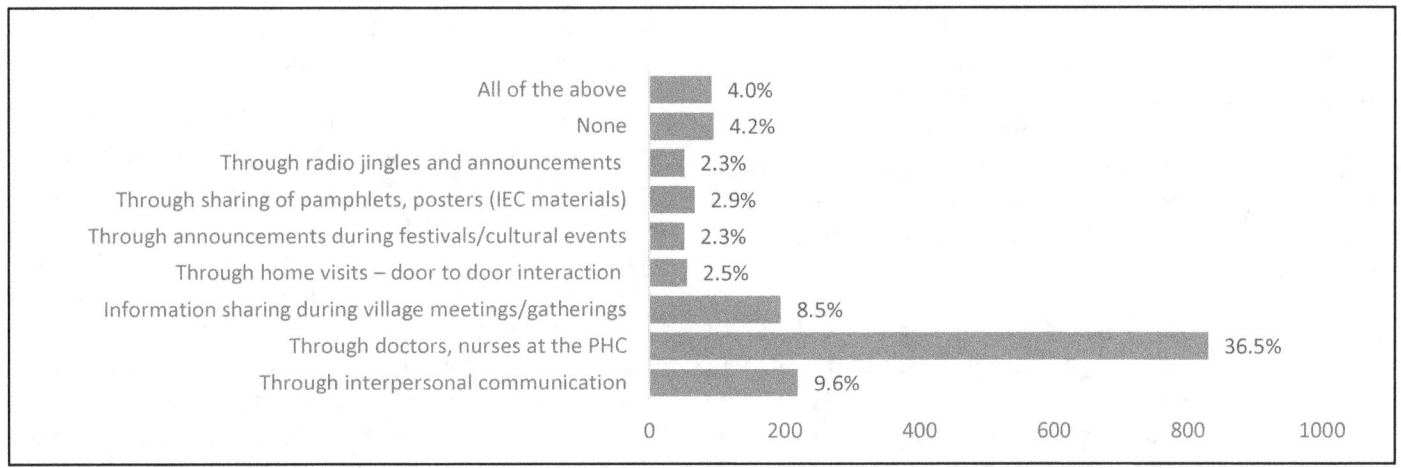

Figure 6: How IHVN communicates with respondents in their villages (N = 2278), *Source: Researcher's Field Survey (2018)*

The respondents said that the inevitability of meeting the village heads and community leaders first on PMTCT is 63.2% when compared to meeting the husbands, which is put at 6.5%. Figure 8 below further illustrates the distribution of the people to meet first if PMTCT information is to be disseminated to the communities:

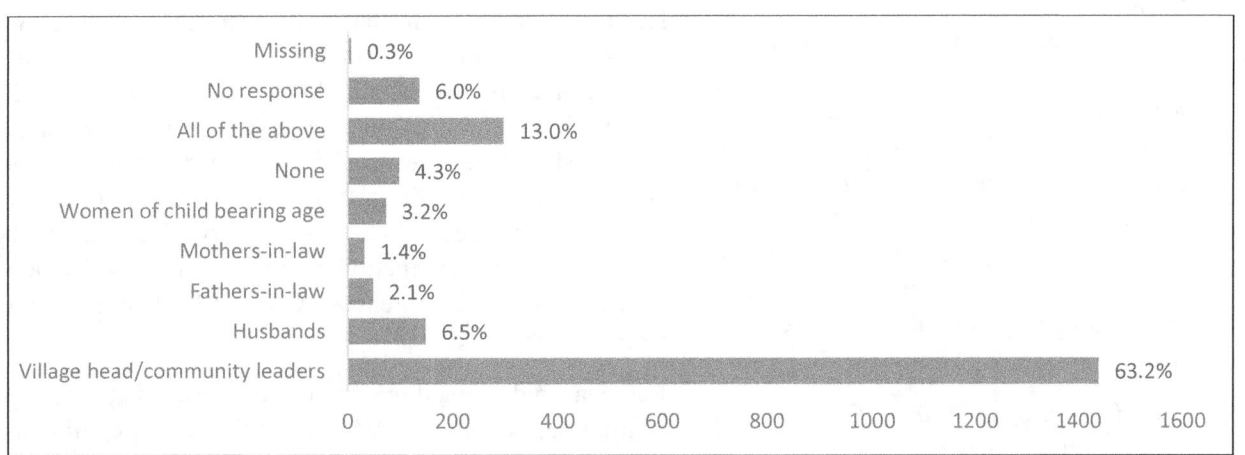

Figure 8: The people to meet first if PMTCT information is to be disseminated to the community (N = 2278), *Source: Researcher's Field Survey (2018)*

Our finding also reveals that when the village head is involved in any matter every member of the community cooperates, because the people "respect him highly for his character, good nature and display of concern for matters that affect his people," Adamu (2018); and "once you come through the chief, the chief will call his elders and that information will circulate the entire community. It has been every effective so far," Bussa (2018).

This study also indicates that the communication channels in use in these villages include drums, trumpets, iron [gong], and mostly word of mouth, and IECs obtained from the PHCs while the communication platforms include markets, religious places, town squares and meeting places within the communities. Others sources of communication include health workers, and non-governmental agencies doing routine outreaches in the communities. Respondents reported that word of mouth by the town crier is most effective in their villages. This can be put forward from these comments:

> Just the mouth. He will say heeee! Be silent and everywhere will be silent, then he will start talking [the town crier]. He will in turn stand at a strategic spot in the community and shout "Heeee" to draw the attention of the people; once he succeeds in getting people's attention, he then will deliver the message to the people and it becomes public discussion. He does this in every area [Angwan] to ensure that one is left out.
>
> *– Rahab Yusuf, during FGD in Old Kutunku, Gwagwalada – Nigeria.*

> Normally in our community, our chief normally pass… if there is any information to pass to the community they normally send a town crier to the whole village to announce [with his mouth] so so people are coming on so so day for this function please make sure you avail yourself maybe to his palace or the community health centre, you will see people trooping in for the programme so I think that is one major way
>
> *– Audi Nyawosa, during FGD inUshafa Village, Bwari – Nigeria.*

Discussion

PMTCT Knowledge and MTCT Prevention

Our finding show that most women of child-bearing age have inadequate knowledge of the mode of transmission of paediatric HIV despite evidence that they are aware of HIV/AIDS and various ways of being infected with the virus and how to prevent infection. Most of them believed that HIV is majorly transmitted to babies through breastfeeding, while a significant number do not have any idea of how the virus is transmitted to children.

Our finding agrees with that of Anigilaje, Ageda and Nweke (2016), who stated that respondents in their study thought that mother-to-child transmission of HIV was only possible during breastfeeding. What this means is that many do not know that the virus can be transmitted to their babies during pregnancy and childbirth as well. The World Health Organisation's four-prong strategy for PMTCT is conceived to bridge this gap. The four elements of this strategy are the prevention of HIV among women of child-bearing age, prevention of unintended pregnancies among women living with HIV, the prevention of mother-to-child transmission of HIV and provision of treatment and care. This finding, therefore, suggests that some women are not accessing PMTCT services so are affected by HIV and suffering in ignorance. The significance of this finding is that more awareness campaigns need to be carried out in these areas to educate them about MTCT, its mode of transmission and prevention.

Communication Platforms and Effectiveness

Most women of child-bearing age in the communities receive health information about PMTCT from the Village Heads who routes information to them through the town criers. Our results confirm that most women of child-bearing age in the Ushafa, IddoPada and Old Kutunku receive health information about PMTCT from the Village Heads who route information to them through the town criers. This finding contrast to the result of a similar work and in the same Federal Capital Territory of Abuja, that the main sources of information about HIV and AIDS among women accessing Antenatal Care (ANC) were health workers (Erekaha, 2015).

Erekaha (ibid) argued that the reason for this is that access to information about HIV/AIDS is limited so community members resort to health workers as platforms to receive HIV/AIDS information for women of child-bearing age. The importance of our finding is the recognition of the role that Village heads can offer in sharing information about PMTCT and galvanizing community members to participate in the uptake of PMTCT services, which hitherto was not fully exploited. Advocacy visits to village heads to buy into HIV intervention programmes is the most obvious involvement of this influential gatekeepers. This study further reveals that school children and literate youths in Ushafa, IddoPada and Old Kutunku are conduits through which women of child-bearing age in these communities receive health information such as HIV/MTCT and how to prevent new infection more than they receive from their husbands, places of worship, neighbours and relations respectively.

Most communication efforts of development agencies and the government are endogenous and driven by the mass media more than indigenous communication tools which the community members attach so much value to. Our finding shows that the closest communication endeavor in this stead is the creation and dissemination of Information Education and Communication (IEC) materials, which again are facility-based than community.

Measures to achieve better PMTCT communication outcomes

The respondents disclosed that there are better ways that IHVN can communicate with community members about the availability and benefits of PMTCT. Our finding reveals that word of mouth through the town crier is the most effective local medium of communication in the communities more than door-to-door, music and dancing. Respondents recommended this medium for better communication outcomes for PMTCT services in rural communities. This finding agrees with Odoemelam and Nwachukwu (2011), who revealed that the use of mass media with all its potential cannot be the best medium for dissemination of HIV/AIDS awareness messages to rural audience.

Therefore, holding the workshops and seminars in facilities would limit the spread of the PMTCT trainings to only women who report to the PHCs for ANC hence the need to take the awareness efforts to village meetings and arenas. From the observation of the researcher during the FGDs, most of the respondents with fair understanding of the mode of transmission of HIV to children were those who had had experience of child birth at the PHCs with the support of their husbands, and not necessarily because of any community conversation around PMTCT. Community conversation on preventing new HIV infection can be enhanced when more women of child-bearing age are empowered through training to know the components of PMTCT and the benefits and how to access the services. In consonance with the social learning theory, this training can be facilitated by mentor-mothers of people living with HIV who will be observed by younger women as they offer care and support to prevent mother-to-child transmission of HIV

in rural communities.

Limitations

Health workers in the primary health centres located in Ushafa, IddoPada and Old Kutunku villages were not involved in the focus group discussions and survey. This was done to guide against this work becoming a facility rather than a community-based study.

Recommendations

Because of the findings, there is need to educate women of childbearing age in rural communities of Abuja about the benefits of PMTCT services using visual/drawing illustrations and pictures in addition to the existing channels in use such as pamphlets, handbills and radio jingles, since most of the rural women in the areas are lowly educated and cannot understand the English language. The local languages of the communities, which are Gbagyi, Gbari and Hausa, should be used in developing and disseminating PMTCT messages to enhance community conversations around PMTCT. Another strategy is that village heads should be involved in development of PMTCT messages and the choice of channels as the only gatekeepers through whom PMTCT information can be passed to the women using word of mouth that is the most effect local form of communication in Ushafa, Old Kutunku and IddoPada.

Conclusion

It has been established that communication platforms and channels are overtly essential for preventing new HIV infection amongst women and children in rural communities, especially local means because the conventional methods have their relevance in urban settlements and settings. It has also been asserted that the nature of communication determines the effectiveness and acceptance of health interventions such as PMTCT. From the findings made we conclude that the benefits and components of PMTCT services are not known in the three communities. Thus, it is imperative to suggest that there is need for the development agencies in the area to seek relevance and effectiveness using community based communication platforms and channels. Importantly, it is necessary for the agencies to also address the issues of language and cultural implications of certain interventions which have militated against communication campaigns for the prevention of mother to child transmission of HIV.

References

Adedokun, M. O., Adeyemo, C. W., and Olorunsola, E. O (2010).*The Impact of Communication on Community Development*.J Communication, 1(2):101-105 (2010)

Anigilaje, E. A., Ageda, B. R., and Nweke, N. O. (2016).*Barriers to uptake of prevention of mother-to-child transmission of HIV services among mothers of vertically infected HIV-seropositive infants in Makurdi, Nigeria*. Patient Preference and Adherence Journal, Dove Press.http://dx.doi.org/10.2147/PPA.S87228

Bandura, A. (1987). *Perceived Self-Efficacy in the Exercise of Control over AIDS Infection.* National Institute of Mental Health and Drug Abuse Research Conference on Women and AIDS: Promoting Health Behaviour, Bethesda

Erekaha, S. C. (2015). *Knowledge, Perception and Practices Relating to Mother-to-Child Transmission of HIV among antenatal clinic attendees in primary health care facilities in Abuja, Nigeria.*Unpublished Master of Public Health Thesis, University of Ibadan, Nigeria

NOUN (2008).*Communication Counseling in HIV/AIDS.* National Open University of Nigeria, Lagos, Nigeria

WHO (2018).*Health Education.*http://www.who.int/topics/health_education/en/

Mefalopulos, P. (2008). *Development Communication Sourcebook – Broadening the Boundaries of Communication.* The International Bank for Reconstruction and Development/The World Bank, Washington

National AIDS and STIs Control Programme (2016). *Core Principles of the New National Guideline for HIV Prevention and Care.*Federal Ministry of Health, Nigeria

Odoemelam, L.E. and Nwachukwu, I. (2011). *Effectiveness of Television in communicating HIV/AIDS control messages in rural communities of Abia State.*Journal of Media and Communication Studies, Vol. 3 (10). Pp. 295-301, October 2011

Patrick, D. (2010). *AIDS Action.* ACET International Alliance and Operation Mobilisation, Middlesex UK

PCRP (2013-2015). *President's Comprehensive Response Plan for HIV/AIDS in Nigeria.* National Agency for the Control of AIDS (NACA), Abuja, Nigeria

ScienceDaily (2018).*New drug capsule may allow weekly HIV treatment.* MIT, Massachusetts http://www.sciencedaily.com/release/2018/01/180109153443.htm

Standard Telegraph (2015).*AMAC, Gwagwalada, Bwari Rank Abuja Top Sex Spots – NACA.*www.standardtelegraph.com/2015/11/30/amac-gwagwalada-bwari-rank-abuja-top-sex-spots/

UNAIDS (2013).*Progress Report on the Global Plan towards the elimination of new HIV infections among children by 2015 and keeping their mothers alive.* Joint United Nations Programme on HIV/AIDS, Switzerland

Interviews

Adamu, H (2018). *Key Informant Interview with daughter of Late AlhajiAdamu Hassan, former Village Head of IddoPada.* Thursday, January 25, 2018 in IddoPada, Abuja

Bussa, D (2018). *Key Informant Interview with Secretary to the District Head, Ushafa,* Friday, January 26, 2018 in Ushafa, Bwari

Ukpabi, B. (2018). *Key Informant Interview with Information, Education and CommunicationOfficer (IEC, Institute of Human Virology Nigeria.* Key Informant Interview, Tuesday, January 9, 2018 in Abuja

Dance in The Yorùbá Family Rites of Birth, Marriage and Death

Felix A. Akínṣípẹ̀
Department of the performing arts, university of ilorin, ilorin, kwara state, nigeria.
Email: felisipe@yahoo.com

&

'Bùnmi Babárìndé-Hall
Administrator, Digital and Emerging Technologies, The Community College of Baltimore County, USA

Abstract

Birth, marriage and death are three vital rites of passages occurring within a family setting in the Yorùbá land. They are life celebrations which bring members of a Yorùbá family together. The Yorùbá social life is closely guided by religious beliefs, so much so that it is sometimes difficult to draw a clear line between the sacred and the profane. Dance occupies an important position in their family celebrations, in religions and communal experiences, and as a form of recreation. Sacred or profane, however, dance plays a most significant role in the life of the people. The reasons for dance are as diverse as the social occurrence. Rites of passage are rituals that mark an individual's transition from one set of socially identified circumstances to another. This paper therefore examines the important roles of dance in three rites of passages in the Yorùbá land hoping, in the process, that the significance of dance in the life of a people can be determined. The paper concludes among others that dance as it occurs during rites of passage functions mainly as means of bringing the extended family together in the celebration of a happy or sad occasion. Dance functions as a reciprocal gesture between children and their parents; while parents honour their children at birth and at their weddings; children in turn honour their parents at death.

Key words: *Dance Rite of passage, Yoruba family, Family celebrate*

Introduction

The Yorùbá, a linguistic and tribal ethnic group, inhabit most of Ọ̀yọ́, Ògùn, Òǹdó, Ọ̀ṣun, Lagos and Kwara states of Nigeria. They all speak the Yorùbá language with dialectic variations. Yorùbá people share a long history of cultural tradition. Common to all Yorùbá people is the belief in Odùduwà as the founding father of the tribe. According to their mythology, the Almighty God called *Olódùmarè* sent Odùduwà to the world with a chicken and some sand. Odùduwà descended on a chain, and with the help of the chicken, spread dry land on the existing waters. The place Odùduwà first founded was called llé-lfẹ̀, the city all recognize as the Yorùbá ancestral home. Odùduwà had sixteen sons each of whom he gave/beaded crown and asked to go and found other settlements. The princes found other settlements and ruled over them. From them, other towns were founded (Akinjogbin Unpublished, 1980: 5-6).

Over the years, the Yorùbá people have survived as an agricultural group. The culture operates under a patriarchal polygamous system in which a man can marry more than one wife. The situation became necessary through the demand for more hands on the farm. As an agricultural society, the Yorùbá people depended on manual labour for increased crop productivity. Many wives therefore ensured many children and more hands on the farm (Ademuwagun,1965:244).

The Yorùbá family is an extended family system made up of all relatives called Ẹbí. The Ẹbí includes grand-parents and great grand-parent, uncles, aunts, and cousins many generations removed as far as one can trace. In the true traditional setting, the family lives in a household Agbo'lé headed by the oldest male who is called Baálé. He is respected by all members of the Ẹbí including their wives and children.

Rites are sets of formal religious ceremonial procedures undertaken and accepted by a group of people or community as a way of doing things. The entire Yorùbá people's lives are shrouded in series of rites especially of birth, marriage and death. (Abioje 2014:11) posits that;

> The funeral rites the Yorùbá perform when grand old people (and adults, generally speaking) die, clearly indicate their belief in life after death. The rites include bathing of the corpse, laying the corpse in state in fine clothes, burring the dead with various articles considered useful on the way and in the spiritual world of the dead.

The Yorùbá social life is closely guided by religious beliefs involving a lot of rites, so much so that it is sometimes difficult to draw a clear line between the sacred and the profane. Sacred or profane, however, dance plays a most significant role in the life of the people. The reasons for dance are as diverse as social occurrence. Harper (1970:71) confirms these social functions when she observes:

> …It is therefore not surprising to find dance as a medium of expression for all levels of the society on occasions of ritual and social significance, and as the most popular form of recreation and entertainment.

Ugolo (2014: 234) also corroborates;

> Dance is particularly necessary and serves as an integral part of community life which takes on many social functions that are sometimes closely connected with customs and rites. Indeed, for some people, dance is the main means of social organization.

Therefore, a house-warming party becomes an avenue for social gathering during which friends and well-wishers dance. Festivals in the Yorùbá culture are closely related to the religious beliefs of the people and dance becomes a medium of worship, thanksgiving and propitiation. On Festival occasions, dance brings all the members of the community together. Occasions which bring the Yorùbá extended family together are closely related to rites of passage, especially birth, marriage and death.

Dance as a cultural phenomenon:

Dance in most African communities plays important role in their culture. It has long been well-known that;

> In the life of primitive people, nothing approaches the dance in significance. It is not mere past-time, but a very serious activity. It is not a sin but a sacred act. It is not mere at or 'display' divorced from the other institutions of society; on the contrary, it is the very basis of survival of the social system in that it contributes significantly to the fulfillment of all society's needs (Rust 1969: 11).

The Yorùbá culture, like other cultures in Nigeria, has a long history and dance has remained an intrinsic part of the culture. Dance is a behaviour within the framework of culture and society. It is "combined inextricably with virtually infinite number of other kinds of behavior" because "dance is culture and culture is dance, and dance is society and society is dance" (Merriam 1974: 9-26). An understanding of a cultural social setting will lead to a better understanding of dance in a culture, just like an understanding of dance can lead to an understanding of why people behave the way they do.

Birth, marriage and death examined in this paper are three vital rites of passage occurring within a family setting. They are life celebrations which bring members of a Yorùbá family together. Rites of passage are rituals that mark an individual's transition from one set of socially identified circumstances to another (Plog and Bates 1976: 230). These occasions include birth, puberty, marriage, parenthood and death.

Dance celebrating birth

Children are very important in the life of the Yorùbá people. They join religious cults in search of children; and much care is taken to protect the lives of the children they already have. The care and anxiety become understandable in a culture which had developed over many centuries without such Western facilities as hospitals and senior citizens homes. Child-parental care is a reciprocal phenomenon in the Yorùbá culture. Children are culturally obligated to take care of their parents when they become too old to take care of themselves. Until the British colonial administrators introduced medical facilities in the nineteenth century, medical care was undertaken by divination priest who are also herbalists.

Furthermore, the increase and continuation of the clan are assured by having children. The arrival of a child into a family is therefore, celebrated with much feasting and dancing. Immediately a child is born, its father sends words to the men in his extended family and to his other male friends and neighbours. That evening, a celebration party called *Ìdáwó Ìdùnnú*, (celebration of joy) is held. Only men are allowed in an *Ìdáwó* party which usually features a night long consumption of liquor especially palm wine, dancing and jokes. Meanwhile the women in the household are expected to busy themselves waiting on the new mother and child.

From the first day until the seventh or ninth day (depending on the sex of the baby), the couple entertains friends and well-wishers with kolanuts, palm wine, and light refreshments. Guests always come bearing gifts of money and children's clothes for the baby. If the baby was a girl, the naming ceremony was held on the seventh day; if it was a boy, it was held on the ninth day. In recent times, most babies are named on the eighth day irrespective of the sex.

The Yorùbá extended family has been broken up in recent years by the need to get salary paying jobs and the flourishing businesses in the big cities. A baby born to any member of the extended family thus becomes a reason for all the other members to come together from wherever they have moved to join their kin in the celebration of the birth of the baby. The naming ceremony day is called *ijó-ìkómọ-jáde* (the day of presentation of the child to the public). For the first time since its birth, the baby is called by a name. There are no limits to how many names a child is given. Some children have as much as ten names; others may have as few as three. No matter how few or how many, however, every child is given an *oriki* a praise name with which a child is called only by close relatives, whenever they want to praise the child or coax him or her to do some jobs around the house or run an errand. The choice of a permanent name, with which the child will be generally known, rests on the child's father, its grandfather, or great grandfather if any of the later is still alive.

The naming ceremony itself is done very early in the morning before sunrise, and it is called *ìsọmọ l'órúkọ*. All the elders of the extended family of the child's father, both men and women, come together to give the new baby a name. Depending on the family tradition, members of the

child's mother's family may also be present at a naming ceremony. Some people even invite friends and neighbours to witness the ceremony. Needed for the ritual are a bowl of cold water, honey, salt, sugarcane (in recent times, sugar has been substituted), kolanuts, bitter kola, alligator pepper, and palm oil. Other items may be added depending on the *orò-ilé* (family tradition).

These items are all food products with significant functions and properties. Honey and sugar-cane, for example, are sweet. With a drop of those on the tongue of the new baby, the prayer is that the life of the child may be filled with such sweetness. Bitter kola has a very bitter taste, but on drinking after, the bitterness gives way to a sweet taste. This is significant in that life is not always sweet and easy. If, however, the child meets with some bitterness of life, may the end of the experience turn into joy. Bitter kola also signifies long life. Palm oil and salt are the most important ingredients in Yorùbá cooking; the prayer accompanying these items asks that the child may have the essential spices of life. Palm oil also signifies calm. Oil poured over boiling water is supposed to calm the bubbles. May the child's life be full of calmness. Kolanut is very important to all rituals in Yorùbáland. It is used for *Ifá* divination, to entertain guests, shared between two people as a sign of friendship, and as part of every sacrifice. On this occasion, the kolanut is used as a symbol to fight evil. Water is a symbol for survival: the baby survived in water (albumen) for nine months while inside its mother; its life on earth is also dependent on water because it is a survival necessity. Thus, a drop of water is also administered on the baby's tongue. This ritual completed, the elders get up in turn, give the baby a name, and put some money in the water.

Names given to a baby are usually carefully thought out and relate to the circumstances surrounding its birth. If a child is born shortly after the death of its grandparents it is believed that the diseased has reincarnated, returning to their clan. A baby boy born after the death of his grandfather is named Babátúndé (father has returned). A baby girl born after the death of her grandmother is named Ìyábọ̀dé or Yétúndé (mother has returned). If a man dies shortly before his wife gives birth to a baby boy, such a child is named Babárìndé (father has come right back). Yéwándé is a name given to a baby girl born to a man whose mother died when he himself was still a child.

Death in a woman's family does not affect the name given to her children since children belong to their father.

Other names allude to chieftaincy titles in the family or recent incidences in the family just before the child was born. With conversion to Islam and Christianity, children's names have also alluded to the faith of the parents. In the past, names alluded to the traditional religion the parents belonged to.

In the evening of the naming ceremony, members of the family and invited guests attend a celebration dance feast. Guests at the early morning ceremony are usually fed with *àkàrà* (pancake made from beans). The evening guests are fed with a variety of food and liquor as they dance. In the past, dancing was usually done to music. They are mainly for entertainment. The evening dance party provides the opportunity for the women of the household to dance, not only in celebration of the birth of the baby, but for the pleasure of their husbands. It is one of the few occasions when the men show their love and affection for their wives in public. As the women dance, their husbands put money on their foreheads. A dance party of this type usually takes place in the courtyard of the family compound. Chairs and tables are arranged in a circle. At one end of the circle is the band stand which provides the dance music. While people eat and drink, others join the dance group that is always in the arena.

Although men and women dance together in the arena, the women do more of the dancing on such occasions as this. Sometimes during a dance party, women dance together in a group and their husbands come into the arena to give them money. Before the end of the party, which usually goes on until about four o'clock in the morning, the mother of the baby is invited to dance in the arena. After a short solo performance, she is joined by other women who honour her by dancing with her. Before her dance is over, the men folks would come into the arena and give her money, immediately leaving the arena after.

The musicians also take advantage of the session. As soon as the money starts coming in, the band leader, who usually does his homework thoroughly with regards to the praise names of the celebrants, and the rich people in the party, starts to sing the praise of the people in the party. Such praise songs usually earn some results; after the people in the arena give money to the celebrant, the musicians also get some attention. Some musicians even prefer not to charge a fee for their services knowing that they could make more money on the spot.

In this way, dance functions not only as a celebration, but also as a means of distributing wealth. Dance becomes a vehicle for women to elicit the public show of affection from their husbands and members of their husband's extended family. Some of the women dance in a group to each of the seated old men in the crowd who must honour them by giving money, no matter how small. If the child is the couple's first born or the first son after a number of daughters, the mother may invite her friends and co-wives to join in buying uniform materials made into *bùbá* and *ìró*. Baby boys are very important to Yorùbá men because it is through them that the man's family name grows. Girls are usually lost to other families through marriage.

From the day the baby is born until forty days after, both mother and child are waited on hand and foot. The fortieth day is called *ìjáde* (outing ceremony). At this time, the woman may finally go out of the family compound to conduct her affairs as before the birth of her baby. The woman and her child, dressed in their best outfits, go out visiting most of the people who had visited them since the baby was, born. With her baby on her back, the woman visits friends and her own relatives. From then on, the child's socialization as a member of the Yorùbá tribe begins. Dance becomes an important aspect of his or her childhood life, because every time the mother dances with the baby on her back, the vibration of her body rhythm becomes transmitted to the child.

Dance celebrating marriage

With variations from place to place, there are three ceremonies involving dance before the wedding day itself. Marriage is the process through which procreation is legalized in most human societies. In the Yorùbá culture, the arrangements necessary to effect the marriage between a man and a woman are commenced as soon as a potential spouse is known. The first ritual is called *Mímọ àna* (a formal introduction between the, two families concerned). Previous arrangements are made for the family of the bride-groom- to-be to go to the family of the bride-to-be for a formal proposal of marriage:

> There are two ways: if the father of a girl has promised to give his daughter in marriage, all that was done was to fix a day when the formal introduction would be... If there was no such promise, the boy or his father or mother must do some spade work, otherwise the gift of palmwine and kolanuts

would be rejected... (Oguntuyi 1979: 17).

The nature of the gift depends on the local tradition of the area.

At this meeting, the man's family make their intentions known, adding that they have found out all that needed to be known about the girl's family, and would the girl's family do the same and let them know if they would have their son as a son-in-law. Marriage in the Yorùbá culture occurs between two families and such a union, it is hoped, should last forever. To make such a permanent commitment, therefore, a thorough investigation is made with regards to physical or mental illness, or incidents of unacceptable social behavior that may be detrimental to the union. Before the introduction ritual is over, the family of the bride-groom-to-be dance for their in-laws-to-be in hopeful anticipation of a favourable answer.

The second ritual is called Ìdúpẹ́ (thanksgiving). After the girl's family members have done, their own ground work and are satisfied with their findings, a message of proposal acceptance is sent to the man's family. In the past, and this still happens in different forms today, the Ifá oracle was consulted to find out if the union between the two families would be successful. If the findings were favourable, then, the proposal was accepted.

On the appointed days the man's family return to their in-law-to-be's family with a few gifts. Ìdúpẹ́ is a show of gratitude for the favourable acceptance of the proposal of marriage. The rituals involved are punctuated with periods of praise songs, composed by the man's family for their future wife. Women from, the man's household make it a point of duty to learn the girl's family oríkì (praise name). As they sing the girl's praise they dance. The betrothal and wedding dates are usually discussed during an Ìdúpẹ́ ceremony. The dowry and other bride-price needed before the girl can officially be married to the man are also fixed on this occasion.

The third ritual occurs shortly before the wedding. This is called Ìdána (betrothal ceremony). In some areas of Yorùbáland, the betrothal ceremony is supervised by the women from each of the two families who will engage in negotiating the bridal price. If the man's relatives believe that they cannot meet the demands of the girl's relatives, they bring some of the articles demanded only in fewer numbers hoping that one of their women have a strong enough bargaining skill to persuade the girl's family to accept what they have been able to afford.

The bride-price usually includes the dowry (money); the latest styles in Aṣọ Òkè (expensive hand-woven clothes); and ether women's wearing apparels; specific numbers of food items like yams, palm oil, kolanuts, bitter kola, salt, honey, and alligator pepper, palm wine and imported liquor. The expensive wearing apparels are to ensure that the young girl after marriage will have decent clothes to wear. In a polygamous situation, a man may hesitate before he showers one of his several wives with gifts. The demand for clothing before marriage gives the girl an opportunity to get as much as she wants from a man without the fear of getting the other wives jealous. The food items are shared among every member of the girl's family. As members receive their share, they say prayers for the girl's happiness in her new home.

Usually, young wives of the bridegroom-to-be's relatives carry all bride-price items in brass trays. The man's family members present form a procession about a quarter of a mile away from the girl's house where many of her own relatives wait to receive the visitors. The bride-groom-to-be does not follow the procession since his relatives must negotiate at this stage. He usually stays in someone's house in the neighbourhood waiting to be sent for when all arrangements have been completed. The bride-to-be is also kept in one room where she is attended by her friends and young wives from her extended family.

The procession formed approaches the girl's house singing and dancing. The dancers' voices and their clapping provide the music. On arriving at the girl's house, the door is found locked. The visitors will have to answer some crucial questions before they are allowed to come into the house. Questions may include what the praise name of the girl they are hoping to marry is? What are her parents' family histories? Could they recite some of the praise names of her two parents' families? When the bride-to-be is from a different part of Yorùbáland from the man, the guests must learn to speak in the dialect of girl's area. This way, the hosts are convinced that the guests have done their homework and are genuinely interested in adding the girl to their family.

As the door opens, the guests burst out singing and dancing until they are seated. To them, this is a step towards getting what they want. Then the bargaining begins. If after examining all the items brought the girl's relatives they accept the gifts, more singing and dancing is done for the successful crossing of yet another huddle. With some of the liquor brought, libation is poured to the ancestors of the two families who could not be present. Prayers ask that the union of the two families be fruitful. Then the guests demand to see their wife.

Three girls have been dressed almost identically for this ritual, and their heads and faces are covered so they are not recognized by the guests. One of these - usually the third girl, is the bride-to-be. The relatives of the bride-groom-to-be must know the essential features of their wife. Most of them would have seen the girl during the introduction and thanksgiving ceremonies. However, most of the people present may never have seen her. When each girl is presented, those of the guests who have memorized some important features and walking mannerisms of the bride-to-be will lead the protest against those of the girls who are not the future wives of their family. From experience, at this little betrothal game, most people know that the first two girls are almost always sent to tease the guests.

At the departure of the second girl, the guests begin to sing and dance in anticipation of the appearance of the third girl who is usually the young wife-to-be. Most of the guests who have had the opportunity to meet the girl lead songs describing some of her features. These songs thus become the guide in looking for features in the third girl that will assure them that she is indeed the girl they have been waiting to see. The atmosphere is always jovial as the girl is unveiled. She is applauded and seated. Older women from the man's family pamper her, wiping non-existing sweat from her forehead, fanning her with hand-made-fan's, and leading songs in her praise.

The bride-groom-to-be who has been waiting in nervous anticipation; is now sent for to join the bride-to-be. The ritual which follows resembles the naming ceremony described earlier, in that the honey, salt, kolanuts, bitter-kola, and alligator peppers are used as symbols to say prayers for the couple. After this, the couple is as good as married because the wedding day only marks the arrival of the girl to her home; however, the girl does not go to her husband's house until the wedding proper is conducted.

The wedding day is called *Ijọ ìgbéyàwó*. Wedding feasts are organized at the homes of both the bride and the bride-groom. The feasting and dancing usually start on the eve of the wedding and continue intermittently until long after midnight on the day of the wedding. Wedding feasts are very expensive. Whereas a child is too young to know the ceremonies that go into its naming ceremony, a wedding becomes the occasion when a person can enjoy all the celebration that goes with the rituals. Dance bands are engaged to supply popular music, and dancing involved in wedding celebration knows no limits. Hundreds of people

are invited and are fed to their hearts' content. Sometimes, more than one band is invited by each family.

On arrival at her new home, she is welcomed by dancing women. A man must not be in the house when his bride arrives. As soon as the music accompanying the bridal party is heard at a distance, the bride groom must go into hiding at a neighobour's house. It is a taboo for a man to see his bride coming into his house. This is why the Yorùbá have the saying: "Ẹni à ń gbé'yàwó bọ wá bá kìí na'rùn" (The person whose bride is being brought must never peep to see). In the past, the wedding day marks the first time the bride steps foot into the man's house. The man did the entire courtship visitation, and it was a sign of bad home training for a girl to visit a man before marriage. In some areas, the girl might even be labeled as promiscuous. This strict rule ensured that the girl remained a virgin until after her wedding.

Before the bride steps foot in the gate, her feet are washed in a ceremonious manner to cleanse her of any bad luck she may be bringing into her new home. The wedding day is very important to a girl. Generally, marriage in the Yorùbá culture, it is a celebration of a happy occasion.

Dance to Celebrate Death

Under normal circumstances everyone is expected to live long, old age starting at about fifty years. Any death occurring before this age, especially where the deceased did not have children is regarded as a death to be mourned. Such death is not celebrated with dance. Where a person lives until old age, the celebration is a way of giving thanks for long life and for the opportunity granted the deceased to live behind children who can now continue life where he or she had ended it. In most of Yorùbáland, people believe that after death, the soul rises to another level where life continues.

People who die young, especially some special class of babies, are believed to go to the third place of rest. These children are called *Àbíkú* (reincarnated children). Some deceased people are believed to reincarnate and be born again by one of the members of their family. The Yorùbá also believe that the soul of the dead ascends to the position of other òrìsàs (gods) where they can now look down on their people. Thus, dance celebrates the attainment of this higher hierarchy by the deceased these souls are represented by the *Egúngún* (masquerades) who are said to come back to the world to judge the living.

Furthermore, dance at a funeral becomes an opportunity for the children of the deceased to honour their parent. Dance functions as reciprocity between parents and children. When a child is born, the parents dance in its honour. Most of the expenses of a child's wedding are borne by his or her parents. Now is the time for the children to honour their parents for all they have received from them over the years. This is one other reason why the Yorùbá value children. Death becomes an occasion for one's children to honour one.

Funeral rites are different from place to place, but dance always becomes an important part of the rituals. There was usually a period of mourning which lasted forty days. After the funeral rites are over, the family of the deceased organizes a funeral party to which a band, like that employed for a child's naming ceremony celebration or a wedding feast, is invited to play. Dance at a funeral party is as elaborate as dancing in celebration of birth or wedding. Just like on the other two occasions children and members of the deceased's family are given money when they dance. And like the other two occasions, death is an occasion which brings all family members together.

In general, the tropical condition of the weather in Yorùbáland allows for dance performance in the open air. All the rites of passage described so far are celebrated with dance feasts arranged outside under the night moonlight and the stars. Because of the expanse of space such setting provides, dance style is always free employing a generous use of space. Dance movements are close to the ground, the giver of life. The body is inclined in a slanting manner forward, and the loose dress style of the people has become a part of their dance performance. Men and women dance holding a panel of their wrapper or garments. Improvisation is freely used within the recognized steps. Aesthetics is mainly judged by how well each individual has been able to interpret the beats of the drums and how freely they are able to move. Dancers get closer to the ground in free abandonment when they have warmed up to the music.

Conclusion

Viewing dance from functional perspective in this paper has allowed us to examine dance in relation to the totality of the culture. Our conclusion is that dance as it occurs during rites of passage in the Yorùbáland functions mainly as means of bringing the extended family together in the celebration of a happy or sad occasion. It also functions as a reciprocal gesture between children and their parents; while parents honour their children at birth and at their weddings; children in turn honour their parents at death. Dance during a betrothal ceremony becomes a non-verbal body language to be recognized by members of a bride-groom's party. Through the study of the movement mannerisms of a bride-to-be her future family can tell her apart from other girls even when their faces are covered. Dance creates occasions for public boasting among men as is seen during an Ìdáwó party when a child is born to a man; it creates an opportunity for women to elicit a public show of affection from their husbands; and an opportunity for a

young wife-to-be to demand for gifts without the fear of arousing the jealousy of other co-wives. On a different level, dance functions in the distribution of wealth in the society. It also provides an opportunity for friends and well-wishers to join in other people's celebrations.

References

Abioje, P. O. (2014). *African Ancestral Heritage in Christian Interpretations.* Ghana: Department of Religion and Human Values, University of Cape Coast.

Ademuwagun, Z. A. (1965). *An Investigation of the Relationship BetweenYorùbá Culture and Formal Education in Nigeria.* Ph.D. dissertation, Boston University School of Education.

Akinjogbin, O. (1980)."The Concept of Origin in Yorùbá History". University of Ife Department of History Seminar Series: Unpublished.

Biobaku, S. O. (Ed). (1973). *Sources of Yorùbá History.* Oxford; Clarendon Press.

Biobaku, S. O. (1976). *The Living Culture of Nigeria.* Lagos; Thomas Nelson (Nigeria) Ltd.

Harper, P. (1970). *Odu* 4. pp. 69 - 89

Harper, P. (1976). "Dances" *The Living Culture of Nigeria.* Biobaku, Sabiru (Ed.) Lagos; Thomas Nelson (Nigeria Ltd.)

Plog, F. and Bates, D. G. (1976). *Cultural Anthropology.* New York; Alfred A. Knopf.

Merriam, A. P. (1972). "Anthropology and the Dance". In: *New Dimensions in Dance Research: Anthropology and Dance - The American Indian.* Comstock, Tamara (Ed). New York: Committee on Research in Dance; New York University.

Ugolo, C. E. (2014). "Hubert Ogunde's Dance Tradition and National Development." In: *Dance Journal of Nigeria.* Vol. 1, No. 1. pp. 231-245.

International Journal of Integrative Humanism Vol 9. No 1. June 2018. ISSN: 2026 – 6286

Sounds of Contemporary Nigerian Music as Social Transformation and Dynamics: An Interpretative Analysis of Jude Abaga's *My Belle and Wild Wild West* Musical Productions

Apeh, Columba Ph. D
Department of Theatre and Media Studies, University of Calabar, Calabar – Nigeria
E-mail: apehcolumba@gmail.com, Apehcolumba1976@gmail.com

Abstract

The main point of this paper is to examine the contributions of contemporary Nigerian music to social change in Nigeria context, taking into consideration two of Jude (M.I) Abaga's musical works – "My Belle" and "Wild Wild West" as interpretative discourse. This study adopts the context analysis method of investigation. Though this inquiry, it is discovered that we need to view human social life in Nigeria context as always structured, but in completely so "structuration" is as much a process of change as a reflection of stability as exemplified in Jude Abaga's musical works". The paper concludes that certain Nigerian contemporary musicians have attempted to expose certain impediments and challenges faced by the Nigerian enclave. The study made recommendations for further inquiry.

Keywords: *Music, Transformation, Social Change, Postmodernity*

Introduction

Music appears to be a universal human activity, either for its own sake or as part of other activities such as dancing, working, playing and worshiping. Much is not the only one of man's activities to be principally associated with sound. Language employs the same fundamental sound elements; difference in pitch, for instance, can be found as a key characteristic of many Nigerian languages. Language and music differ in organization and purpose, not in basic material; the sounds of language are primarily for conveying specific concepts, the sounds of music are not. Of course, language and music may overlap. Poetry can emphasize the musical values of language, while music can express all manner of emotions and even specific ideas – but then only by associating with something non-musical (Boudon 32).

Though much of Nigerian musical history remains *Terra incognita* from the sociological viewpoint, the results so far obtained require constant coordination of effort is not to be wasted. Many questions associated with Nigerian contemporary music are unanswerable, both for lack of adequate data and lack of an appropriate framework of theory and relevant hypothesis. Yet the macroscopic picture has begun to emerge and it is already time to attempt an assessment of what the major changes mean in the social lives of Nigerian populations.

The phenomenon of social change as pertinent to contemporary Nigerian music is iniquitous. Although earlier sociologists often treaded stability as normal and significant social change as an exceptional process deserving special explanation, scholars currently expect to see some continuous level of change in all social organizations, including contemporary music. Sharp, discontinuous changes are of course rare, but still a normal part of social life (Giddens 106). According to Boundieu on the above premise, asserts that;

> … we deserve to see human social life as always structured, but incompletely so. "structuration" is as much as a process of change as a reflection of stability. Indeed, the existence of stable social patterns over long periods of time requires atleast as much explanation as does social change (98).

Cumulative social change must be distinguished from the universal processional aspect of all-social. Sociologists both study the form of particular transactions and develop models to describe the dynamics of large-scale statistical aggregations of such processes. Sometimes, specific process of social life undergoes long-term transformations. These transformations in the nature, organization or outcomes of the processes themselves are what is usually studied under the term "social change". On the above backdrop, Calhaun writes that;

> Human social history is given its shape by cumulative social change. Many of these are quite basic, like the demographic transition or the creation of the modern state; others are more minor, like the invention of the handshake as a form of greeting (39).

Cumulative social changes may take place on a variety of different scales, from the patterns of small group life through institutions like the Business Corporation or church to overall societal arrangements. Significant changes tend to have widespread repercussions, however, and so it is rare that one part of social life changes dramatically without changes, occurring in others (Durkheim 73). While some important changes are basically linear-like increasing population – others discontinuous.

Foucault, has emphasized basic transformations in the way knowledge was constituted and an order described to the world of things, people and ideas. His work has recently been taken as support for the claim that the modern period has ended. Theories of postmodernity "argue that at some point the modern period gave way to a successor (92). Lenski et al asserts that where modernity was rigid, linear, and focused on universality, postmodernity is flexible, fluidly multidimensional, and focused on difference (22).

Some postmodernist theories emphasize the impact of new production techniques, while others are more exclusively cultural. The term "postmodernity has often been applied rather causally to point to interesting features of the present period without clearly indicating why they should be taken as revealing a basic discontinuous shift between periods (Wallenstein 67).

At sake in debates over the periodisation of social change is not just the labeling of periods, but the analysis of what factors are most fundamentally constitutive of social organization.

In a nutshell, contemporary Nigerian music play a dominant role in social changes and dynamics in the 21st century Nigerian Milieu. For example, it is very common to see a teenager not able to chant the Nigerian national Anthem, but could memorize and sing popular music tracks they hear either when such is being aired, or from their senior folks around them. A typical scenario is one which teenagers repeat songs refrains or choruses like *"If you do me I do you"* (P-Square); *"Shake up your bum-bum"* (Timaya); *"Mummy Fall Yakata for bed" (Zule zoo);* *"Enter d place weda U no go Carry Belle too* (Tuface Idibia); *"Take Banana" (Dbanj); and Partoranky's* *"Money dey find me"* among others.

The above backdrop affirms that contemporary Nigerian music has been adjusted to foreign cultures, considering the progression of Nigerian music from traditional folksongs, high life tunes, fuji, Afro Juju, reggae, disco raga., Afrobeats and Hip Hop, show evidence of change and its effects on the contemporary Nigerian milieu to concur with Attah's view that change in culture may arise either from invention made within a particular society or by virtue of inter-societal contact and the consequent of borrowing or diffusion of cultural items from one society to another (57).

Since contemporary music and the society is ultimately related and connected with the latest and most trendy civilization, its influence on the society should always be a strong point of consideration. In spite of the morally decadent status quo of the Nigerian contemporary music scenario, a few musicians have still proven to be strong agent for social watch as exemplified in the musical works of Jude (M.I). Abaga.

Indepth Analysis of Jude Abaga's *"My Belle"*

Chorus

My Belle o, my Head o (4x)

Verse 1

Mommy don't cry Imam makes sure you say we no die Imam go hussle and we go try Hunger hook man for neck, shey na bowtie `Whatever it takes, me I no shy If na heaven food dey, make we go sky E better now make I sit down, make I no try I go even buy ticket make we both fly Mama, if it

means say, make I turn slave, kuta kente Anything just to make clean pay You never see food chop since Wednesday Make I wash car, sell gala, shine shoe Shey na work, anything I no mind do, I go do better work, even times two Cos it's not easy, it's not easy, it's not easy
(Repeat chorus)

Verse 2

Chale, no vex, Anything for your boys, make we go flex.No work make we do, so no cheques, Aaah we sef wan rock Rolex. Do something for your boys, we are loyal.You be king, you be chief, you be royal. Alaiye you go scatter them total, International star, no be local eh ha.If we get work, wey go bring better food make we take chop. No be road we for stand, we for dey shop, If for say things connect like we network If for say school fees dey, we for dey class. You sef no say Warri no dey carry last. But as things dey na, we no fit chop grass. At all at all, nah him bad pass
(Repeat chorus)

Bridge

Naija people, just surviving Okada riding, police bribing. Pastor preaching, pay your tithings School fees paying, food providing. Impure water, no electric So much traffic, see the life is hectic. Sewage leaking, there's air pollution. Rats are everywhere, no solution Roads with potholes, people dying, All the bastards politicians lying University, degree pursuing. Fuel scarcity, people queuing. Black market, petrol impurity. Armed robbery, there's no security, Fuel prices, Niger Delta. Religious crises, then no shelter

Verse 3

Oga stop there. Abi u never see road block here. Na we be the police search and stop here. If you wan pass son gotta drop here
U no dey see gun abi u no well. If you form actor, u go go cell. See behind counter, no be hotel You go do 3 nights before u go bail But if you want move You sef know wetin you suppose do. Do am quick quick make I no expose you Nyem something make I hold or I'll hold you Hey Sergeant Collins, make you come check Search am quick, search him bag and him pocket. Any exhibit wey we come get.Then alarm go blow on una trumpet (Repeat chorus till fade)
(*http://www/freenaijalyrics.com/ m-i-my-head-my-belle/*)

Analysis

The song is written and sung in pidgin or 'Nigerian English" language to the understanding of a wider percentage of the common Nigerian citizens, the song in content habour the multiple problems that clouds the minds of ordinary Nigerian citizens as they strive to survive the hard situation in the country. the persona start by crying out his pitiable status quo – *"My Belle o, my head o",* which paints a picture of the persona struggling between his empty stomach state, borne out of days of hunger and starvation; and struggling to think out plans how to proceed from his stagnant standpoint. The persona, out of strong determination, further consoles his crying mother by saying "If na heave food dey, make we go sky". He has made up his mind to take unimaginable steps just to put food on the table. He further clarifies issue by telling the mother that even if it means becoming a 'slave' just to make money, be it car-washing, selling of gala etc. "Cos, it's not easy".

In verse two, the persona, now a school drop-out, is run into by his friend who has now made it big in life. He hails him and pleads that he (Chale) should just provide anything they may feed on since they have become victims of circumstance with no jobs. That:

> "If we get work, wey go bring better food make we take chop No be road we for stand, we for dey shop if for say things connect like we network if for say school fees dey, we for dey class".

The jobless ones as school dropouts have become beggars. The musician-persona, in clear terms paints a picture of how the Nigerian corruption situation has entrenched the country into decadence on the socio-political economic, educational and even religious fronts – ranging from bribery, unnecessary church tithings, the unhealthy state of living with 'impure water' and no source of electricity, sewage and air pollution as a result of gas flaring, roads with potholes and the eventual accidents which results in many death – things that would ordinarily be in abundance, considering the buoyant Nigerian economic state.

Lastly, the musician-persona gives a third person account – a typical example of how corruption has ripped the country of its glory. Here, he gives a scenario of security officials compelling a driver for a bribe:

> Oga stop there Abi u never see road block here. Na we be the police search and stop here…You sef know wetin you suppose do. Do am quick quick make I no expose you Nyem something make I hold or I'll hold you Hey Sergeant Collins, make you come check search am quick, search him bag and him pocket. Any exhibit wey we come get Then alarm go blow on una trumpet.

The supposed boss in the stop-and-search road block group orders the driver who supposedly is with an exhibit to stop. The police boss now orders the sergeant to search the suspect's bags and pocket. Instead of arresting him, opts to demand for bribe and allow his pass. Lastly, the boss warns the driver that the instant he refuses to pass, 'then alarm go blow'.

Critical Analysis of "Wild Wild West"

Chorus

Better get your gun, Get your vest Cos in J town is the wild wild West, Down here everyone curse, no one less Nobody care, nobody notice, so know this, Until you feel the gun blast Nobody gon' sleep & nobody gon' rest, Down here everyone curse, no one bless cos in J town is a wild wild west

Verse 1

Yeah, I just wanna cry, I just wanna know why people struggle they unify Wanna blame somebody middle ginger in the sky Let it linger while the anger, then I'm feeling vaporized. I just wanna pick up my gun and start to run were the evil once pondered upon their cranium. Put the gun against their temple, Squeeze the bullet into their mental curses on my dental so vengeful, but with my pencil I stenciled the pain, try my best to show the world events full of shame, J town was peace they try to cancel the name, But even when the fire burn the stand still remains. The wing came and restart Our religious our came, When I held I was like oh! God not her again. But in faith we remain open for the day break, Do whatever that it may take, I hear somebody saying…

(Chorus)
Verse 2

Yeah, wishful is, my memories of peaceful bliss, Now streets full of deceitfulness Evil is now around where all of my people lives, need a hero quick, J town I miss how you were, Tell me, how did this occur? Now memories of peace are in blurr. I repay and you were so pretty I swear, Driving through the city thinking this is not her, she seems so strange when did she change, Blood on her street, smoke in her sky, Cant feel her heart beat no hope in her eye. Orphans, coffins, bastards, caskets, mass burials, How we goona move past this? The Sun about to set. I'm getting ready for the war, I fear it isn't done yet!!

Chorus
(http://www.afrobeatslyrics.com/lyrics/wild-wild-west.html)

Analysis
The first two lines of the chorus speaks volume:

Better get your gun Better get your vest Cos in J town is the wild   wild West Down here everyone curse, no one bless Nobody care, nobody notice, so know this, Until you feel the gun blast   Nobody gon' sleep and nobody gon' rest Down here everyone   curse, no one bless Cos in J town is the wild wild west.

The musician-persona warns that everyone should get their gun and their bullet-proof vest because it is a 'wild wild west' (a 1999 American film with intense gun shootouts) scenario – a shootout zone where one can kill and be killed, even without anybody noticing, Jos was the hub of mentioned is Jos town. As at the time of release, Jos was the hub of suicide bombings, ethno-religious crisis, and this has continued cross the central and northern part of the country to date where innocent citizen are lost in hundreds and thousands and properties worth millions off naira,

He goes on to lament thee bewildering state off the continuous disunity among people. He wants to take up a gun and find whoever is responsible for the quagmire shaming this once a very peaceful place. He further consoles himself that will not hesitate to let the world know what has become of the town,

Try my best to show the world events full of shame, J   town was peace they try to cancel the name.

He finally put a glimpse of hope saying: But in faith we remain hoping for the day break. The musician-persona, in verse two, throws-back to his wishful memories of when J town was very peaceful and was in love with. As he drives through the streets, he sees blood on her streets and smoke in her sky. He then ponders over how this came into occurrence that his lovely J town is now replete   with Orphans, coffins, bastards, caskets, and mass burials. He finally expresses hiss sincere fears that the 'war' (bombing and killings) is far from being over.

Influence of these Songs on the Nigeria Society

Music has been an effective means of transporting information that has been used for centuries as a reliable mechanism to communicate and teach the masses. By this, we African musician is burdened with expectation; he or she is like an African creative (dramatist), who tries to avoid the big social and political issues of this society contemporary Africa will end up being completely irrelevant. In line with the above excerpt, the African, nay, Nigerian artist in this case a singer, takes up one social challenge off updating , informing the populace, and bringing to consciousness their collective worries.

The two musicians investigated for the purpose this research was purposefully selected on the ground that each of them conforms with the above premise, and contain a considerable number of audio-visual elements. Music video, as a medium, communicates intended and unintended message through its audio and visual components such as song texts/lyrics, dance movements, gestures, facial expressions, and costume/clothing, among others' (Odogbor 338).

The music video for M. I's 'My Belle' and wild wild west had, by January 2011, received 71,719 and 26,913 views on Youtube, just inn their first months of release , which suggests its popularity among many individuals. Both songs at the time of release were hits on radio stations across the country and lasted for years. This can be likened to Tuface Idibia's. For instance; G.T the Guitarman's Dreamer; Idris Abdukareem's 'Nigeria Jaga Jaga; African China's 'Mr President', with very strong and vivid lyrics, painting a true picture of the   web of correction which has by-produced hardship faced by Nigerian citizens for instance, the verse of African China's 'Mr. President' reads; 'Food e no dey, my broad water no dey, our country no good o!

The Chorus Echoes

Mr. President, led us well If you be governor, govern us well If you be senator, senate am well If you be police, police well well No dey take bribe Also, G. T. The Guitar man's 'Dreamers' in his chorus, pose series of questions; "when I'm gonna be what I want to be When am I gonna see what I want to see? Time is ticking and I can't wait no more. Do dreams ever come true in this part of this world?"

Jude Abaga, also in his popular trace 'Craze', treats same social issues as contained in 'My Belle'. The first verse captures thus:

…let's face the fact That the people are slim and thee governor's fact And the people laboring, only thee oga relax People struggle and toil, others chopping them all, We know the lowest and the poorest Are living in grotesque

These musicals all well describe Nigeria, nay, Africa and the positive changes it needs too make.

Conclusion

Nigeria music, through its audio-visual contents, influence the thinking, perception and behaviour of the viewer-listener society. For instance, many Nigerian music videos have contents that present what may be the odd side of the county in relations to its image. Mundy (259 - 260) points out the stunch influence of music videos:

…Music videos take us beyond conventional notion of television, representation and spectatorship. In its knowing, s elf-reflexive direct address to spectators who are deemed to be always there, music video constructs a dreamscape, replete with images that the spectator internalizes and which she or he finds reproduced and reverberating beyond the world of the TV set (and other viewing problems)

In this regard, both M. I. Abaga's "My belle" and "" wild wild west"" audio-visually triggered the patronage of the Nigerian citizenry because they are not just music for its purpose but music for informational and educational purposes. They have, however, addressed social issues bothering the larger Nigerian society which the common, poor citizens constitute. This cuts across all angles of the society - politician, social, economic, educational, security and even religious.

The artists in focus is very passionate about the current state of Africa and are the few outspoken Nigerian celebrities when it comes to social issues. Their passion is evident in his activism towards social change, quite unlike most Nigerian music artist, who produce their tracts basically for commercial purpose, and so they pay little attention to the educative and informative values that will bring about societal transformation positively.

In a nutshell, what kind of Nigerian contemporary music production could be legitimate for accomplishing social change in the 21st century Nigeria? In contemporary Nigerian music an effective tool for accelerating or achieving social reform, or can it be used to prevent the disruption of Nigerian society?? Is Nigerian contemporary music productions even justified to achieve either of these objective or area there always better alternatives available than music?? Is the use of contemporary music in relation to social change a phenomenon unique to the 1960s and 1970s periods in Nigerian musical history? If not, what lessons, if any, are contained in our Nigerian?

It will be tempting to try to provide an easy answer to the complex moral and social questions raised by the issue of contemporary Nigerian music and social change. This paper did not provide all such answers. Indeed, it may have raised many additional questions. Hopefully, this paper will cause you (Nigerian) to examine your own values and attitudes and enable you to eventually try to attain some tentative conclusions considering sounds of contemporary Nigerian music ass social transformation and dynamics.

Recommendations and Suggestions for Further Research

Based on the premise that much is a driving force in the society, because across the types and genres of music, it is evidence that music reflects and create social conditions – including the factors that either facilitate for impedes social change. Since music can induce social change, it is therefore pertinent that its context be very informative, educative and entertaining as well.

Secondly, Nigerian musicians can change the society (positively or negatively). This demands strong consciousness of what they sing and how they communicate to the audience as others would by large influence contemporary Nigerian societies (audience). Seemingly, presently especially within the hip hop/Afrobeat genre of Nigerian music, the music including has been inundate the Nigerian populace with a more noisy and far less informative or educative songs, which to a large extent has not morally satisfied the expectations of the public.

Thirdly, the song text/lyrics of songs from most Nigerian music should be conceived and managed such that they have no less effect than offering the general viewing/listening public positively impactful contribution to the growth and well-being of individuals and society. Nigerian musicians who are the principal actors in this case should always have this at the back of their minds.

Based on the above backdrop, Nigerian music should propagate are authentic methodology of its communicative values, presentation, presentation and promotion of cultures and values, in this regard, instead of using music for self-appraisal or esteem. Also, the Nigerian music and video censors. Board has a huge role to play in the regard of controlling and monitoring the content of the kind of music consumed by the public as well as enforce laws guiding these.

The Nigerian communication commission should provide strict bane on radio and television stations who default these laid down laws. These way, musician would be conditional to record didactic musical contents which will in turn educate, inform and entertain the masses.

Works Cited

Boudon, R. *Theories of Social Change.* Cambridge: Polity Press, 1996

Bourdieu, P. *The Logic of Practice.* California: Oxford University Press, 1990.

Calhoun, C. "Culture, History and the Problem of Specificity in Social Theory, in S. Seidman and O. Wagner,(eds)., *Postmodernism and General Social Theory.* New York: Basil Blackwell, 1991.

Durheim, Emile. *The Decision of Labour in Society.* New York: Free Press, 1993.

Etta, F. A. *Monograph on Social Change: Social Problems and Social Work.* Calabar: Success Printing Press, 2009.

Foucault, M. *The Order of Things: An Archeology of the Human Sciences*. New York: London House, 1973.

Giddens, A. *The Constitution of Society.* Berkeley: University of California Press, 1996.

http://www.afrobeats/lyrics.com/lyrics/wild Wild-West. htm.

http://www.feenaija lyrics.com/m-my-head-my-belle.

Lenski, G., J. Lenski and P. Nolon. *Human Societies.* New York: McGraw-Hill, 1990.

M. I. "My Belle". Youtube, 2009, web 12th December, 2015.

Mundy, John "postmodern and Music Video". Critical survey vol. 6, No. 2 *Television Drama-TV and Theory* (1994) Berghalm Books, 259-266. Web. 18th April, 2013. (http://www.jsfor/stable/14555828).

Odogbor, P. O. *The Potentialities of Dance and Other Elements in Nigeria, Popular Music Videos to Influence Children.* Dance Journal of Nigeria, Vol. 1, No. 1, 2014.

Wallerstein, I. *The Modern World System,* 3rd volume. San Diego: Academic Press, 1988.

International Journal of Integrative Humanism Vol 9. No 1. June 2018. ISSN: 2026 – 6286

Re-thinking Discipline and the Creative Process in Performing Arts

Dr Chris Nwaru

Department of Theatre Arts, Faculty of Humanities, Imo State University, Owerri

Email: chrisnwaru@yahoo.com

Abstract

This paper takes a look at the creative process which is a disciplined process. As a process that lifts man to the divine, it requires a strict discipline within the essence of man if he is to achieve attunement with the creative energy of God, the Supreme Creative Artist. For it is in the degree that man's soul is attuned to the source of his being that he is able to catch a glimpse of the nature and activity of the Creator of the universe, the Creative Principle which brought him forth into expression and which stirs in him the urge to re-create as a secondary creator.

The Creative Process

The creative process is a dynamic spiritual process which emanates from within the individual as man quests for an understanding of the meaning of existence and eternal Truth. It is only a glimpse of ultimate reality that we can catch. But the degree and intensity of the individual soul essence determines his closeness to the source of life and consequently the amount of light that is shed on his creative intelligence for the new creation of the art piece which should come from him. If he is peripheral, his perception of the human condition will be peripheral and consequently, the depth of his art piece will be shallow and of little consequence. In fact, peripheral artists are usually unable to observe the dynamics of their environment and incapable of understanding the inner meanings of their society and the import of its cultural reality.

The Artist

An artist is a thinker, a seer, an extra-ordinary perceptive observer of the human condition, a seeker of truth, a sensitive register of societal temperature, a visioner with a high level of intuitive power, and operates within a super-mundane wave-length. Some scholars have defined the artist as a maker of beauty, next to God, the original creator, and therefore he lives and exists in a state of perfect order, self-control and discipline.

One must state at this point that all that call themselves artists are not necessarily so. There are two levels of artistic manifestations, namely, Fine Art, and Vulgar Art.

Fine Art

Fine art represents the soul essence of the artist and the high level of his spiritual and moral maturation as well as the high level of his intellectual development. His creation thus has depth in its intuitive insight, meaningful level of thought and perception, a healthy quality of soul essence, and a positive level of moral consciousness. Emerging from an artist of this quality of divine essence, truth unfolds in an art piece such that elevates man to the noble and the divine, man's intellect sharpened, his soul edified, and his mundane self elevated to the ethereal. Janet Wolff (1993, p.7) observes that 'the artist is a kind of super human who manages to live outside of his society and to bring from his retreat some kind of pure reflection on society'. Wolff's observation indicates that this notion places the artist as an illuminated genious. And in the medium of the theatre, the spectator emerges after a good performance, lifted purified and edified in his soul essence. He emerges with a better understanding of life and better equipped to face the odds of life. He may not know what tomorrow may bring but he knows who holds tomorrow.

The theatre, like the place of worship, is an arena where the eternal and perplexing questions are asked and enacted. But while, at the place of worship, the worshipper may be less questioning with submission, to the Supreme Creator in faith and total obedience, the theatre throws the issue of the human destiny, and the human condition open as a protagonist grapples with the dynamic forces of life. At the end of the experience, the audience gains a better insight into life and re-assures himself that there is more to know about ultimate Truth. Rob Pope (2005, p.76). asserts that such creativity has the ability to respond to conditions, biological and social, in ways that are healthful and 'healing' rather than harmful and destructive'. The experience has a purifying and edifying effect.

Vulgar Art

On the other hand, vulgar art is early, vulgar, bestial and unedifying. And because it stays entirely on the physical level of awareness, it expresses on a low level of abstraction and shrinks the brain of the artist and the audience alike, causing their moral sense become numb, their soul essence turned negative, their level of artistic sensibility turned pornographic, and the arena of the theatre turned into a place of escape for the unserious, loafers and the vulgar. Concerning the creation of vulgar art Bert O. States reveals that the artist is human and can only see in parts, he writes about the Phenomenologist attitude in the realm of art making and theatre. He recalls that:

"For the Phenomenologist's, there is no such thing as a 'Divine Standpoint'. It is demonstrated with the example of the perception of a mailbox. From where we look at the box, we can never see every side of it, anyway, we are able to describe the look at the box or to visualize it entirely in our mind". Phenomenologists comment that to complete our perception of the world, there is always a part of the process called "apperception", that is the creation of our mind to complete the perception of material object or ephemeral arts (Bert O, 2007, p. 371).

However, at the conclusion of such performance, the members of the audience leave the venue more bestial than they came, more defocused on the essence of life, less intellectually alert, and more dehumanized. The venue of the theatre whose function is to alert man to his place in creation and cause him a level of restlessness when he swings away from the pendulum until he restores himself back to his noble place becomes a lewd arena where man

falls into the lower depths of life. Fine art heals and restores humanity while vulgar are dehumanizes and destroy; Fine art instills discipline and the beauty of the soul while vulgar art instills indiscipline, immorality and the ugliness of the human soul.

Every theatrical performance, be it drama, music or dance engage the audience on a reasoned, artistic level of focus on a moral question that threatens life. The fine artist, the true artist, digs deeps and incisive on the issue without equivocations and artistically unearths all aspects of the issue as he aims for a glimpse of ultimate truth. And to achieve the needed insight, he himself must be a disciplined individual in his soul, his mind, moral awareness, and in his physical self. Without this he will be unable rise to the transcendental level of perception to communicate vision meaningful life in his work.

The issue of the creative proves does not apply only to the playwright, music composer or choreographer. It also applies to the performer on stage and production crew backstage. Theatre life is a much-disciplined life. Perhaps, it would be of gain to take a look at what usually take place at the department of Theatre Arts, University of Ibadan some years back and perhaps recently, which most times is referred to as a military camp. It is a training ground where the performing artists in training are disciplined. They are handled as follows:

1. They are introduced to the discipline through an initiation /production exercise. Water from the shrine of stage is splashed, as it were, on them as a foretaste of what the Theatre Arts course is all about. Those who cannot cope run away from the department at that point. Those who cannot run for whatever reason, decide to stay and face the fireworks. After the initiation exercise, each one is sworn into the discipline in the manner of how freshers are sworn into the university system at matriculation initiation exercise.

2. A prepared Code of Conduct and Theatre Ethics are given to each student to learn and observe throughout his training period in the department.

3. He observes strictly production rules, codes of conduct and ethics, failing which he is punished according to his offence. Moral laxity is quickly punished, and the use of artificial stimulants is vehemently discouraged.

4. Theatre is a group art, hence the emphasis on the love for the theatre over-riding the love for self. Unco-

operative spirit is quickly destroyed or the student leaves the department for another university.

5. Self-praise is minimized by a de-emphasis on curtain calls which give ovations that might inflate individual's ego.

6. Punishment of artists with irresponsible inclinations, particularly to rehearsal times and lack of appreciation of order of priority in terms of theatrical production over-riding personal programme and desires.

7. Strict observance of the notice board for an update on the notices and events in the department.

8. Being accountable for items used for productions; any loss or damage is paid for by the artist who used it. Performance may be over, but production is not over until all items used are returned to their proper places.

9. Production and administrative staff being united and in one voice on issues with transparency in truth and justice.

10. Consciousness of the healing role of the theatre in the society as it repudiates man when he strays; humanizes and civilizes him when he drifts to bestiality and moral death.

Wrong Notions and Practices on the Art

There is a dangerous philosophy in contemporary Nigeria that believes that anybody can be a performer so it is those without much brain that get into it. And with that definition people who should not be found in the theatre as artists are there. This philosophy should be vigorously resisted and such drifters into the theatre be removed without any delay. Art is a new life, a new creation. A non-artist in the arena of an artistic experience is a poison that can kill the new life. Such poison must be vomited with quick dispatch.

Another destructive philosophy sees art as a cultural show and is thus only useful at big government events to entertain government officials and their guests, serve as a meaningless interlude at a moment when nothing meaningful is happening at a meeting, symposium, etc.; serve as a sideshow for dinners, house-warming, birthday parties or christening of a child of a government V.I.P.; serve as an interlude at soccer match or political rally. These activities are the equivalent of the popular airport painting which is quickly slapped on the canvas by non-artists for quick money from foreign visitors. Such kills art and makes non-sense of the artist. It also gradually reduces the intellectual, moral and spiritual levels of the spectator's

maturity, sublimity in his soul and turns him eventually into a shallow being with no centre that holds. The ultimate of such a decline is seen in the shallowness of the people's cultural heritage in the way man leaves images of himself and the nobility of his soul for posterity to remember him by. As Akinbiyi ably articulated in his lecture in on the "Spirit of The Artist", a people's level of maturation is strongly reflected in their culture. For most threatening to the realization of the completeness of being is the inability to appreciate and live one's cultural ethos. 'Thus, for a man to mature he must encourage the maturation of his culture.' (1993, p. 15).

Lisa Moran, Curator Education and Community Programs in Island observes that the wrong notion and practices of the art in Island resulted to some other types of performances as she states:

> The proliferation of performance art in the 1970s resulted in the emergence of new forms and categories of performance art. Prompted by the political and social upheaval of the 1960s, activist-based performances, such as activist art, street art and guerrilla theatre, sought to draw attention to political and social issues through satire, dialogical and protest techniques (Moran, 2005, p.6).

Finally, the reduction of the art of the theatre to mere entertainment has been the death-blow to the proper development of the theatre in the contemporary Nigerian scene. Traditionally the medium of the theatre was primarily a healing and corrective agent for the society at large and for the individual. The Mbari fertility and creative essence embody the main essence of creativity in its ability to die and regenerate a new life for the healing of the Land, the preservation of life, the rebirth and re-newel of life. In that process the old edifice must undergo certain levels of creative traumas so that the weight of the mundane, the negative and the unproductive may be shaken off and destroyed in order that a renewal or rebirth of life may occur for the health of the society and the individual citizen. That was what art was also meant to do in the society. And this was responsible for the reason why art, particularly the art of performance, is what the places of worship use to life the worshippers closer to their God, as well as it being used at the swearing in or a new President of a country, at the Court of law which is a performance arena with the judiciary standing in for the Supreme Deity in dispensing justice. For the same reason for art of performance is used to express man's attunement to God at festivals, communal celebrations and at rites of passage in births, deaths, marriages and significant stages of human development and maturation.

Conclusion

The artist of today has derailed himself or has lacked enough discipline stay on the rail and keeps impostors out. We are now terribly invaded t inconsequential intruders who seized the artistic mantle from the artist ard wearing it without sanctity and without vision.

References

Akinbiyi, N. (1993) 'The Spirit of The Artist'. In: The *Nigerian Guardian.* Saturday, May 29th, 1993, Pp. 15

Amadi, Elechi (1982) *Ethics In Nigerian Culture.* Ibadan. Heinemann Educational Books Ltd.

Bert O, States (2007) 'The Phenomenological Attitude'. In: Critical Theory and Performance. J.G. Reinelt and J.R. Roach (eds). The University of Michigan Press, 371-379.

Goldsmith, Joel (1977) *The Art of Mediation.* London: George Allen & Unwin Publishers Ltd

Moran, Lisa (2005) 'What is Performance Art. In: *Education and Community Programme.* Island: Island Museum of Modern Art (IMMA).

Pope, Rob (2005) *Creativity: Theory, History, Practice.* London, Routledge.

Sofola, Zulu (1992) 'The Artist And The Tragedy of A Nation'. An Inaugural Lecture. Ilorin: University of Ilorin Press.

White, R. S. (1982) 'Innocent Victims: Poetic Injustice'. *Shakespearean Tragedy.* London: The Athone Press.

Wolff, Janet (1993). *The Social Production of Art, 2nd edition.* London: Macmillian Press.

Fake News, Misinformation, Disinformation and Deception as Communication Channels of Democratic Governance in Nigeria

Oshega Abang Ph. D

Department of Mass Communication, University of Calabar, Nigeria

Email: abangoshega@unical.edu.ng

Effiong Edet Okon

Department of Linguistics and Communication Studies, University of Calabar, Nigeria
Email: effiongedetokon54@gmail.com

Abstract

Following the aftermath of the 2015 general elections in Nigeria, the media landscape has been inundated with fake news, disinformation, misinformation, and deceptions. What is intriguing being the fact that both the ruling and the opposition parties are unrelenting in the propagation and dissemination of messages with dire consequences to security concerns and political stability. The public is daily fed with inciting messages, allegations and counter-allegations all of which have severe implications on political stability and sustainable democratic infrastructure given the precarious balance and our core nascent democracy. This paper is a content analysis of some of the message propagated to either discredit or incite ugly situations that have dire consequences given the heterogeneous and precarious balance Nigeria as a nation finds herself.

Keyword: Fake News, Deception, Misinformation, Denials, Disinformation

Introduction

The 1999 constitution of the Federal Republic of Nigeria (as amended) provides in chapter 2, the duties of the citizens and in chapter 4, the rights of the citizens. For instance, section 14 of the constitution states that, "Nigeria is a country based on the principles of democracy and social justice"; while section 15 emphasizes the need to promote integration by encouraging free mobility of the people, goods and services. Democracy, Social Justice and Social Integration depends heavily on information and enlightenment, awareness creation and sensitization, using the media and other approved but credible channels for information dissemination, in line with Karl Deutsch (1970 p.217) concept of communication in politics. (Deutsch, 1970, p.217)

Information in any democratic society has six principal uses which include but are not limited to: Decision-making; Political participation; Education and awareness creation; Conflict management and resolution; Nation building; and Intra and international relations (Bangura, 1996, Abang 2015, Abang, 2017).

In such societies, information not only assist government in the process of steering and co-ordinating human efforts towards the attainment of set goals, but it also serves as the process in making decisions through a chain-link and network of communication channels. This explains in part why contemporary democracies though, salubrious to democratic stability lay great emphasis on the fact that rights, freedoms and liberties should be constitutionally guaranteed and conventionally accepted (Ikpe. 2010, p. 375).

Acquisition of information is most beneficial to the citizens in the areas of voting as well as in the perceived influence that they enjoy through government policies, programmes and infrastructural development. On the other hand, information is critical in governance and every political system performs its functions by way of information dissemination, awareness creation, sensitization and public education. The belief is that, without a continuous exchange of knowledge, attitude and values, neither society nor politics would be possible. Besides, the main business of governance and of leadership is the ability to communicate and influence people's opinions, as well as, the ability to communicate their agenda, policies and strategies to the citizens using the media (Hague and Harrop, 2003 p. 95).

Specifically, dissemination of information using various channels of communication is the web of human society, and all social processes are analyzed in terms of structures, content and flow of communication. Put in other words, the structure of information with its more or less well-defined channels, is in a sense, the skeleton of the social body which envelopes it, while the content of such information serves as the very substance of human intercourse (Pye, 1965 p4).

The dissemination of information (fake, misinformation, disinformation) in terms of flow therefore, determines and often impact on the pace, stability and harmony in any dynamic social-political and economic development of a nation. In this regard, information dissemination refers to all processes of communication (including facts, opinions, beliefs and biases) exchanged by the citizens or by the government in the course of institutionalized political communication (Harrop, 2003; McQuail, 1992; Pye, 1965).

Indeed, the enhanced awareness of the important role of information in democratic societies has been demonstrated by the steep rise in the use of information technology (ICT) in varied social processes worldwide. This development is consistent, with the established position that information or the media helps to cause attitude change and, by so doing, ensures sustainable socio-economic and political transformation in a nation (Agbaje, 1991 p. 12).

Prognostic views

Nigeria is a constitutional state comprising 36 states and the Federal Capital Territory Abuja, with 774 Local Government Areas, consisting of several ethnic nationalities with over 500 languages and dialects. For some time now, Nigeria and Nigerians are severely being stressed not only because the structures that should make the country function as an indivisible nation are said to be faulty, but also because, the more welfare Nigerians expect from the leadership, the less they get; the more they are told or informed about collective security, peaceful and harmonious co-existence, the more they are harassed both by the security apparatus of government as well as by the hoodlums who are the products of inequities, deprivation, and urban denials (Abang, 2014, Olukotun, 2000; Oyovbaire, 2001). As a political entity, Nigeria has been in political transition since 1849 when John Beecroft was appointed British Consul for the Bights of Benin and Biafra. Since then, there have been several experimentations with different forms of governments and governance of the many desperate nationalities that occupies Nigeria's geo-political space (Momoh, 2012 p.36).

At present, Nigerians are overcrowding the democracy highway which they are walking on; and the highway now seem to be developing bumps and manholes and craters all of which are yelling for attention. Visibly, the citizens are agitating, and the agitations are impacting negatively on Nigeria's democracy and democratic governance which has been in a precarious balance since the 2015 general elections. The ready explanation for this has been the undisciplined behavior of the political class and stakeholders; allegations and counter allegations of mis-governance, corruption and corruptive influences; decaying infrastructure; poverty and unemployment are being lebelled on each other for the roles they played or failed to play to make the nation strong, or in building a strong and virile economy (Yusuf, 2014; Brown, 1982). Outside of these, there are also, some security challenges and the aggravating issues of insurgency and terrorism carried out by the Islamic sect-Boko Haram that propagates ideas and philosophies which challenge the very foundations of peace, national security and political order on the basis of religion and a denunciation of western education in a secular state.

Next to these, the nation is bedeviled by recent clashes between herdsman and farmers over the issue of cattle colonies, beside the worrisome issues of the abduction of school girls in Chibok, Borno State and Dapchi in Yobe State.

Against this background, there is no gainsaying the fact that, information propagation and dissemination in such precarious situations necessitate proper management, deep analysis and evaluation. This paper is therefore focused on fake news, misinformation and disinformation as channels of national disintegration:

Objectives of the paper

The objective of the paper is to among other things;

(i) Explore the possibilities of establishing an acceptable process between the media (information packaging); dissemination (channels of communication) and their implication on political stability.

(ii) Evaluate whether the messages (contents) disseminated are aimed at building or destroying the fabrics of the nation's political and security infrastructure – That is, whether fake news, misinformation or disinformation can strengthen or destroy a democratic society and their institutions?

In doing this, the paper will unravel why government institutions and functionaries sometime take delight in deceptions, denials and misinformation of the citizens. It is basically a content analysis of some selected messages published or broadcast by citizens on trending issues to elicit reactions especially their attitudes and responses towards critical national issues, vis-à-vis the intended or the unintended consequences and effects of the information propagated or disseminated.

Thematic views

One of the misconceptions held by many people is that, "In countries whose constitutions says that, it is illegal to bridge the right of individual and of the press to speak freely, it would be right to think the freedom to have access to any piece of information is something taken for granted". Indeed, such a view is wrong. History, it could be said, is replete with examples of many democratic governments and their functionaries in both developed and developing nations who always give a feeling of concern about empowering citizens with information to serve as checks on governments (Best 1996, p.15). For instance, the end of the cold war seem to have turned attention of the global community to among others, two critical issues (i) communal and intra-state conflicts and (ii) security challenges and political instability within nation state (Bassey, 2010 p.76).

In Nigeria for example, the Freedom of Information Act 2011, suffered setbacks and denial of assent by President Olusegun Obasanjo before it was passed into law in 2011 and assented by President Goodluck Jonathan even when Nigeria is said to be one of the freest developing nation with a fairly well-established media industry (Uche, 1989; Agbaje, 1992; Jibo, 1996). With over 250 public and privately owned electronic media and about 70 print media establishments including magazines, the media landscape in Nigeria could be said to be adequate outside the problems of elite contradictions and manipulation of the media within an atmosphere of socio-political turbulence (Jibo, 1996.p5).

The effects of such manipulations have resulted to situations whereby when a national issue enters the public domain, the communication lines though, not all the times, take tribal, religious and political position on it. Such divides in the polity have remained and may remain deep to the dangerous extent that public policies and opinion will defer to them, while the media as channels of information are also skewing their reports and analyses to accommodate the interest of its adherents (Abang, 2017.p.80). The result today is that, the Nigerian media as a veritable tool of information and communication are replete with genres such as fake news, misinformation, disinformation, Deception and Denials.

Conceptual Clarifications

Fake News; These are news articles or items that are intentionally and verifiably false. They have political, social and economic implications and are usually propagated to mislead the reader or audience on critical issues of national concern.

Misinformation: This can be classified as false or inaccurate information, especially that which is deliberately intended to deceive. Misinformation is simply wrong information irrespective of whether it is deliberate or accidental, a genuine mistake or criminally intended as in gossips and other misleading information used to confuse or misdirect people with manipulative instincts such as hoaxes and fake news.

Disinformation: This is out rightly false information that is spread deliberately to deceive. The word disinformation did not appear in the English dictionary until the late 1980s. It is propagated to create tension or outright blackmail. For instance, Russian tactical Weapon office in 1923 conducted active intelligence operations during World War II and during the cold war era (Bithman, 1985 p. 49) to deliberately deceive and mislead people.

Denials: It is the plural of denial. It is the action of denying that something happened, or that something is not true. Denial are associated or followed up with counterstatements, rebuttals, retraction and abjurations. In ordinary English usage, Denial is to assert that a statement or allegation is not true, for the purpose of this paper, denials are synonymous with defense mechanisms in which confrontations with national issues or security challenges are avoided by denying their existence.

Deception: This is the act of propagating a belief that is not true, or is not the whole truth-deception can involve dissimulation, propaganda, and sleight of hand, as well as distraction, camouflage or concealment. deceptions are common in television series aimed at shoring up government achievements, photoshoping and outright mischief.

Theoretical Considerations

Across the globe, there is a great deal of consensus on how the media should report on political and security issues. Despite differences in media and political structures, clear majority of Nigerians seem to agree that, it is never acceptable for a news organization to favour one political party over others in their news reportage.

Though the media landscape has changed dramatically over the past decades, through digital sources, there have been a tremendous increase in the reach of social media and public engagements. Sourcing for news or information–whether through Google, Facebook, Twitter, WhatsApp or Local media websites, has become ubiquitous, and Smartphone alerts and mobile applications now bring the latest developments to people instantaneously around the world. (Pew Research, August, 2017).

Observably, new digital platforms have also come with innovations that enable novel forms of communication and greater reach than at any point in human history. For instance, disinformation and hoaxes that are popularly referred to as "Fake news" are accelerating and affecting the way individuals interpret daily developments. Put in other words, as the overall media landscape has changed, there have been several ominous developments. Rather than using digital tools to inform people and elevate civic discussion, some individuals are now taking advantage of social and digital platforms to deceive, mislead, incite or harm others through creating or disseminating fake news and disinformation.

In their book "**Propaganda and Persuasion**", Garth Jowel and Victoria D'Donnell (2007) characterized disinformation as a cognate that was developed from the same name given to a "KGB" black propaganda. They stressed that, disinformation games are designed mainly to manipulate the decision-making elite, and to receive no good publicity. Disinformation in this regard include the distribution of forged documents, manuscripts and photographs, or spreading dangerous rumour and fabricated intelligence. Although the terms Fake News, Deception, Misinformation and Disinformation have been popularized only recently, they have hitherto been extensively covered by academic literature in Political Science, Economics, Psychology and Computer Science as in the works of Flynn, Nyhan, and Reifler (2017), in their recent overview of political misperceptions, especially on how new information affects political beliefs. For example, (Berinsky, 2017; DiFonzo and Bordia (2007); Taber and Lodge, (2006); Nyhan, Reifler, and Ubel (2013); Nyhan, Reifler, Richey, and Freed (2014). Have all dwelled on how rumors propagate while Friggeri, Adamic, Eckles, and Cheng (2014), in their effects of Media Exposure (Bartels 1993, Della Vigna and Kaplan 2007, Gerba and Green 2000 and Gerber, Gimpel, Green and Shaw (2011). All focused on fake news and deceptions that have political implications and inciting. All of them are very instructive given the Nigeria political landscape with special attention to the 2015 general elections.

Writing on military ethics and emerging technologies, David Danks and Joseph Danks (2014) stressed that, the ethical implications in using disinformation has significant degree of philosophical debate over issues that relates to the ethics of war and the use of technologies in information gathering and dissemination.

Similarly, studies in psychopathic fiction reveal that, scenarios are always created whereby positive information about themselves and negative information about others are usually created, casting others in bad light. Example of these are not far to seek, in Iraq, Saddam Hussein, who, while a malevolent dictator, had not lied to the world about having no "Weapons of Mass Destruction" (WMD), but had Western democracies headed by George Bush of the United States of America, and Tony Blair of the United Kingdom succeeding in instilling enough fear, uncertainty and doubts in the media and the general populace to convince most that Saddam Hussein was "Duplicitious" and did in fact, have the Weapons of Mass Destruction. Such successful deception resulted in the launching of the Iraq war with little opposition and the hanging of Hussien, having been convicted by the International Criminal Court.

Corroborating this, Abram Shulsky (2017.p.4) observes that, the United States of America is now having difficulties employing denial and deception campaigns because of the open media which frequently exposes any major operation undertaken militarily or diplomatically.

Although legal restrictions sometimes tend to hamper governments and intelligent service; there are exceptions during or in wartimes when some measures of martial laws are imposed. Research, however reveals that authoritarian governments frequently employ denials and deceptions campaigns both domestically and internationally to manipulate domestic opposition and foreign governments.

While it could be said that during peace time, intra-state and inter-state deceptions have little traction because the level of trust between the different ethnic groups or nation states is usually low, therefore, being caught in a lie would be ruinous. Thus, leaders in democratic societies during such periods move up the ranks largely by employing political deceptions. In so doing, they may not be familiar with deceiving the people for personal gains, but may have considerable political capital and public trust following their programmes (Mearsheimer, 2011. P6). Put in other words, with a comparatively high level of trust, democratic leaders successfully indoctrinate the public with deceptions such a fear mongering and illusions such as "Being God sent" leaders to redeem the people or that they

as leaders are reluctantly responding to the yearnings of the people to lead them. (Godson, 2017.p12). Obviously, false or inaccurate information especially that which is deliberately intended to deceive are those often entangled in a web of secrecy and misinformation (Hutchinson, 2004, Donald, 2005, David, 2014).

Diagnostic Considerations

Across the global community, and Nigeria in particular, public functionaries and government institutions are usually faced with the burden of rebutting media reports. The ready explanations are that there is, if any, a thin line that distinguishes misinformation, deceptions, propaganda and disinformation even when the degree in terms of overlap may be subject to debates. Besides, there seem to be no universal definition of these terms not only because they all refer to misleading content found on the internet and especially on social media, but also because they consist, and include producing tailored false content which are usually targeted at the views, concerns and preferences of social media users whose pages can generate tens of thousands of interactions.

Often misinformation, disinformation and deception hardly meet the definition of propaganda whose motives in some cases are political concerns rather than financial benefits but tied to a large audience with an agenda. In this regard, political relevance does hardly provide or serve as lessons since they seem to validate political perceptions and worldviews. Specifically, if an information campaign or machinery uses falsehood and emotional appeals not to persuade or attract, but to distract, disrupt, divide, confuse and damage a target audience's understanding of political cohesion, then it will more closely align itself with disinformation and its undermining functions.

In contemporary democratic dispensation, the Nigeria political landscape is said to be very precarious. With political stability standing in clay feet due partly to the near absence of cohesion in the polity based on agitations for restructuring of the country, the resort to misinformation, false news and disinformation by those in opposition not minding their dire consequences has become a political pastime as political pundit daily pour out venoms with little or no regard to their consequences and national interests. Though the resort to the use of social media by the opposition is traced to the denial of access to public owned media establishments by the leadership or the ruling party, the act has not only given the opinion a shot in the arm, but it has quite often whittled the positive impacts expected of these media organs.

Under such circumstance or situation, the opposition party's denial of access to public owned media or the deliberate play down of their views according to them, sometimes lead them to embark on misinformation, deception and misinformation, purposely to discredit or ridicule the leadership or government in power. Examples of these are not far to seek. Following the aftermath of the 2015, and prior to the 2019 general election campaigns the then opposition party, All Peoples Congress (APC) propagated the following media stunts:

- "BBOG" Bring Back our girls. It was quite extensive and misleading
- Fake and misleading information on the seizure of several Millions of dollars meant for the purchase of arms in South Africa just to discredit the leadership.
- Disinformation and misinformation on the ceding of Nigeria's territories in the North East to the Boko Haram insurgents to discredit the ruling political party.
- Fake news and misinformation on the high level of corruption and corruptive influence as in the oil subsidy scam perpetrated as acts of misgovernance
- The aviation intervention contracts misappropriation and misgovernance; and the continuous assurance that the APC government will rescue chibok girls within 6 months if elected into office.

These issues were canvassed and propagated internally and externally with remarkable effects as manifested in the defeat of an incumbent President, despite huge sums of monies used in the campaign for re-election of the ruling political party.

The leadership at the time led by the People's Democratic Party (PDP) also engaged in deceptions and denials as in these media stunts.

- Opposition party Presidential candidate has no West African School Certificate.
- Opposition party involved in hacking, forgery and printing of fake voter's cards.
- Mohammad Buhari Opposition Party Presidential candidate to lead the Boko Haram team for

negotiations with the Federal Government on the release of Chibok girls.

- All peoples Congress is a religious organization with an agenda to Islaminize Nigeria.
- Dapchi school girls kidnap is a conspiracy- failure of governance

Issues such as these, beg the questions whether the, propagators and disseminators of misinformation and deceptive information ever have the unity of the country in mind or, whether they consider such misinformation and deceptions as good for nation building, balkanization or for the restructuring of the country?

The worrisome issue here is that, fake news and misinformation are usually propagated through the social media, even when the people are aware of the increasing and unprecedented scrutiny which the press, its members and the media generally are receiving. The media are criticizing and questioning the activities and conduct of many institutions and their functionaries, yet as channels through which deceptions, Misinformation and disinformation are processed and disseminated, they have not and may not, be able to conduct themselves in ways that are above reproach especially in the courts of public opinion (Angwe, 2014. P.44).

It seems to have been accepted quite reluctantly by media scholarship and practice that, the media is a powerful instrument and an agency for setting and executing its own agenda for its own target audience. (Oyovbaire, 2001), but it needs to be stressed that, in all circumstances and especially that during electioneering campaigns restraint is needed or required in the propagation and dissemination of misinformation, disinformation and deceptive information.

This is because, misinformation and deceptions are like gossips that information cheaper to propagate and disseminate tan hard credible, and authoritative. Moreover, stakeholders cannot costlessly infer accuracy since they enjoy partisan news. Misinformation and deceptions sometime generate utility for some people, as well as impose private and social costs by making it more difficult for them to infer the true state of the nation.

Social media as a source of political information

The Nigeria political environment offers several reasons why social media platforms have become conducive for deceptions, false news and misinformation. These include but not limited to;

- On social media, the fixed costs of entering the market and producing content are vanishingly small;
- The format of social media-thin slices of information viewed on phones or news feed windows – can make it difficult to judge an articles veracity; and
- Facebook friend networks are ideologically segregated, and people are considerably more likely to read and shares articles that aligns with their ideological positions, whether the stories are false or not.

The implications here are that, people who get news from facebook or other social media platforms, are less likely to receive evidence about the true state of the world. For instance, the Nigerian political landscape readily offers several possible explanations for a preponderance for a Pro-People's Democratic Party (PDP) engaging in fake news, misinformation and disinformation; and the All People's Congress (APC) with a propensity for deception and denials. This is because the more there is a high decline of trust in the mainstream media among the populace, obviously increases the relative demand for information from nontraditional sources, since the general perception is that the mainstream media tends to favour the leadership of the ruling party, because "He who pays the pipper, dictates the tune".

Basically, the leadership now and the opposition then, and it is also applicable now that the roles have been reversed, have simply been more compelled to enjoy or like deceptions, misinformation and fake news to be freely disseminated to the public not minding public sensitivities and sensibilities.

For instance, with less than 10 months to the 2019 general elections, the social media in Nigeria have been propagating inciting hate speeches critical of the collective existence of Nigeria as a sovereign state.

Only recently, there were gory pictures of supposedly innocent Nigerians massacred along the "Benin Ore" road by herdsmen with an appeal to the general public to stay away or not to ply the Benin-Ore road (https://post-Nigeria.ng).

And in a source attributed to Dailygobewatch.eu. Nigerians are given to understand that: Sergeant David Bako who claimed to be a deserted soldier and one of the abductees of the Dapchi school Girls in Yobe has circulated messages believed to be authoritative and credible on how the Dapchi girls were abducted. The message has been widely circulated with the sole aim of discrediting the administration of President Mohammadu Buhari.

The message states in part: "Dapchi girls, Boko militants did not come with a single gun, they exchanged pleasantries with community leaders and left after dropping the girls." (https://bit.ly/2ps9NSV).

Similarly, https://newsexpressngr.com/News/51205 has also disseminated stories such as; "How the Buhari administration is fuelling and escalating killings by Fulani herdsmen.

If these are misinformation or outright disinformation, the federal government on its part has not done much to allay the palpable fear among Nigerians.

For instance, Daily Sun of Tuesday March 20, 2018 ha a caption. Jonathan blew N150bn days to 2015 elections.

$500m Recorded Abacha loot missing: EFCC to quiz ex-finance minister (The Nation, Friday 19/1/18).

Stories such as these, create the impression that the federal government strives on deceptions and denials especially now that the social media is inundated with stories on issues such as;-

- Why the army withdrew troops from Dapchi few days to the abduction and the rebuttal
- Defence minister rebuttal to the allegation that he gave a specific date for the release of the girls.

Summary and Conclusion

The geo-political space called Nigeria has for some time now been inundated with inciting stories, allegations and counter-allegations by the leadership of the ruling political party (APC) and that of the opposition People's Democratic Party (PDP). The allegations including conspiracy theories, have been disseminated to the public, who for sometimes, now rely on social media for information instead of the traditional media.

International Journal of Integrative Humanism Vol 9. No 1. June 2018. ISSN: 2026 – 6286

Reliance on the social media is attributed to the fact that, information propagated and disseminated especially by the public owned media establishments are either deceptive or outrightly misleading. Secondly, the opposition party and other stakeholders outside governments believes and sometime reason that, since they have been denied access to public owned media services, the only option left to them is the resort to social media that has large followership and at low cost to them.

According to Mark Twain (1866) "if you don't read the newspapers… or listen to Radio and Television, you will be termed uninformed; if you do read the newspaper or listen to the Radio and Television, you will be misinformed".

Mark Twain's observation became more apt in the aftermath of the 2011, before, during and after the 2015 general elections in Nigeria. During this period, the geo-political landscape changed dramatically. Through digital sources, there was, and has been a tremendous increase in the propagation and dissemination of deceptive, fake and unverifiable sources of information, misinformation and disinformation.

Fake news and sophisticated misinformation campaigns have become very problematic in democratic systems, and there is growing concern on how to address the issues without undermining the benefits of digital media. In order to maintain an open, stable democratic system, it is important that governments should introduce News literacy and strong professional journalism in the country.

Next to this, the news industry should be made to provide high quality journalism practice in order to build a public trust to correct fake news and disinformation without legitimizing them. Specifically, individuals should follow a diversity of news sources, and be skeptical of what they read and watch especially now that fake and deceptive news and misinformation are generated by outlets that masquerade as actual media sites but promulgate false, deceptive or misleading accounts designed to deceive the public.

Finally, the general public is in dire need of information that will help them to make sense out of complicated developments as well as to enable them to deal with the ever-changing nature of social, economic and political events. Many areas are going through "transformation and mega-changes" and these shifts have created enormous anger, anxiety and confusion. In a time of considerable turmoil, it is vital to have a healthy fourth estate that is independent of public authorities.

Taken together, these steps would further quality discourse and weaken the environment that has propelled deception, misinformation and disinformation in the global community and Nigeria in particular.

References

Abang, O. (2015) Sensitive Information Gathering and Dissemination: AN Assessment of Doctrinal Roles the Military and the Media in Nigeria. LWATI: Journal of Contemporary Research vol. 12.

Abang. O. (2o17) Dominance and Control of Public Media Broadcast: A Study of the Imbalances in Information Flsow. NDUNODE: vol. 12(1). Pp 291-300.

Adamu, Roy (2017) Disinformation: A primer in Russian Active Measures and Influence Campaigns. Briefing to the US Senate Committee on Intelligence. https://www.ussenate.retrieved 30/3/2017.

Agbaje, A. B. (1992) The Nigerian Press, Hegemony and the Social Construction of Legitimacy, New York: The Edwin Mellen Press.

Bangura, A., Isayas, D. Smith, G. and Thomas, M. (1996). Political behavior. New York: University Press of America.

Bassey, C. and Oshita, O. O. (2010). Governance and Border Security in Africa.

Best, C. (1996). Press Development in Nigeria, Jos: Midland Press Ltd.

Bithman, L. (1985). The KGB and Soviet Disinformation: An Insiders View, Pergamon-Bassey: pp49-50. ISBN 0-08-031512-0.

Borugault, L. (1995). Mass Media in Sub-Saharan Africa. Bloomington, Ind.: Indiana University Press.

Brendan Nyhan, "Why the fact-checking at Facebook Needs to be Checked", New York Times, October 23, 2017.

Brown, L. "An Untraditional View of National Security" in Reichart, A. (ed); (1982).American Defence policy, Saltimore: John Hopkins University Press.

Deutsh, Kart W. (1970). "Political Communications and the Politicall System". In Louis D. Hayes and Ronald D. Hedlund (eds). The Conduct of Political Inquiry: Behavioural Political Analysis. Englewood Cliffs, N.J: Prentice-Hall.

Donald C. F. Daniel (2005) "De nails and Deceptions", In Jennifer E. Sims; Burton L. Gerber (ed). Transforming US. Intelligence. Georgetown University Press.

Hague, R. and Harrop, M. (2003). Comparative Government and Politics: An Introduction. New York: Palgrave.

Hustchinson, William (2004) "The Influence of Maskirovka on Contemporary Western Deception theory and Practice", Proceeding of the 3rd European Conference on Information Warfare and Security. ISBN 0-954-7096-2-4.

Jason Schwart, "Study: Taggig Fake News on Facebook Doesn't Work", Politico, September 12, 2017.

Jibo, M. (1996). Politics Mass Media and National Development, Lagos: Malthouse Press Ltd.

John J.Mearsheimer, "Why leaders lie," in Carlos Lozada (ed). The Washington Post, April 15, 2011.

Joseph Kahne and Benjamin Bowyer, "Educating for Democracy in a partisan Age: Confronting the Challenges of Motivated Reasoning and Misinformation's American Educational Research Journal, February, 2017.

Kessler, C. S. (2000). "Globalization: Another False Universalism?: Third World Quarterly, vol. 21(6),pp 930-941.

Marc Fisher, John Cox and Peter Hermann, "Puzzagate: From Rumor, to Hastag, to Gunfire in D.C" Washington Post, December 6, 2016.

McQuail, D. (1992). Political Communication" In Mary Hawkesworth and Maurice Kogan (eds). Encyclopedia of Government and Politics vol. 1. New York: Routledge.

Nic Newman, "Digital News Sources", Reuters Institute for the Study of Journalism, 2017.

Pew Research Centre, "Digital News fact Sheet", August 7, 2017.

http://post – Nigeria retrieved on 23/3/18

Dailyglobewatch.eu retrieved on 23/3/15

http://bit/y 2psgnsv retrieved on 25/3/18

Daily sun newspaper www.sunnewsonline.com Tuesday, march 20, 2018

The nation newspaper www.the Nationonline.ng. Net. Friday January 19,2018 p4

https://www.google. Com. Ng reneged 24/3/18.

International Journal of Integrative Humanism Vol 9. No 1. June 2018. ISSN: 2026 – 6286

Peaceful Co-Existence in Nigeria: An Analytical Study of Christian Perspective of Neighbourliness

Chibuzo Ikechi NWANGUMA, PhD

Dept of Philosophy Religion, Mountain Top University, Km 12 Lagos-Ibadan Expressway, Ibafo, Ogun State.

Nigeria. Email: chibuzonwanguma@gmail.com

Abstract

Peaceful co-existence in Nigeria has consistently been proven almost impossible amidst the various efforts to live together in harmony as a people; and this has been due to the activities evil men who have consistently taken undue advantage of the endemic ethnic biases or religious bigotries in the society to perpetrate their evil agenda. Given the religious stance of the issue, this study was poised to explore a scriptural approach in unraveling the matter. Basically, the method adopted in carrying out the study was an analytical appraisal of the selected text as Paul's theme in the passage was assessed vis-à-vis the subject matter of the work. The peace in Nigeria was termed negative, where the peace in existence is mere absence of direct violence, war, or fear etc. or anything worse than such as affirms the study. Basically, the deduction of the study was that the issue could not be who a neighbour is but what the problem is. Men of mischief were seen taking undue advantage of the ignorant, idle, and indigent youths to accomplish their nefarious selfish interests; and the counsel of this work is that such must not be accommodated: the appropriate quarters even the government must resist them squarely especially since the Government's primary assignment is to ensure safety of lives and properties of the citizens though such may be hard for them to do on the ground that most of the ills in the society are often caused by majority of them in government.

Key Words: *Peaceful, Neighbourliness, Co-Existence, Self-defense, Nigeria*

Introduction

The last two lines of the Nigerian National Anthem read, "One nation bound in freedom peace and unity." When one reads or sings this or even hears such being sung, the thinking will be such that the nation is a place where maintenance of peace is a common thrust especially as the cultural and the philosophical ideology behind the white colour of the nation's flag is "peace and unity," as it were. And, looking at the situation of things in the nation especially in relation to peace, one will hardly be wrong to term such conclusion as a mere cliché. Quite pathetically, ill-willed fellows among the elite class, out of their selfish interest, having known the influence of religion and ethnicity in the country, stylishly engage the weak in creating near-absence of peace among peoples of Nigeria at will especially through the means of xenophobia and religious bigotry. As true as this assertion could be, none

among the perpetrators has once accepted responsibility for this, but Nigerians know. Even the international community knows. Such has significantly affected the security situation of the nation-state of Nigeria. That is, it is no longer news to wake up any day and hear of anything that has to do with loss of lives on account of the attacks of some gunmen or armed men here and there. If it would not be through means of Boko Haram scourge in the north, it could be that of the Hausa-Fulani herdsmen across the nation or even that of kidnappings all over the place, harassing unsuspecting innocent citizens and even foreigners alike. Worst of it all is the fact that the kingpins of these barbaric acts especially that of the Boko Haram scourge could succeed in using the world's most acclaimed institution (religion) about morality as well as peace-making, to foment such dastardly acts.[42]

---

[42]Chibuzo I. Nwanguma, "Re-Reading 'Living in Peace with our Neighbours' Rom. 12:17, 18) in the Light of Security Challenges in Nigeria" *Insight: Journal of Religious Studies*, Vol.10, (2014), 67

Looking at this study from the point of view of Paul's words in Romans 14:19 "… pursue the things which make for 'peace'" and Galatians 3:28 "There is neither Jew nor Greek…) in relation to peace, togetherness, and security issues in Nigeria," it will be necessary to say, from the very outset, that the selected passages are essentially all about relationships the Christian is expected to keep with those within and outside the Christian folds particularly, in context of this study. While one might think the passage is Pauline, it will be pertinent to state, from this onset, that the passage rests basically on the sayings of Jesus, known to Paul through oral traditions which Matthew eventually documented in the acclaimed Sermon on the Mount (Matt. 5-7). This was why this author, in another study on a related theme sees working on the subject matter as a challenging task especially in connection with "… the relative nature of the main key word in the title 'peace' and the same renders this work most herculean" particularly, when the statement of Jesus, "Peace I leave with you, my peace I give unto you, not as the world giveth, give I unto you" (John 14:27, KJV), comes to mind.[43] This statement, therefore, provides two distinct types of peace, namely, the world's peace, and Jesus' peace. The implication of this saying of the Lord which is evident across New Testament literature is the main task of this paper.

The Problem

As implied in the introduction above, one would wonder whether Nigerian peoples ever understood what they were embarking on before they declared themselves a people. This puzzle comes about when one ponders on the issue of "living in peace with neighbours" in the country where lives and properties of people are not safe in market place or places of worship for the sheer sake of belonging to a particular ethnicity or religion. Thus, men of mischief have virtually succeeded in using ethnicity and religion to make living in peace with neighbours almost impossible especially where petty misunderstanding that ensues between two members of different ethnicities or religions inadvertently, inter-ethnic or inter-religious quarrels or riots that end up claiming lives in tens, hundreds, or even thousands suddenly results. As one thinks about all these, a question like could such not be politically motivating quickly comes to mind. For instance, if it is not news of killing in churches or any public outfit capable of attracting multitudes of people and thereafter burning houses, it will

be that of Hausa-Fulani herdsmen encroaching upon people's farms, school compounds and even raping people's wives and daughters across the country. All these make peaceful co-existence very difficult if not impossible. Since April 2014, the Chybock girls' story has always been an uninterrupted headline news on national dailies that one would wonder the veracity of the saga especially, whether a political party is not using this to score political points? Wherever such abounds as case seems in Nigeria, one will hardly believe there is unity or peace.

Looking at the issue critically, the counsel of Paul in Romans 12:17-18 on "pursue the things which make for 'peace'" vis-à-vis other relevant passages in the Bible stimulated by studying the passage (Romans 14:19), particularly the New Testament passages, was considered very cogent for the problem especially given that Paul himself, as it were, lived like some of those involved in the mayhem live today (cf. Acts 9:4-6; 22:3-18). Certain underlying realities of the passage led to references to other relevant New Testament verses and the outcome constituted the thesis and conclusion of this paper.

The Word Peace: A Definition

The word peace could mean several things to different people. Basically, it can mean want of war or liberty from any form of upheaval. However, to some people, especially the average Nigerian, particularly among the Igbo, one will hardly talk about peace and forget about war. To such the raw material which peace producers take to peace factory is war during which the feelings and thinking of all as well as their abilities and capabilities would have been known. Could such be what Jesus had in mind when He said, "Peace I leave with you; my peace I give you, not as the world gives do I give to you. Let not your heart be troubled, neither let it be afraid" (John 14:27). However, He also said in another place that He never brought peace to the world but war…, that relatives would turn against their own for His sake (Matt. 10:34). Could this explain why the obvious challenges in religion world or what?

What then is Peace? Usually, the term could be defined as:

    a.   freedom from war, or the time when a war or conflict ends

---

[43] Ibid, 68

b. a calm and quiet state, free from disturbances or noise

c. a state of mental calm and serenity, with no anxiety

d. freedom from conflict or disagreement among people or groups of people

e. a treaty agreeing to an end of hostilities between two warring parties

f. the absence of violence or other disturbances within a state.

In the same vein, Dzurgba[44] defines it as freedom from quarrel, strife, conflict, rioting, disorder, hostility violence or war." He adds that "it is freedom from fear, anxiety, uncertainty disturbance or tension" and that "it is an atmosphere of calmness, security and safety."[45] These two definitions aptly represent the various definitions on this concept. Peace also includes "personal wholeness, soundness and wellbeing as well as general prosperity."[46] Common in the definitions is the frequent occurrence of the word "healthy" or "newly healed" interpersonal or international relationships, prosperity in matters of social or economic welfare, and the establishment of a working political order that serves the true interests of all. But, Vine approaching it from New Testament perspective, describes it as a) harmonious relationships between men (Matt. 10:34; Rom. 14:19), b) between nations (Luke 14:32; Acts 12:20), c) friendliness (Acts 15:33; 1 Cor. 16:11), d) freedom from molestation (Luke 11:21; Acts 9:31), order in the State (Acts 24:2), f) harmonized relationships between God and men accomplished through the Gospel (Acts 10:36; Eph. 2:17), and g) the sense of rest and contentment consequent thereon (Matt. 10:13; Mark 5:34; Rom 1:7; 3:17).[47] The correspondence between these definitions and the etymological terms *pax*, *shalom*, and *salaam* forces one to wonder what came over Nigeria and Nigerians especially, as one remembers the national anthem of the country and the last sentences of the stanzas in particular. This will be addressed later in this paper.

As earlier stated in the foregoing paragraph, the immediate ancestor of the word peace is *pax*,[48] a Latin word meaning "freedom from civil disorder." and our English word came into use in various personal greetings from c.1300 as a translation of the Hebrew *Shalom*. The translation is however, imprecise because the verb means a lot to the Jews. Primarily it means "to be safe or un-injured in mind or body (Job.8:6; 9:4)." Shalom can better be described thus:

> This word is normally used when God is keeping His people safe… it also means to be finished or to be completed …. Other meaning of this word could mean to be in peace with one another (Ps. 7:4-5), to make a treaty of peace (Joshua 11:19; Job 5:23).[49]

The word peace is a cognate term with the Arabic *Salaam*[50] with multiple other meanings as explained above. The New Testament word ei)rhvnh, *eir¢n¢*, means everything stated above except a state of concord, peace, harmony between governments, e)pwta~| ta^ pro\`$ ei)rhvnhn, *ep¢t¹ ta pros eir¢n¢n*, ("ask for terms of peace," Lk. 11:21), and harmony in personal relationships (Matt. 10:34).[51] One can deduct from all these that:

(a) Peace is all about total soundness, that is, soundness in all aspects of life viz. health, intra-personal and inter-personal relationships as well as social or economic matters or well-beings;

(b) Given that Christianity, Judaism, or Islam use or apply the word as a religious maxim

[44] A. Dzurgba, *Contemporary Ethics: Theories and Issues*, (Ibadan: John Archers (Publishers) Ltd, 2007), 36

[45] Ibid

[46] Chibuzo I. Nwanguma, "James' Concept of Wisdom (James 3:13-18): A Veritable Tool for Peace and Conflict Resolution in Nigerian?" *African Journal of Biblical Sties* Vol. XXXII, No 1 & 2 (2014), 186

[47] W. E. Vine, *Vine's Complete Expository Dictionary of Old and New Testament Words*, (London: Thomas Nelson Publishers, 1996), 464

[48] S. Zodhiates et al (eds.), *Hebrew-Greek Key Word Study Bible*, (Chattanooga: AMB Publishers, 2008), 2013

[49] An Unpublished anonymous writer whose work made much sense to this writer

[50] Ibid

[51] Fredrick W. Danker *A Greek-English Lexicon of the New Testament and other Early Christian Literature*, (3rd ed. Based on Walter Bauer's *Griech=Duetsches-Worterbuzu Den Schrieten Des Nuen Testaments Und Der Fruhchristlichen Literatur Sixth Edition ed. Kurt Aland Barbra Aland, with Victor Reichmann and on previous English ed. By W. F. Arndt, F. W. Gingrich and F. W. Danker*), Chicago: University Press (2000), 287

International Journal of Integrative Humanism Vol 9. No 1. June 2018. ISSN: 2026 – 6286

or dictum, the concept it portrays or communicates is both true and divine, and a necessity for human existence.

This could perhaps explain why the author of the later Nigerian national anthem makes reflection of it (peace) a concluding sentence in each of the two stanzas of the anthem. But the peace in Nigeria can only be better perceived in relative terms. The image is most apparent in the analogy of Bakut as he quotes Johan Galtung (1990 and 1996). Here peace is classified as 'negative' and 'positive'. In his words:

When peace is said to be 'negative', it means that the peace in existence includes only the absence of direct violence, war, fear and conflict at individual, national, regional and international levels. On the other hand, when peace is said to be positive, it means that peace in existence, in addition to the above, also includes the absence of unjust structures, unequal relationship, just and inner peace at individual level.[52]

The former rather than the latter in this citation is true of the kind of peace that exists in Nigeria. Better put, the peace that exists in Nigeria is far worse than the so-called negative peace and this is why Jesus' or Christians' perspective of the term neighbour and such will be attended to later in the study. However, if all will cooperate on the major things rather than on private ends and prejudices, peace and unity will tend to emerge rather than strife and disunity[53] because emphasizing the positive is an incomplete, but nonetheless fairly accurate, description of what can be done. Thus, if men aim at the great objects proposed by the Christian religion, they will live in peace. If they seek to promote their private ends, to follow their own passions and prejudices, they will be involved in strife and contention.

Leaving in Peace with Neighbours (Rom. 12:17-18): An Exegesis

The passage, in Greek text, reads thus:

17 mhdeniV kakoVn a)ntiV kakou~ a)podidovnte$, pronoouvmenoi kalaV e)nwvpion pavntwn a)nqrwvpwn:**18** ei) dunatoVn toV e)c u)mw~n, metaV pavntwn a)nqrwvpwn ei)rhneuvonte$|: (Rom 12:17-18)

As noted in the introduction, Paul in his narrative counsel, moved from relationships between believers to relationships with those who do not know God, who themselves may even be enemies of God as well as that of believers. In vs17a, for instance, he says mhdeniV kakoVn a)ntiˆ kakou~ a)podidovnte$ ("Do not repay anyone evil for evil"). While this gives no option to reason that is, thinking of the application of the *lex talionis* (an eye for an eye, a tooth for a tooth)[54] concept, going by the force of the verb a)podidovnte$ and a)ntiv, *apodidontes and* anti ("giving back," "instead of") and that of kakovn, and kakou~ ("bad") however, the remainder of the verse is open to more than one interpretation.[55] The believer is apparently left with the choice of reacting like any other person would want to do, but like Harrison and Hanger would put it, since Christians are constantly under the scrutiny of both the unsaved persons and fellow Christians, they must be careful with respect to what they do; their conducts must not betray the high standards of the gospel.[56] Again, the verb pronoew~, *pronoeœ* ("thinking of beforehand") which is translated "be careful" in NIV but literally translated "to think of beforehand," implying that the believers' conducts must not be regulated by the improper habits that characterize the conducts of the world, but that in all conditions, the actions of the believer must be such that reflect the gospel they preach and represent the body of the saints as worthy ambassadors of Christ.

With the conditional clause ei) dunatoVn toV e)c u)mw~n, ("If possible, so far as it depends on you") which entails that living in peace with people is dependent on one's ability v18, Paul ended this passage with an exhortation that is even more difficult to follow especially

---

[52] B. T. Bakut, "The Environment, Peace and Conflict in Africa" in. S. G. Best (ed.) *Introduction to Peace and Conflict Studies in West Africa*, (Ibadan: Spectrum Books Ltd., 2006), 235

[53] Martins G. Collins "Peace" Retrieved from the wed on Friday, 15th December, 2017, ttps://www.bibletools.org/index.cfm/fuseaction/Bible.show/sVer seI

[54] Solomon Andria, "Romans" in N. Weanzana and S. Ngewa (eds.), *Africa Bible Commentary Series*, (NC: Hippo Books, 2012), 232

[55] Everett F. Harrison and Donald A. Hanger, "Roman" in T. Longman III & D. E. Garland (eds.), *The Expositor's Bible Commentary* (rev Ed.), (Grand Rapids, Zondervan, 2008), 192

[56] Ibid

in context of hatred. Thus, the charge to live at peace with everyone is hedged about with two qualifying statements. The, if clause, as shall be seen below, implies that situations may arise when living in peace, ei)rhneuvonte$, (*eir¢neuontes*) with all may really be difficult or even impossible. Much will be extensively discussed on this in the subsequent segments below especially in the segment on the contextual interpretation. Whatever the position in the subsequent sections, however, the truth, nevertheless is, anything the believer is confronted with while on his pilgrimage journey here on earth now, either in Nigeria among the heathens and the Boko Haram insurgencies and attacks, or anywhere in the world, the hostility now may not be severer than what it was when the church had the emperors of Rome and the unfriendly Jews to contend with all over the empire when this counsel was given. If they could maintain their standards as believers amidst all odds, the present believers in Nigeria and anywhere could do better.

Christians' Perspective of the Word Neighbourliness: An Explanation

The Christians' perspective of neighbourhood actually came to the bear as Jesus their Lord, answered the question by "a certain lawyer" in Luke 10:25 as to what to do in order to inherit eternal life. Jesus' answer was simple, "what is written in the law? What is your reading of it?" (v26). By Luke's choice of the word "tested Him," one could see that the lawyer had idea of what to say but Jesus as a wise Teacher, would not fall into his trap. He rather chose to answer him the way He did. The lawyer's choice to answer Jesus' question from Deuteronomy 6:5 and Leviticus 19:18; and his follow-up question to Jesus brought about what one can rightly call the Christians' idea of neighbourhood.[57]

According to Gundry, this question of the lawyer "who is my neighbour" "attempts to draw Jesus into the rabbinic debate over whether the term 'neighbour' includes non-Pharisees and personal enemies."[58] Jesus, in His parable, decided not to answer this question the way the scribe expected it but perhaps put it right, "To whom can I be a neighbour?" because this latter question arises from an attitude which recognizes anyone in need as a neighbour.

The choice of such phrases like "a certain man from Jerusalem," a certain priest," "a Pharisee," and "a Samaritan" makes the discussion difficult for the lawyer. With respect to this, Gundry further writes that the Samaritan had equal reason to pass by the injured and possibly dead man, however, for Samaritans likewise avoided defilement from the dead – and perhaps even more reason, because chances were the victim was a detestable Jew. Consequently, when the Samaritan discovered the man was an injured Jew, he treated the wounds with indentation continues overleaf wine to disinfect them and olive oil to soothe them, tore bandages from his own turban or linen undergarments to wrap up the lesions, went on foot as the Jew rode the donkey (the slower pace exposing them to greater danger of further attacks by bandits), paid enough money to an innkeeper for two weeks of convalesce, and pledged unlimited credit for any expenses – all without hope of reimbursement since Samaritans had no legal rights in Jewish legal courts.[59]

Subsequently, the narrative vis-à-vis the parable of Jesus, a neighbour, contrary to the popular definition of "one of two or more people that are near one another," or "those living in the house next to mine," the term "neighbour" means one who is available to help at the time of need regardless the distance in race, or age, or place of abode. The person may be of different race, and can even often disagree with one with respect to either religious views or in general world-views. The summary of Jesus' parable on "who my neighbour is" is that everyone is a neighbour to as many as are willing to go His way.[60] The story however, is not only on neighbourhood but it includes Jesus' idea of love. This is shown in the question He asked the lawyer at the end of the parable and the answer which the lawyer by means of circumlocution answered, "The one who showed mercy on him" (Luke 10:37). Thus, religious persuasion, inclination or ethnicity of whatever, human beings made by God are precious to Him and anything done to assist anyone at any given time is of paramount importance to God. To the Christian, everyone regardless the faith or race is such that deserves the best attention at all times. The same is a neighbour.

---

[57]Chibuzo I. Nwanguma, "Re-Reading 'Living in Peace with our Neighbours', 70

[58] R. H. Gundry, *A Great Survey of the New Testament* (rev. ed.), (Grand Rapids: Zondervan Publishing House, ND), 156

[59] Ibid , 157

[60] T. Nelson, *The Word in Life Study Bible: Discover the Truths of God's Word for Your World*, (Nashville: Thomas Nelson Inc., ND), 258

Living Together in Peace with Neighbours: A Contextual Clarification

Basically, Paul's theme in the entire passage (Rom. 12:14-21) as one looks at it holistically, on a general note, is a focus on the Christians' commitment or service to the society both within and outside Christian community especially the latter. Christians are here exhorted to maintain good relations with non-Christians through praying for their welfare, empathy with their joys, sympathy with their sorrows, and respectful and forgiving attitudes towards them. According to Gundry, if non-Christians still practice persecution amidst the believers' favourable disposition towards them, "God Himself will judge them and vindicate His people (Rom. 12:14-21)."[61] In the light of this passage, especially vs. 19-21, Zodhiates et al, referring to one of the imprecatory Psalms, Psalm 109:1-29, assert that the Christian can decisively do something, at least, to pray that God should intervene and punish them. Contrary to the age long view that imprecation "was only proper in the Old Testament times … that New Testament grace demands that believers are never to pray in the manner to invoke the wrath of God upon the wicked", they start airing their view in this regard with this rhetoric question, "is not the command to love one's neighbour also found in the Old Testament (Ex. 23:4, 5; Prov. 20:22; 24:17)? Did not the Lord even then proclaim that vengeance is His (Deut. 32:35, of Rom. 12:19)?[62] They add

> In the same manner note that David, the author of most imprecatory prayers of the Old Testament, was unwilling to hurt Saul, one of his worst enemies, even when he was delivered into his hand. Even more convincing is the fact that there are instances of such imprecation in the New Testament (Acts 1:20; 5; 8:20-23; 13:10, 11; Rom. 11:9 (cf. Ps. 69:22, 23; 2Tim. 4:14).[63]

Further to the analogy of Zodhiates and his colleagues as regards imprecation with respect to the text under review is the implication of the lacuna in the first clause of vs. 18, "if it is possible, as much as depends on you" (NKJV). The clause certainly implies that the ability to bear or endure a pain varies from person to person, from time to time. What happens in a situation when while a party desires peace, the other does not seem to like the peace? The Lord's instruction to the disciples quickly comes to play here: "And when you go into a household, greet it, if the household is worthy, let your peace come upon it. But if it is not worthy, let your peace return to you" (Matt. 10:11-13). One can only live in peace with his neighbour as much as he can - only to the extent of his ability. Again, if the statement of Jesus in Matthew 5:39b is literally read, the common interpretation is non-retaliation but if closely examined in context of this topic, one is left with the responsibility to use his initiatives. There could be need for instant justice by the recipient especially if the slapping reoccurs after the second slap. The reason is particularly because the Lord did not say what should happen after the slap on the other check. Discretion is ultimately needed before the slapper kills the individual.

While the Christian will hardly be advised to strike back, the silence of the Lord with respect to what happens after the strike on the second cheek calls for discussion. The principle of natural justice and of course self-defense or self-protection is hereby implied. The slap receiver has right to either run away, call out for help or defend himself. To this Nelson would say "… some circumstances call for resistance and self-defense. The Law specifically sanctioned self-protection when there was no other apparent recourse (Ex. 22:2). Likewise, Jesus Himself protested when slapped (John 18:22-23)."[64] While no one has the right to take laws into his hands, it will also be nice to note in this connection that Jesus did not totally deny principle of *lex talionis* (law of retaliation). Against modern popular misunderstanding, the *lex talionis* safeguarded justice by not allowing excessive punishment as well as by insisting on punishment; Jesus' instruction to "go two miles" instead of "one mile" in Matthew 5:41 is one of His characteristic way of ensuring peace and one of His hyperboles as opines Gundry.[65]

Bringing this to the context of our discussion, it is on record that several peace talks have taken place between Islamic leaders who have always claimed non-party to what have been happening and the Christian leaders who have been at the receiving end of the mayhem to no avail. For instance, Isidore Nwanaju dedicated a section of his six hundred and thirty-five-page book *Christian-Muslim Relation in Nigeria* in which details of the several efforts

---

[61] R. H. Gundry, op cit, 283
[62] Zodhiates et al, op cit, 1088
[63] Ibid

[64] T. Nelson, op cit., 28
[65] R. H. Gundry, op cit., 138

on this issue were well documented.[66] If the Muslim leaders know nothing about the happenings and peace talk with them seems to yield no result, peace talk is therefore out of the approach. The issue on ground is that of terrorism, and the people involved are not known. Their demand is what no one can grant them..., that Nigeria should be Islamised.[67] One will therefore be right, at this juncture, to adjudge Ahiamadu right when he said that obedience to Divine instructions in Nigeria would be difficult "because of a diversity of loyalties to various divinities ... Hence, the question of the quality of justice and peace inherent in Nigerian has been an elusive one ..."[68] as one looks at the issue holistically. For instance, a statement credited to Abubakar Shekau, leader of Boko Haram in 2012, according to Nigerian Christian Elders Forum (NCEF) at a meeting in reference to Boko Haram insurgency and Fulani Herdsmen harassment across the country demanding some explanations from the Muslim leaders who claim that those groups are none Islamic sects, reads thus:

> It is between Muslim and unbelievers (arna). It will stop when Islamic religion is the determinant in governance in Nigeria or, in the alternative, when all fighters are annihilated and no one is left. I warn all Muslims at this juncture that any Muslim who assists an unbeliever in this war should consider himself dead.[69]

It then becomes necessary to advise that:

1. Christians or Nigeria cannot seek peace with them because they are not neighbours by all standards of Christian neighbourhood and neighbourliness as already explained above.
2. Christians cannot take laws into their hands by fighting back because the Bible especially in New Testament does not encourage such.
3. The Government should use its agencies to fight such an ungodly position to a halt because it has the capacity to do so both as empowered by the constitution and the scriptures (Rom. 13:1-7).[70] Thus, they should come out of their hidings and get the issues resolved.

Nonetheless, it seems the government itself is highly handicapped in this regard. Why? From all indications, the probability is high that virtually all in government are the progenitors of corruptions and terrorisms in the society. Thus, asking them (those in government) to fight or forestall them (the terrorists and corrupt practices) is like telling one to dissolve an institution he constituted which is practically impossible. Consequently, the resort is prayer for God's intervention in His own way; for only Him can overthrow the wicked the way He does (Hag. 2:22). In history, He brought Pharaoh and his army down and saved His people (Ex. 14:25-31), He dethroned Saul (1 Sam 13:13-14; 15:22-23), He sent Nebuchadnezzar to the animal kingdom for a long while (Dan 4:31-33) and brought his dynasty down (Dan 5:25-31). He also had Herod eaten up by worms while alive till he died (Acts 12:21-23). All these He did in His own way. In any of the cases, humankind was freed: this is why His intervention is just very urgent in Nigerian case and Nigeria must be freed.

At whatever level of government, its responsibility is essentially to protect the citizens and maintain peace and order, and since this is not in place, the cry of Nigerians is God, send us the Messiah. This is particularly because the concept of self-defense is not necessary in the context of Nigerian Security Challenge. The reason is essentially because those involved in the act are non-visible, and they are generally seen to represent a people or even a government. They have made Lebanon non-governable and are trying to overthrow the government of Nigeria.

Conclusion and Recommendation

In conclusion, this work was poised to address the issue of peaceful co-existence in Nigeria taking cue from the counsel of St Paul on "Living in Peace with our

---

[66] Isidore Nwanaju, *Christian-Muslim Relations in Nigeria*, (Lagos: Free Enterprise Publishers, 2005), 324-501
[67] Ola Ojo, a discussion on the subject matter, Ajebo on 19th June 2017.
[68] Amadi E. Ahiamadu, "Justice and Peace Exemplified by the Gibeonites (Josh. 9-10): Implications for Sustainable Peace in Nigeria," *African Journal of Biblical Studies*, Vol. XXXII, No 1 & 2 (2014), 79

[69] Nigerian Christian Elders Forum, "Islamisation: Nigeria on Theories of Jihad" a Meeting by the Sect consisting of Several Christian Leaders on the looming Jihad in Nigeria, Vanguard News, 11th September, 2017 (Posted to My MTN Line)
[70] Chibuzo I. Nwanguma, "Re-Reading 'Living in Peace with our Neighbours', 73

Neighbours" in his Romans account as stated in chapter twelve, verses seventeen and eighteen vis-à-vis other relevant Biblical passages stimulated during the work basically in the New Testament. Generally, it was established that the peace that is prevalent in Nigeria was a negative or partial one in the sense that it is such that exists to avoid obvious trouble and such has been in existence for as long as one can remember. Thus, the study revealed, it has been persistent essentially due to the nefarious activities of mischief makers among some influential men in the country who have consistently taken undue advantage of the ignorant and indigent idle youths to create avoidable troubles in the society using the tools of ethnic sentiments and religious bigotries which they know are glaring in the nation. As indicated above, such has been on for as long as one can remember, perhaps, right from the early days of the country. It was also deduced that the issue has been such that has defied several peace and conflict resolution solutions so far engaged to curb the menace.

To address this issue, more working concerted efforts have to be made by leaderships and members of the two main groups, religion and ethnic regions, identified in the course of this study as the most susceptible to those vicious men who for selfish interests have not ceased to use them to foment troubles in the country. In the first instance, it will be advisable that the leaders be told that they have to be sincere to themselves in intra-religious as well as intra-ethnic matters, and in inter-religious issues as well as inter-ethnic matters. This is important because only sincerity can help to solve the problems especially given that the activities of most of these leaders have gotten to the point that one begins to suspect that they are allies and cronies of the mischief makers identified in the study. The second advice is more like the first. Let them, the leaders, cultivate the habit of telling their followers the truth and nothing but the truth and this will certainly frustrate the evil activities of the selfish influential men who use their followers to perpetuate their vices. The third thing to look at is the issue of job and wealth creations so as to empower especially the youths who have always been used to do all the evils. Also, there is the need of educating the youths on insisting on seeing the children and relatives of elites joining them in the mayhem the former would want them to embark on. Of course, what will make such insistence worthwhile is job or wealth creations. Above all, the Christian leaders in particular should necessarily consider prayer therapy. This writer strongly believes that the main cause of all these are some spiritual forces. The same Paul suggested such in another letter of his, "Put on the whole armour of God, that you may stand the wiles of the devil. For we are not contending against flesh and blood, but against the principalities, against the powers, against the world rulers of this present darkness, against the spiritual hosts of wickedness in the heavenly places" (Eph. 6:11-12, RSV). The issue has gotten to the point that one has to resort to prayers and chances abound that such brings about the desired results.

Bibliography

Ahiamadu, A. E., "Justice and Peace Exemplified by the Gibeonites (Josh. 9-10): Implications for Sustainable Peace in Nigeria," *African Journal of Biblical Studies*, Vol. XXXII, No 1 & 2 (2014)

Andria, S., "Romans" in N. Weanzana and S. Ngewa (eds.), *Africa Bible Commentary Series*, (NC: Hippo Books, (2012)

Bakut, B. T., "The Environment, Peace and Conflict in Africa" in S. G. Best (ed.) *Introduction to Peace and Conflict Studies in Africa*, Ibadan: Spectrum Books Ltd. (2006)

Dzurgba, A., *Contemporary Ethics: Theories and Issues*, Ibadan: John Archers (Publishers) Ltd (2007)

Gundry, R. H. *A Great Survey of the New Testament* (rev. ed.), (Grand Rapids: Zondervan Publishing House (ND)

Harrison, E. F. and Hanger, D. A., "Roman" in T. Longman III & D. E. Garland (eds.), *The Expositor's Bible Commentary* (rev Ed.), Grand Rapids: Zondervan (2008)

Martins, G. C., "Peace" ttps://www.bibletools.org/index.cfm/fuseaction/Bible.show/sVerseI (2017)

Nelson, T., *The Word in Life Study Bible: Discover the Truths of God's Word for Your World*, Nashville: Thomas Nelson Inc. (ND)

Nigerian Christian Elders' Forum, "Islamisation: Nigeria on Theories of Jihad" a Meeting by a Sect consisting of Several Christian Leaders on the looming Jihad in Nigeria, Vanguard News, 11th September 2017 (Posted to My MTN Line)

Nwanaju, I., *Christian-Muslim Relations in Nigeria*, Lagos: Free Enterprise Publishers (2005)

International Journal of Integrative Humanism Vol 9. No 1. June 2018. ISSN: 2026 – 6286

Nwanguma, C. I. "James' Concept of Wisdom (James 3:3-13): A Veritable Tool for Peace and Conflict Resolution in Nigeria?" *African Journal of Biblical Studies*, Vol. XXXII, No. 1 & 2 (2014)

Nwanguma, C. I., "Reading 'Living in Peace with our Neighbours' (Rom. 12:17-18) in the Light of Security Situation in Nigeria, *Insight: Journal of Religious Studies*, Vol. 10, (2014)

Ojo, O., A discussion on the subject matter at Ajebo in Ogun State, Western Nigeria on 19th June 2017.
Vine, W. E., *Vine's Complete Expository Dictionary of Old and New Testament Works*, London: Thomas Nelson Publishers (1996)

Zodhiates, S. et al (Eds.), *Hebrew-Greek Key Word Study Bible*, Chattanooga: AMB Publishers (2008)

Okon E. Etim (Ed). Igbo Traditional Religion, Culture and Security. Calabar: Afri Penticost Press, 2016.

Onwa Anibe, R. "The Human Person and Immortality in Igbo Metaphysics. *In African Philosophy*. Ed. R. A. Wright. New York: University Press of America, 1984.

Ozumba, G. O. *A Colloquium on African Philosophy*. Calabar: Jochrisam Publishers, 2004.

Uka, Emele M. *"The Theology of African Traditional religion"* in *African Traditional Religion and Philosophy*. Ed. Etim. E. Okon. Calabar: University of Calabar Press, 2013.

Zecariah, Aleyanma. *Modern Religious and Secular Movements in India*. Bangalore: Theological Book Trust, 2003.

International Journal of Integrative Humanism Vol 9. No 1. June 2018. ISSN: 2026 – 6286

Towards Effective Deployment of Theatrical Performance to Address Anti-Social Behaviours In Ahmadu Bello University, Zaria

Imoh Obot Sunday PhD

Email: imohobot2000@gmail.com

&

Ogakason, Rasheed Oshoke

Department of Theatre and Performing Arts, Ahmadu Bello University (ABU), Zaria

Email: rashmanson@yahoo.com

Abstract

Theatrical performance is one of the tools deployed to address social issues in Nigeria. However, the trend in the university today shows that the university community is not fully benefitting from the efficacy of theatrical performances to address anti-social behaviours among students. The aim of this study was to investigate the extent of use of theatrical performance to address anti-social behaviours in Ahmadu Bello University with the view to adopting same by the university authority as one of the instruments to address student's anti-social behaviours on campus and also possible militating factors. Relevance Theory by Paul Grice was used. Survey research design was deployed and the population included undergraduate students of Ahmadu Bello University, Zaria. It was established that theatrical performances are occasionally enacted as measures to discourage students from involving themselves in anti-social behaviours during orientation programmes and during special events. These performances were not enough to adequately address anti-social behaviours among students. The study recommended that the University authorities need to consciously deploy performances to address anti-social behaviours and factors militating against the deployment of theatrical performances should be addressed with the view to making frantic improvements in strengthening the essence of theatre practice, especially in the area of providing adequate funding.

Keywords: Effective Deployment, Theatrical Performance, Anti-social Behaviours and Ahmadu Bello University.

Introduction

The use of theatrical performance to address social issues in Nigerian universities is becoming a topical issue (Ayakoroma, 2013). Although university has been the custodian of theatre practice as a discipline since its inception in University of Ibadan much of it use has been in outside communities and necessary within the university community. These is perhaps because, it is largely seen as an academic exercise and even community theatre, which is part of the courses offered in theatre departments is seen in that light. This to a large extent has limited the relevance of theatre especially in its bid to address social issues.

Theatre was introduced intoNigerian University as a course of study in the University of Ibadan in 1961, for manpower development and capacity building in various areas of theatre making such as acting, stagecraft, directing, play writing, music and set design. In view of this, it can be deduced that it was not primarily designed to address social issues especially within the university community. Over the years, society evolved and theatre as a discipline embraced several new dynamics, and University lecturers began to deployed theatre as an instrument of social change in form of Theatre for Development (TFD) and Community Theatre (CT), encouraging governments, development agencies and NGOs to embrace it in their development projects. To corroborate this, Olalekan, Akashoro, and Shaibu (2010:107) state that "there exists an obsession among theatre and literary scholars to prove that theatre, whether in the literary or performative form has a contribution to make to the development of the society".

In spite of these achievements, it seems that the university theatre is yet to effectively accommodate contemporary realities especially in deploying it to address numerous social challenges within the university community such as students' anti-social behaviour. Amongst measures taken by the university authorities to address students' anti-social behaviours, the prominence of theatre is uncertain (Ayakoroma, 2012). This paper examined the deployment of theatrical performance to address students' anti-social behaviours in Ahmadu Bello University, Zaria (ABU). It also identified possible militating factors that hamper it usage.

Conceptualising Anti-social Behaviours in Nigerian Universities:

Okeshola andAdeta (2013:99) assert that "anti-social behaviours are actions which can affect academic processes, social order and relationships among members of the university community and have widely and wildly crystallised into one of the contemporary problems on hand". Anti-social behaviours in Nigerian universities include: cultism, drug addiction, examination malpractice, robbery, stealing, obscene dressing, sexual promiscuity, rape, and falsification of results" (Amaele, 2013:32).

Anti-social behaviours in no small measure violate the norms and values of tertiary education especially the university which include contributing to national development through high level relevant manpower training; developing and inculcating proper values for the survival of the individual and society; developing the intellectual capability of individuals to understand and appreciate their local and external environments; acquiring both physical and intellectual skills which will enable individuals to be self-reliant and useful members of the society; promoting and encouraging scholarship and community service; forging and cementing national unity; and promoting national and international understanding and interaction (Nwabueze1992:1).

These menaces to a large extent have contributed to reducing the quality of university education in Nigeria. Cultism leads to rustication or expulsion of guilty students and outburst of violence on campus which might leave many students wounded, maimed or killed. Drug abuse leads to madness in most cases if not properly handled, loss of sensory perception, low retentive memory and above all it can act as a motivating factor to criminality. In the same vein, examination malpractice invariably leads to churning out of half-baked graduates and making it difficult for Nigerian students to study abroad, reason being that the western countries have lost confidence in our educational system.

In reaction to the devastating effect of anti-social behaviours in Nigerian universities, various university authorities have deployed several measures to address the issue. A cursory look at these measures is important for this paper. It has been observed that stringent security measures have been put in place in most universities to checkmate entry by fake students. In order to curb examination malpracticesthe use of Identification Card (ID) has been enforced and can make it difficult for "ghost' or "mercenary" to have easy entrance (Amale, 2013). Also, creation of disciplinary committees/panels of enquiry is found in Nigerian universities to screen and verify academic documents, thesis and dissertation, with the purpose of prescribing punishable measures such as expulsion, rustication and suspension to defaulters.

Furthermore, the use of Information, Education and Communication material (IEC)such as flyers, posters, billboards and display boards is fast becoming prominent in Nigerian university campuses. A few examples billboards have been observed in Ahmadu Bello University campuses (Samaru and Kongo) with various messages against cultism, sexual immorality, drug addiction and indecent dressing.

Also, worthy of mention is that university security units have had to collaborate with leaders and vigilantes of local communities where tertiary institutions are situated in order to assist by providing genuine information about individuals and groups whose activities are questionable (Amale, 2013). This is because the security measures have become stringent on campuses and that makes cultist to relocate to nearby communities. One of such measures taken by Ahmadu Bello University in 2012 was the introduction of *"Local Hunters"*. The former Vice Chancellor of Ahmadu Bello University, **Professor Abdullahi Mustapha, in**an interview stated that: "We are using local hunters to fight cultism. Even if there are cultists now, they don't operate in the university because of the activities of the hunters who trace them to all their hideouts" (Daily Trust, 2012).

Despite these measures, eradicating anti-social behaviours on university campuses is far from actualization. Against this backdrop, scholars have provided theories to explain this situation. Sub-Culture Theory states that wherever a subculture is allowed to develop, eradicating it becomes extremely difficult because it becomes rooted in some way in every new generation. The Nigerian experience suggests that these three theories are indicative of the causes of cultism. The only issue of concern with respect to the political economy theory is the notion of equality in society. The theory seems to suggest that without equality, which itself means different things to different people, cultism will always exist (Amaele, 2013).

Furthermore, Differential Association Theory formulated by Edwin Sutherland in 1939 proposed that through interaction with others, individuals learn the values, attitudes, techniques and motives for criminal behaviour. According to this theory, the environment plays a major role in deciding which norms people learn to violate. To corroborate this assertion, Amaele (2013) asserts that:

> The principle of differential association asserts that a person becomes delinquents because of an "excess" of definitions favourable to violation of law over definitions unfavourable to violation of law. What this means is that an individual will become a criminal because they are exposed to more favourable criminal behaviour. In other word, criminal behaviour emerges when one is exposed to more social message favouring misconduct than pro – social messages. This can be seen in environments with poor socio-economic conditions which may encourage negative views towards the law and authority.

Form the above statement, it could be deduced that criminal behaviour is learned, it is learned in interaction with other persons in a process of communication. This would mean an individual is influenced to participate in criminal behaviour through watching and interacting with other individuals who are engaging in the criminal behaviour. The principal part of the learning of criminal behaviour occurs within intimate personal groups. When criminal behaviour is learned, the learning includes techniques of committing the crime, which are sometimes very complicated, sometimes simple and they learn the specific direction of motives, drives, rationalizations and attitudes for committing a crime.

Conceptualising Theatrical Performance as an Instrument for Social Change

The use of theatrical performance to address social issues is not a recent practice (Brocket, Oscar, and Ball). Theatre has been a viable medium of communication, expression and intervention especially addressing or facilitating diverse cultural, political, moral, economic and developmental issues in the world. According to Umukoro (2008:47):

> Theatre is perceived to be a miniature model of society. Succinctly put, it is a microcosm of an identifiable society. It functions basically like a mirror in reflecting images within its environment. The impact of performance and theatre as a whole is incontestable. The use of theatre for conscientization and change haveexisted over the years.

From the above, it is important to note that the determining factor as to the relevance of a theatrical performance is its ability to communicate effectively and in view of this, Umenyilorah (2014:34) asserts that:

> Performances are designed to pass across a particular message to the audience through verbal and non-verbal means; even in cases of entertainment, the underlying aim is to send a message. In view of the above, theatrical performances is a means of communicating messages to the people. Because of the strength of the theatre and theatrical performances, Playwrights have written plays to address several nagging issues in the society such as: gender, politics, religious crises, ethnicity, unity and need for peaceful coexistence. Examining a few of these plays is imperative.

In the same vein, Jegede (2014:38) asserts that theatre is:

> A research-driven approach for promoting and sustaining behaviour change in individuals and communities, and is implemented through the development and distribution of specific healthy and robust messages via a variety of communication channels.

Consequently, theatrical performance is a research driven approach that has been used over time to achieve social change in the society. It is important to note that the use of theatrical performance to address social issues is not a recent practice. Theatre has been a viable medium of communication, expression and intervention especially addressing or facilitating diverse cultural, political, moral, economic and developmental issues in the world (Abah, 1984). Thus, the affinity between theatre and society is both strong and cordial. As far back as the Greek era, theatrical performance constituted part of religious worship, expression of civic pride and indication of cultural superiority (Brocket &Oscar). However, the use of theatre for social change as assumed other nomenclature, such as Community Theatre (CT) or Theatre for Development (TFD). Nonetheless, the essence remains the same: driving community development. These are forms of theatre, particularly evolved from the university, where theatre practitioners avail their theatrical skills to assist communities to rise above their economic, development, social and cultural challenges (Abah, 1984).

Ahmadu Bello University and Theatre Practice

Ahmadu Bello University has been one of the proponents of the concept of theatre for community development. The history of theatre as a discipline in Ahmadu Bello University (ABU) is that of a balance between academic theatre and theatre for social development (Dandaura,2014). This means that apart from theatre studies, theatre scholars and practitioners have used theatre for community development purposes. For example, Samaru Theatre Project and Community Theatre, a form of theatre for conscientization began in 1976 at the Ahmadu Bello University, Zaria, by a group, known as the ABU Collective. The group comprised Michael Etherton and Brian Crow, and Nigerian theatre artists, such as Salihu Bappa, Steve Oga Abah and Tunde Lakoju. These theatre practitioners were determined to avail their theatre skills to addressing the community problems that beset Zaria. Since then, the work of theatre practitioners in ABU have contributed to the evolution of Theatre-for- Development field in Africa as most or other workshops adopted the ABU methodology (Dandaura,2014).

The practice of theatre for social change is predicated on psychological immediacy which is one of the strengths of theatre. This means that there is a living presence of the actors and the audience within a performance environment.

Actors and members of the audience have the opportunity of influencing on another. Also, theatre draws from the interactive relationship of performers and spectators (Brockett and Ball, 1998) and that makes it being three-dimensional in natureAyakoroma (2012). These qualities, make theatrical performances fully packed with diverse potentials that if properly deployed can enhance behaviour change.

Similarly, theatre is therapeutic in nature; meaning that it is capable of correcting students who have been involved in one form of anti-social behaviours or the other; that is, if the university disciplinary committee decides not to punish them by rustication or suspension. For instance, a cult member may be subjected to playing different roles in a theatrical performance that depicts some of the cult activities. By playing such roles, those students can see themselves in different lights. Also, while playing such role (character), he might be surprised or ashamed that he participated in such acts. This is considered as a window of purgation that can go a long way in providing an opportunity for such students to re-examine their conducts in the university. Thus, marking the beginning of the journey to behaviour change.

The Concept of Relevance Theory

Relevance Theory was propounded by Paul Grice in 1989. It states that "language communication is not an encoding and decoding process alone, but more importantly, a conduct of getting inferences from context" (Grice, 1989). The first principles of this theory is that a communicator or performer seeks the attention of an audience (viewer) by indicating that the communication or performance is relevant to the audience's interest. It means that human cognition tends to be geared to the maximization of relevance. Thus, the communicative dimension of this theory is that a performance gets its optimal relevance when it is germane enough to be worth working on; and moreover, when it is the most relevant utterance that the performer is willing and able to perform.

Secondly, Relevance Theory further stipulates that meanings must be interpreted within a context. This implies that a performance should be put in context or be situated within what is realistic and contemporary in the society whereby the audience can relate to as they experience the performance. Thus, the effectiveness of a medium to communicate and live up to expectation. Its essence is measured by its ability to remain relevant to the society. Grice's emphasis of relevance is pivotal to communication (Grice 1989).

Data Presentation and Analysis

To examine the deployment of theatrical performance in Ahmadu Bello University to and the militating factors in addressing anti-social behaviours among students380 copies of the questionnaire were administered to undergraduate students of Ahmadu Bello University, Zaria and 373 copies were retrieved. Therefore, this analysis was based on the duly filled and returned copies of 373 questionnaire.

Table 1: Respondents' Socio-Demographic Characteristics in Ahmadu Bello University, Zaria

S/N	Variable	Characteristics	Frequency	Percentage (%)
1.	Sex	Male	204	(54.7)
		Female	169	(45.3)
		Total	**373**	**(100.0)**
2.	Age	15-20	125	(33.5)
		21-26	202	(54.2)
		27-32	46	(12.3)
3.	Faculty	**Total**	373	100.0
		Education	13	(3.5)
		Environmental Sciences	72	(19.3)
		Law	59	(15.8)
		Medical Sciences	26	(7.0)
		Natural Sciences	24	(6.4)
		Pharmaceutical Sciences	17	(4.6)
		Social Sciences	34	(9.1)
		Management Sciences	16	(4.3)
		Engineering	38	(10.2)
		Veterinary Medicine	33	(8.8)
		Agriculture	13	(3.5)
		Total	**373**	**(100.0)**
4.	Level	100	110	(29.5)
		200	99	(26.5)
		300	114	(30.6)
		400	50	(13.4)
		Total	**373**	**(100.0)**
5.	**Attended Performance**	Yes	170	(45.6)
		No	203	(54.4)
		Total	**373**	**(100.0)**

Source: Researcher's Field Survey, 2016

Table 1 above shows that 57.4% of the respondents were male while 45.3% respondents were female. 54.2% of the respondents were in the age bracket of 21-26. Also, majority of the respondents representing 30.6% were students in 300 levels followed by 29.5% from 100 level cutting across the respective departments and faculties.

45.6% of the respondents admitted that they had attended theatrical performance in the university theatre while 54.4% said that they had never attended. This implied that more students had not attended performance and there was a need to increase the level of awareness. It also shows that majority of the students who did not attend were from 100 level.

Table 2: The use of Performances to Address Anti-social Behaviours in Ahmadu Bello University, Zaria.

S/no	Features	Degree of Agreement				Total (%)
		Strongly Agree (%)	Agree (%)	Disagree (%)	Strongly Disagree (%)	
1	During orientation programme for new students	146 (39.1)	143 (38.3)	14 (3.8)	70 (18.8)	373 (100.0)
2	During academic/workshop Performances	178 (47.7)	77 (20.6)	70 (18.8)	48 (12.9)	373 (100.0)
3.	During special events where performances are enacted for commemoration	187 (50.1)	108 (29.0)	78 (20.9)	00 (0.0)	373 (100.0)

Source: Researcher's Field Survey, 2016

Table 2 showed that 146 respondents, representing 39.1% strongly agreed and 143 respondents representing 38.3% agreed that performances addressed issues of anti-social behaviours during orientation programmes. Also, 178 respondents (47.7%) strongly agreed and 77 respondents (20.6%) agreed that performances during academic/workshop performances were also instances that performances were deployed to address anti-social behaviours on campus. In the same vein, 187 respondents representing 50.1%strongly agreed and 108 (29.0%) agreed that performances to commemorate special occasions also addressed anti-social behaviours among students.

Table 3: Factors Militating against the Deployment of Theatrical Performance to Address Students' Anti-social Behaviours in Ahmadu Bello University, Zaria.

S/no	Features	Degree of Agreement				Total (%)	Mean	Remarks
		Strongly Agree (%)	Agree (%)	Disagree (%)	Strongly Disagree (%)			
1	The use of theatrical performance is limited to academic functions	72 (19.3)	144 (38.6)	100 (26.8)	57 (15.3)	373 (100.0)	2.6	**Agree**
2	Over reliance on Coercive instead of behaviour change approach	73 (19.6)	194 (52.0)	41 (11.0)	65 (17.4)	373 (100.0)	2.7	**Agree**
3	The use of theatrical performances outside academic function as distraction	49 (13.1)	167 (44.8)	116 (31.1)	41 (11.0)	373 (100.0)	2.6	**Agree**
4.	Poor funding to enact performances to address social issues on campus	124 (33.2)	124 (33.2)	40 (10.7)	57 (15.3)	373 (100.0)	2.9	**Agree**

Source: Researcher's Field Survey, 2016

On factors militating against the deployment of theatrical performance, 38% of the respondents and 19% agreed and

strongly agreed respectively that the use of theatre was limited to academic exercise. Also, 52% of the respondents and 19% of the respondents agreed and strongly agreed that direct involvements of university security, religious institutions, guidance/counselling, and the disciplinary committees contributed to the underutilization of theatrical performance as measure to address anti-social behaviours on campus. Furthermore, 48% of the respondents agreed and 13% strongly agreed that adding the use of theatrical performances to encourage social change to the curriculum was capable of bringing about some form of distraction to academic exercise. In the same vein, 124 of the respondents 33.2% strongly agreed and 124 representing 33.2% agreed that non- provision of funds to enact extracurricular performances with focus on social change can limit the use of theatrical performance to address anti-social behaviours among students.

Findings revealed that 77.4% of the respondents agreed that it was during orientation programmes for incoming students that theatrical performances were officially deployed to advice students to refrain from anti-social behaviours on campus Apart from this period, other theatrical performances were for academic purposes. Furthermore, findings show that 63.3% of the respondents agreed that academic workshop performances were helpful in addressing anti-social behaviours among students. Although, the intention of the workshop performances was not to address anti-social behaviours but to teach students. It was further revealed that, theatre curriculum, in the universities under study stipulates that each level (100-400 levels) present play performances at the end of each semester and these performances were publicised for audience to watch and the choice of plays were mainly for academic exercise as earlier said.

Performances enacted to commemorate special events in the universities under study occurred occasionally. Usually, the university authority is at liberty to draft the department of Theatre and Performing Arts into creating a performance to mark such occasions. The performance could be an improvisation or an existing play. In this regard, findings revealed that such performances were not enacted for the purpose of addressing anti-social behaviours in the real sense of it. In view of this, it means that the use of theatrical performance to address anti-social behaviours among students was grossly inadequate.

On the aspect of factors responsible for in-effective deployment of theatrical performance to address anti-social behaviours, it was found that theatre was primarily restricted to academic functions was mentioned. It could be deduced that in holding tenaciously to this assertion, the aspect of community development initiative of theatre would be considered as secondary or non-existent. However, it is a known fact that the primary purpose of theatre as an academic discipline in the university is to impact theatrical knowledge to students. In so far as theatre is set primarily to achieve academic purpose, consciously or unconsciously, it addresses anti-social behaviours and social ills in the society. Therefore, both academic and social purposes are achievable at the same time.

Furthermore, 71.6% of respondents accepted that since the university authorities have adopted measures such as internal security and have setup disciplinary committees to punish students who indulge in various anti-social behaviours, among others, it was needless to also co-opt the department of Theatre and Performing Arts into the mainstream process. To a large extent, this could serve as one of the major reasons why the university authorities have not particularly repositioned theatre to be integrated as one of the measures to address anti-social behaviours. It is important to note that deploying coercive measures alone is not enough to address anti-social behaviours; a blend of coercive and persuasive measures can achieve more results and arguably, theatre is an effective persuasive measure in this regard.

In addition, poor funding was also considered as a militating factor against the use of theatrical performance to address anti-social behaviours among students. It is important to note that for the department of Theatre and Performing Arts to enact more performances, adequate funding is required. Findings showed that 67% of the respondents attested to the fact that poor funding was a major factor militating against the use of theatrical performance to address anti-social behaviours among students.

So far, findings have revealed that the use of theatrical performance to address anti-social behaviours among students in the universities under study is grossly inadequate. Based on the high level of awareness in the university community as a result of the impacts it has generated over time which clearly shows that theatrical performance has the capacity to bring about social change if effectively deployed. This being the case, it therefore connotes that theatrical performance is relevant and recognised in ABU in line with Paul Grice's Relevance theory, which says that the essence of a discipline is measured by its ability to remain relevant to that society in terms of what is communicated, how it is communicated and why is it communicated. It also means that the audience understand the mode of communication. That means there is the process of coding and decoding; the process of sending and receiving. Further explanation can be given that a performance gets its optimal relevance when it is relevant enough to be worth working on and moreover, when the performer is willing and able to perform.

Conclusion

It is important to note that the university authorities have not consciously deployed theatrical performances to address anti-social behaviours or other social challenges within the university community. The use of theatrical performance in whatever platform in the university is for academic purpose, even the community development projects (community theatre) that students carry out as part of their field works and workshops are on the basis of capacity building and manpower development. In view of this, the potentials of theatre are not fully harnessed. Therefore, since society has moved on and theatre as a discipline has evolved, it is imperative for the university authorities to find new expression for theatre to thrive. This is where the relevance of theatre lies in a world that is overtly result oriented. Therefore, the University authorities need to consciously deploy performances to address anti-social behaviours and also factors militating against the deployment of theatrical performances should be addressed with the view to making frantic improvements in strengthening the essence of theatre practice, especially in the area of providing adequate funding.

Reference

Abah, O. (1984). The *Points of Divergence in the Samaru Project: A Paper Presentation*. Zaria: Department of Theatre and Performing Arts, Ahmadu Bello University, Zaria, Nigeria.

Amaele, S. (2008). *Cultism in Tertiary Institutions in Nigeria*. Ilorin: Indemac Print Media.

Ayakoroma, B. F. (2012). Theatre Practice in Nigeria: To be or not to be? Being a Paper Delivered at the *International Theatre Day (ITD)* at the Cyprian Ekwensi Cultural Centre, Abuja-Nigeria.

Brocket, Oscar G. (1980). *The Essential Theatre*. New York: Holt Reinhart and Winston.

Communication Technologies (2013). ICTs in a Private Christian Mission University, Southern Nigeria. *African Journal of Business Management.7.31:*3078-3089.

Dandaura, E. (2011). The Transmutations of Development Theories and Theatre for Development Interventions: In: ResearchgateEvolution of Development Theories and Theatre for Development Interventions. (2011). Retrieved 20 October, 2017 from https://www.researchgate.net/publication/2581069 98

Grice, H. P. (1989). *Studies in the Way of Words*. Cambridge MA: Harvard University Press.

Jegede, E. (2014), The Heart of Change: Communication and Communication Use in *PATHS 2 and UNICEF in Nigeria*. PhD Thesis, ABU Zaria.

Nwabueze, N. (1992). *The Nature of Social Problems and Social Policy*. In: Nwabueze, N., and Oyekanmi, F. D. (Eds). *Social Problems and Social Policy in Nigeria*. Lagos: Osko Associates, University Theatres in Nigeria. *Management Science and Engineering*, 4(2): 51-61

Okeshola, B. &Adeta, K. (2013). The Nature, Causes and Consequences of Cyber Crime in Tertiary Institutions in Zaria-Kaduna State, Nigeria. Department of Sociology, Ahmadu Bello University Zaria, Nigeria. *American International Journal of Contemporary Research, 3(9):98*

Okwu, O. J. (2006), A Critique of Students' Vices and the Effect on Quality of Graduates of Nigerian Tertiary Institution. *Journal of social science, 12 (3):*193-198

Olalekan, G., Akashoro, J. K. and Shaibu, H. (2010). Theatre and Development: Opportunities and Challenges in a Developing World. Kamla-Raj, J. Communication, 1(2): 107-112 (2010)

Omonijo, D. O., Nnedum, O., Anthony U., Fadugba, O. Akinrole, O, Uche, Onyekwere, C. &Biereenu-Nnabugwu, M. (2013). Social Vices Associated with the Use of Information Communication Technologies (ICTs) in a Private Christian Mission University, Southern Nigeria. *African Journal of Business Management.7(31):*3078-3089,

Umenyilorah, C. U. (2014). Theatre as Tool for Development in Nigeria.*Journal of Humanities and Social Science.* 19(6): 34-40.

Umukoro J. (2008). Environmental and Cultural Factors in Design: A Paradigmatic Approach to Stage Costuming in Indigenous Nigerian Drama. In: Yerima, A., and Duro, O. (Eds.) Trends in the Theory and Practice of Theatre in Nigeria. Lagos: *Society of Nigerian Theatre Artistes* 47(57).

www.ingramcontent.com/pod-product-compliance
Lightning Source LLC
Chambersburg PA
CBHW081201280526
45791CB00006B/2153